W9-DBW-007

EMOTIONAL FITNESS

JANICE BERGER

In Collaboration with Harry Hall

Prentice
Hall
Canada

A Pearson Company
Toronto

Canadian Cataloguing in Publication Data

Berger, Janice
    Emotional fitness: discovering our natural healing power

ISBN 0-13-018182-X

1. Mental health. 2. Emotional maturity. I. Hall, Harry (Harry F.). II. Title.

RA790.B473 2000   158   C00-930176-3

© 2000 Janice Berger
All Rights Reserved. This publication is protected by copyright, and permission should be obtained from the publisher prior to any prohibited reproduction, storage in a retrieval system, or transmission in any form or by any means, electronic, mechanical, photocopying, recording, or likewise. For information regarding permission, write to the Permissions Department.

ISBN 0-13-018182-X

Editorial Director, Trade Division: Andrea Crozier
Acquisitions Editor: Paul Woods
Production Editor: Jodi Lewchuk
Art Direction: Mary Opper
Cover and Interior Design: Gord Robertson
Author Photograph: Ted Simonett
Cover Image: The Special Photographers Co./Photonica
Production Manager: Kathrine Pummell
Page Layout: Dave McKay

1 2 3 4 5 WC 04 03 02 01 00

Printed and bound in Canada.

Visit the Prentice Hall Canada Web site! Send us your comments, browse our catalogues, and more. **www.phcanada.com**.

A Pearson Company

This book is dedicated to my mother, Muriel,
who did not have the same opportunity to heal as I did
and
to my children, Karl, Paul, Lisa and Alice,
who have taught me so much
and brought me such joy.

CONTENTS

ACKNOWLEDGMENTS

My heartfelt gratitude goes to my longtime friend and colleague Harry Hall for his exceptional contribution to this book. It has been such a privilege to collaborate with him and I am indebted to him for the time he was willing to spend on what was initially my project alone. His wisdom, steadfastness and his eagerness to be clear has produced a more useful and better organized book than would otherwise have happened. As well, his inimitable sense of humour has kept me laughing as usual.

I owe my thanks and appreciation to many others as well. Kathy Doerner gave many hours of solid assistance and her continued enthusiasm for sharing knowledge about our natural emotional healing power. Karl Berger, Terence Tse and Lisa Berger have concretely contributed to the production of the book and their confidence in me has touched me deeply. My faithful assistant Susan Winterton has kept me functioning and organized as my normal work schedule shifted and changed to accommodate my writing. My walking companion of fourteen years Dianne Gibson has listened to all my ups and downs and has helped where she could. Helle Moeller, Paul Berger, Anne Nares and Nancy Woods read the fledgling manuscript and offered their valuable early opinions. My dear friend Jean Harrison encouraged me from the beginning to write this book and has offered her support and substantial assistance all along the way as she always has in my life. Ann Goldring assisted me with her writing skills in the early stages of the book. Paul Woods of Prentice Hall was astute and enthused from the beginning. My thanks also goes to the many people over the years who have suggested that I write.

In order to protect my clients' rights to confidentiality and privacy, the examples used are all composites and no one found in this book corresponds to any actual living person, except for the example of my experience and me.

It is always amazing to me how much similar experience we share and yet how uniquely ourselves we all are. I am grateful to my clients of the past twenty-five years who have inspired me with their courage and tenacity and who have proven to me over and over again the existence of our natural healing power and the possibility of emotional fitness.

INTRODUCTION

MY BROTHER DIED. Ten years later, I began to say good-bye.

Ron was my only sibling, but I did not have time to grieve. Within thirty-six hours of the plane crash that took his life I gave birth to my second son, Paul. I missed the visitation and the funeral, the sharing of experience through talk and touch that would have helped me begin to heal. Instantly my time was filled with caring for a new baby and seventeen-month-old Karl, helping my parents cope with their loss, and supporting my husband, who took over my brother's business. There was no time for me.

I experienced only brief release for my grief: the unbidden and sudden tears whenever I heard Ron's favourite song "You Are My Sunshine," the embarrassing tears whenever I met someone who spoke of him, the lonely tears as I walked my newborn in the middle of the night.

The loss of my brother was not my first encounter with the death of someone important to me. When I was a young girl my grandfather, who often used to take only me to the movies, died. There was the war: my much-admired cousin was killed in combat; a family friend was killed in a practice manoeuvre; another cousin was taken prisoner of war. Neighbours, friends, and my family looked grim, and I was scared. Although it was acknowledged that I might have troublesome feelings about these events, my family did not know how to give me the room and support to feel and express my feelings. I did not know I needed to feel so much more so I shut down my feelings and just carried on.

At age seventeen, well past those anxious years, my dear friend Johnny died violently in a motorcycle accident. My friend's mother said, "Johnny wouldn't want you to cry." Again, nobody knew how to give me support so that I could grieve enough—weep and sob, even rage, until I did not need to do it any more.

Feeling fully was contrary to my conditioning. I have come to know that *feeling all that happens to us is the key to letting go and to being fully alive.* I have come to understand that this is our natural emotional healing power that exists to keep us emotionally fit. Knowing this has made such a difference in my life.

I needed to grieve my brother's death and feel my loss. I needed to deal with—that is, *feel*—all the unfinished business from my relationship with my brother: my resentment that Ron had never let me into his life, my anger and hurt from the times he had punched my arm or belittled me, my anguish because he did not really like me, my sorrow that we were just getting to know each other when he died. I needed, as well, to feel the sadness evoked by the earlier loss of a beloved friend and I needed to grieve all the losses, small and large, that I had been unable to feel completely.

The opening to my own emotional life came through my desire to be a good parent. My earlier traumas had begun to reveal themselves in telling moments with my children. I would be irritable but would not really understand why. I remember my excitement when I discovered Thomas Gordon's *Parent Effectiveness Training.* Gordon talks about labelling feelings so that we can express them. I began to label my feelings specifically: hurt, disappointment and frustration, for example, not just amorphous irritability. When I did this I began to know what was bothering me. It was only then that I could do something about it. Labelling my feelings began to open me up to myself.

Through my reading of Arthur Janov I began to acknowledge my overreactions and my underreactions—what Janov calls "hallmarks of neurosis." I needed help to deal with the feelings that were surfacing. I was fortunate to be directed to Dr. Mary Lou McIntosh, whose practice focused on deep emotional processing.

My life began to change. I began to feel deeply the loss of my brother, not only as an adult when he died, but the loss I had suffered as a little girl when I put so much need on my older brother who did not like me at all. I put my need on Ron because my father was largely absent from my life. Ron disliked me and acted out on me because no one was hearing how he really felt when this little sister intruded into his life. Completing emotions that belonged to past incidents allowed me to integrate my experience rather than keep it split off from my awareness. In my therapy I relived both lesser and greater traumas in my life, I felt and connected with my repressed emotions and as a result I was able to feel more fully in the moment. I learned that feelings *whatever they may be* deserve a lot of room. I was opening to the potential of my life.

This has continued to be an ongoing process for me: listening to my feelings, feeling again and again their impact on me, giving them space. When I am filled with feelings that will not go away, feelings that want to stay around, I am able to recognize that these feelings are likely supported by pain from my past. With this understanding I am able to continue to complete feelings and become clearer about my life in the present.

In my twenty-five years as a therapist I have been privileged to know many courageous people who have enhanced their lives, often dramatically, when they were able to risk change by allowing themselves to feel. I have come to understand that emotional health and a sense of freedom within are possible for those who wish to take the time necessary to connect with themselves and the truth of their lives—a simple process, but not an easy one.

In recent years the physical and sexual abuse of children has received considerable attention, yet the more subtle damage children suffer—emotional abuse and various degrees of neglect—has not been acknowledged for what it is. I have had many clients who feel ashamed because they believe their abuse was not severe enough to result in the problems they are having. One client was besieged with self-doubt and could connect this feeling to his mother's insidious put-downs but said, "It's not as if she took a belt to me or anything." I asked, "Would you deny your injuries if you were hit by a car, not a Mack truck?"

We misunderstand our suffering; we perpetuate pain by trying to avoid feelings instead of going into and through them. The simple question "How are you?" could be so helpful, yet it rings insincerely and expects no answer. The question "How do you feel?" is seldom asked. Perhaps we do not ask because we are afraid of the response; we would have to be courageous to listen to what we are afraid to hear.

How much healthier we would all be if we could ask each other, "How does that make you feel?" and listen to the response.

Our culture teaches us to ignore our emotions and our real needs, even to be ashamed of them. Instead we are offered false solutions, hints of higher self-esteem if we consume. Television advertisements lure us to believe we can find joy in the purr of a new sedan, fulfillment in a pot of spaghetti sauce and adventure in a bottle of beer. For pain we have a choice of pills. But imagine instead if we could alleviate our stomachache by connecting to the anxiety producing this discomfort. Imagine discovering that we could lessen the pain in our shoulders by feeling through all the "shoulds" we carry there. There are many benefits to this process: being able to be ourselves with our spouse, having a bit of self-doubt from time to time but not being overwhelmed by it, not needing to self-righteously judge others, feeling clear to make choices.

There is no mystery to psychotherapy, nor do we necessarily need to go into therapy to access our natural healing power. I ask my clients, "What was that like for you?" and I listen. We can ask ourselves such questions as "How do I feel about that?" "What do I need?" "When have I felt like this before?" and pay attention to our gut response. Whether we do it on our own or with a skilled therapist in intensive therapy, the movement toward emotional fitness begins in the same way: we learn to feel our emotions fully, connect with their roots and take the risk of accepting the responsibility to change our behaviour in order to honour our self. The more we achieve this, the less energy we use holding our feelings, pretending and hiding our true selves.

The process of completing held feelings by feeling them as fully as possible instead of repressing them is the way we "let go." Although this may be challenging and is certainly not a quick fix, I have a profound belief in the potential of all people to move toward wholeness. I have worked with many individuals who have shown enormous courage as they have changed their lives despite great odds. *I have seen the power of the human spirit.*

I believe our lives can be different. We can feel more alive and centred in ourselves. It is possible to learn to access and facilitate our own natural emotional healing power.

This book is the fulfillment of my desire to open doors for everyone willing to take responsibility for their own healing and willing to risk taking steps toward positive change.

Part I
Keys for Emotional Well-Being

The core of emotional health is our ability to experience the whole spectrum of human emotions and to experience them fully. The more we can experience emotions fully, the more we will develop a strong sense of self—that is, we will know who we are. The more we can risk being who we are, the more emotionally fit we will be.

Feeling as fully as possible is not only the key to knowing who we are, it is also the key to letting go of harmful thoughts, feelings and actions. It is the key to living in the moment and feeling alive.

We readily accept and appreciate that our bodies have a natural healing power to deal with physical injuries and disease; less understood is our natural ability to heal from the suffering of emotional distress.

We all have this capacity to heal. Just as we can assist our bodies to heal physically with good nutrition, proper rest and exercise, we can also assist our natural emotional healing power by understanding how it works and facilitating its functioning.

Sadly, we have been seduced away from taking advantage of our natural healing power. We have been conditioned to stay up in our heads, to use our cognitive ability only and to ignore and shut down our feelings.

When we do not appreciate this human asset we cannot cooperate with it, we cannot help our children access it and humans continue to suffer. Many of us are caught in a web of self-doubt and self-denigration. Many of us spend considerable energy pretending to be someone we are not, pleasing others, trying to live up to others' expectations, trying to be perfect. Some of us cover true feelings by being aggressive, demanding or domineering. We repeat mistakes, second-guess ourselves, continue unsatisfying jobs and unrewarding relationships, get jerked around by big feelings or feel depressed. We may not know that our lives can be different.

The cycle of distress is perpetuated when we stamp the imprint of pain and emotional injury from our past on our children. This does not need to be the case. *We can all learn to access our natural emotional healing power in order to live more healthy lives.*

Moving toward emotional fitness is an ongoing process—a becoming. It is not a panacea for perfection; it is moving toward wholeness.

As whole persons, we are open to all of ourselves and all of our feelings.

I

OUR NATURAL EMOTIONAL HEALING POWER REVEALED

I magine feeling good about yourself and feeling in charge of your life, saving energy by being open, direct and honest in your communication and seeking others who are able to be this way too, feeling free inside and exercising choice in making decisions, facing conflict openly and standing up for yourself. Imagine allowing and accepting all of your feelings and coming to know and like who you are.

What is our natural emotional healing power?

Our natural emotional healing power is our capacity to feel through whatever is happening to us. We all possess this capacity. It is available to us at *any* age. Many of us do not know how to use it because it was interfered with or unsupported when we were infants and young children. If we did not know how to use it then, we have difficulty allowing our children to use it to have their feelings now.

Think of a baby with its whole body involved in a raging cry. This baby is engaged with its innate healing power and is healing. I believe an infant will recover from any hurts, emotional or physical, by spontaneously and totally discharging its emotions if it is supported and not stopped. In her book *The Aware Baby* Aletha Solter notes that "Babies learn to suppress their crying very easily if they are not given the necessary undivided attention when they cry."

We would not suffer so greatly as adults if, as children, we had been allowed to have our feelings and to experience them fully with support. If we had been allowed to fully discharge our feelings at the time of traumatic incidents (whether major or minor) we would not carry the residue of these feelings into our adult life. Our natural emotional healing power would have worked.

Without this complete discharge, the accumulation begins and our natural healing power keeps attempting to help us finish the feelings. This is why a three-year-old may be inconsolable because someone gives her the blue cup instead of the yellow. She is crying about all the accumulated disappointments of her young life and her reaction seems out of proportion to this minor incident. But if she is allowed to cry all that she needs to now, with a parent's loving presence, then her next upset will more likely be just about that upset. She will have cleared out the accumulated pain.

Fully experiencing our emotions brings relief, completion and insight and allows us to move on in our lives. Many of us do not know that suppressing and repressing our feelings causes our suffering. We *suppress* our feelings when we deliberately hold them back; we *repress* them when we unconsciously hold them. Knowing that we cannot get over our pain until we get into it is an essential key to emotional health. It is not the pain itself that causes our suffering; it is blocking the pain that hurts so much. This kind of suffering can be compared to a boil that needs to be lanced: when the boil is pierced, there is immediate relief. So too is there relief when we get into our pain. It will be "yucky"; there will be work to be done to clean it all up, and there no doubt will be a scar left, but scars do not hurt.

Completing feelings means feeling them when they arise until we are free of them. This means taking the time to feel as soon as possible after the feelings present themselves. It is obvious that we cannot follow all our feelings in public places, but we do need a safe place in our home that we can retreat to. Needless to say, the older we are when we start to cooperate with our natural healing power, the more accumulated pain we have to clear. Still, it is better late than never. Even people in their sixties and seventies who have had a lot to grieve about their lost potential would not want to return to the confusion and suffering of their lives before they learned to feel more fully.

Our natural emotional healing power is potent and ever-present. It continually affords us the opportunity to deal with our incomplete feelings and is constantly trying to function to heal us. Again and again we find ourselves triggered by similar people and situations. The same feelings recur. However, we have not always known that their recurrence is our opportunity to finish with them. Unless we know how to use our natural healing power, it will cause us trouble. We will feel jerked around by our feelings or depressed and not in charge of our lives.

There is more and more scientific evidence to support the existence of this power. For example, researchers have found a chemical difference between emotion-induced tears and irritant-induced tears from wind or onions. William Frey, a biochemist, has concluded that tears help to relieve stress by eliminating certain stress-related chemicals from our body. Arthur Janov and Willliam Frey found the stress hormone ACTH as well as endorphins in tears, which "help remove the biochemical aspects of stress and are therefore a biological necessity." The point is that *emotionally induced tears heal.*

The ability to experience feelings is a central part of what makes us human and this ability is now being linked scientifically not only to emotional health but to physical health as well. As neuroscientist Candace Pert writes in her recent book *Molecules of Emotion,* "Health and happiness are often mentioned in the same breath and maybe this is why: Physiology and emotions are inseparable." She also notes that "sometimes the biggest impetus to healing can come from jump-starting the immune system with a burst of long-suppressed anger."

Our culture has not encouraged us to trust ourselves and to cooperate with our natural healing power; rather it has taught us that we need to know external things in order to solve our problems. True knowledge and understanding come when we have felt through the held feelings that have unconsciously influenced our decisions and led us to sabotage ourselves in various ways. This does not mean that we do not use our brains to solve our problems; it just means that we are freer to use our brains well. Our natural healing power frees us in this way.

Each life is like a tapestry

In the tapestry of our lives each thread stretches back as far as we do. Along these threads of our experience there are knots of held feelings. These are feelings we were unable to complete; that is, feel completely because we did not feel safe enough to do so. They reside as unfinished business inside each of us, awaiting their opportunity to be unravelled and resolved. As we go about our daily lives we get triggered and catapulted unconsciously back to another time when we were unable to finish with the feelings. When we remain unaware that this is what is happening we do not understand ourselves—and we do not take advantage of our natural healing power at work. We are tied in knots. We are exhausted.

In the 1930s world-famous neurosurgeon Wilder Penfield first stimulated certain cells of the temporal lobe with an electrode and dramatically demonstrated that memories exist in their entirety. His patients would relive events and emotions from the past while conscious—they would see the images, hear the sounds, smell the smells, and laugh and weep. They ceased to be in the memory when the electrode was removed. *We begin to make sense of our lives when we understand that everything that has ever happened to us is still with us today.*

Trusting in our natural emotional healing power

It is difficult to trust in a power that has been so ignored, misunderstood and even ridiculed in our culture. Yet more and more evidence suggests that suppression and repression take effort and so take a toll on our bodies, leading to stress-related disorders. In her very helpful book *Women's Bodies, Women's Wisdom* Christiane Northrup notes that "if we don't work through our emotional distress, we set ourselves up for physical distress because of the biochemical effect that suppressed emotions have on our immune and endocrine systems."

We learn to trust our intrinsic healing power the more we notice it working for us. Many of us have had some experience with the relief that comes when we finally say something we have needed to say. We have experienced feeling better after crying or expressing anger. When we have discharged our feelings and made connections that make sense of our lives, we have newfound energy. We come to understand that this feeling power keeps us clear about our lives, keeps us living in the moment and keeps us living without pretence or illusions. This does not mean we will always be happy, but it does mean that we can come to appreciate feeling our full range of emotions. It means we will be more authentic; we will know who we are and we will feel alive.

Feelings as signals

Since our culture has adulated logic and reason and denigrated emotions, few of us have learned to really listen to our feelings and to use them as guides for our lives. When there is a decision to be made it is more likely that we will stay up in our heads, listening to the "shoulds" and "shouldn'ts." We may wonder what others will think of our decision or we may concoct elaborate rationalizations to support what we decide to do. A war goes on between our head and our gut.

We need to be aware of the lack of coherence between our minds and bodies and use it to pay attention to what is really going on. Sometimes this will alert us to guilt feelings that are appropriate for the present because we may be avoiding obligations that are real in our relationships. On the other hand, guilt may be present because we carry a load of it from our past, which weighs us down. Many of us have a very active voice within us that edits and censors our feeling response to the world. However, *feelings are not right or wrong, they just are.* It is imperative that we stop judging our feelings and instead treat them as important signals worth listening to and feeling to their fullest.

When we suppress the reality that our feelings are signalling to us we split off from them, and therefore from our true selves. We do not know who we are or why we really do what we do. We just keep going. Our natural healing power keeps presenting us with our feelings in our relationships, in our perplexing, obsessive thoughts and drives, in our anxieties, in our depressions and in our frightening dreams. We cannot get our lives the way we want them to be. This is when we need to take notice and then acknowledge that we have been blocking our innate ability.

Can I always trust my feelings?

Feelings are always accurate but they are not always appropriate to the current situation. If the strength of the feeling is too big, then we can become aware that the bigness of that feeling is coming from somewhere back in our experience. If a feeling of rage comes up when our child annoys us, for example, we must use our intelligence and our caring to take responsibility for the size of that feeling and to know that our child is not responsible for it. Our big feelings are something we need to own as ours and to explore further, away from our children. Trusting that our feelings mean something, even though they may not be appropriate in the current context, gives us access to our natural emotional healing power.

Our natural emotional healing power is revealed in our over and underreactions

Overreactions are feelings that are bigger than the current situation calls for. There is a pinball effect wherein the current situation ignites old pain, reminding us of incomplete feelings, unfinished business that needs our attention. When these old unfinished feelings bounce off each other and resonate with the present feeling we often feel bewildered by our own responses.

> Sarah offers to drive her aunt to a funeral and to stay with her for support during the service, although the deceased is a complete stranger. At the graveside Sarah finds herself sobbing. She is hugely embarrassed and has no idea why she is so overwhelmed with sadness.

Like Sarah, we may feel confounded by our feelings when they are big and inexplicable. We find ourselves yelling at the kids when we know they do not deserve it, we cry at work and do not know why, or we rage without reason. We may feel swamped with yearning, seduced by adulation or overwhelmed with anxiety. These overreactions push us to heal old wounds through our natural healing power and can be welcomed. When we notice these overreactions, feel them as fully as we can and connect them to their source, they begin to lose their intensity. Parents who continue to shout at their children need to take responsibility for the size of their anger. Sarah needs to trust that her tears do mean something; our natural healing power requires that Sarah allow the sad feelings to be felt, for only then can she begin to make a connection with what her feelings are really all about.

In their book *Giving the Love That Heals* Harville Hendrix and Helen Hunt state, "When a parent does experience intense, nonrational, mystifying reactions to certain encounters or experiences with his children, that's a signal that he needs to ask himself some questions." This is an opportunity for us to take responsibility for our feelings and engage our natural healing power. When we suspect or know that our feelings are too big for the current situation we can say to ourselves, "I wonder what this is all about for me?"

Underreactions, although much more difficult to recognize, also herald unfinished business. Underreactions involve an absence of emotions where one would expect to have feelings, a lack that results in passive behaviour.

Underreacting is an enormous protection, saving us from the overwhelming feelings underneath. When we understand it as a protection we can notice it and feel its defensive strength. When we do this enough we loosen it and begin to be able to feel the underlying feelings. Our healing process begins when we start taking responsibility for our underreactions.

It is quite common for someone who generally underreacts to eventually blow and overreact. This happens when the feelings simply cannot be contained any longer. Breakouts and breakdowns are the price we pay for living a life of underreacting. Underreacting is a dangerous defense since our natural emotional healing power, contained, will find a crevice to explode the repressed feelings into our world. The uncontrolled nature of these feelings frightens us and those nearby. We most often do not use it as an opportunity to cooperate with our healing capacity because we have internalized the need to clamp down on it. When we do cooperate with it, however, we reverse this unhealthy, cyclical process and begin to heal.

We may not know when we are underreacting, and friends and family who care about us might tell us when we are tolerating something that is definitely not good for us. If we find ourselves defensive when they do this it is another signal that there is something here needing our attention. Our defensiveness is a protection against feeling something we do not want to feel. When we admit this to ourselves we can notice our defensiveness and our underreaction, and realize that there are feelings being held back.

We underreact and tolerate something unhealthy because it is familiar to us; we learned to tolerate a long time ago because we had no control as children. One of my clients was completely permissive with her children and had a chaotic and unhappy household as a result. When she connected with how her needs and wants had never been attended to in her young life and how it made her feel that they were unimportant, she realized that she was tolerating and that this was harmful not only to her children but to herself. She gradually felt more entitled and became more responsible for setting boundaries for herself and her children. With the help of her husband and her children she was able to work out a more fair approach to sharing responsibilities, a way in which everyone's needs could be addressed.

Indifference, the inability to enjoy and passive behaviour patterns all point to underreacting. Yet responding appropriately to a situation is made more difficult in our culture by the fact that underreacting is often seen as a virtue.

For example, when someone does not cry at a funeral of a loved one it may be said that she behaved well; Jackie Kennedy was described as "magnificent" at her husband's funeral. Crying is perceived as weak and the one who does not cry is considered the "strong one." This confusion about strength and weakness in our culture keeps us valuing underreacting. We are often uncomfortable with displays of feeling because witnessing such displays unconsciously takes us closer to our own pain, which we are wanting to keep out of our awareness.

Although many of my clients come to see me because they are overwhelmed by feelings they do not understand, others come because feeling flat and blue overwhelms them. Depression is a kind of underreacting; sitting on feelings that are too painful to experience. When we hold in painful feelings we deaden everything; we cannot feel our joy and love if we are depressing ourselves by holding anger or sorrow.

> When Angela entered my office she had been depressed for about two years and was confused and discouraged about feeling this way. She was married to a successful man who provided her and her family with every material comfort. She felt ungrateful because she continued to feel bad despite her husband's efforts to please her.
>
> As Angela unravelled her feelings from the past she began to realize that by trying to make her mother's life right she had never had the chance to be who she was. She had never allowed herself to know the rage she felt about her father's compulsive gambling or her mother's need to escape to her job and leave Angela to care for the other children. Angela bitterly resented her parents' adulation of her husband and their lack of recognition of her. As she felt through the very difficult feelings from her past, her rage and her sorrow, she began to come alive to the possibilities of her own life. She began to take risks to be herself, to look after herself and enjoy her life.

It is common to feel depressed and not know why. We often feel ashamed because there seems to be no apparent reason for us to feel this way. Like Angela, we may have everything we have been led to believe will bring us happiness, yet we feel terrible. Little feelings have large roots; we will alleviate our depression when we connect with and fully feel the feelings that we are repressing.

Raw wounds

I'm not good enough . . . I'm bad. . . I don't deserve . . . It's my fault . . . I'm unlovable. . . It must be me; there must be something wrong with me . . .

Raw emotional wounds are often hidden from our conscious awareness and we flinch as people in our lives may unwittingly flick salt in them. This reaction is actually our natural healing power being revealed—and we can engage with it. Unfortunately, when we do not understand this we often get stuck in blaming those who trigger the pain of these old wounds.

Jessie habitually sought appreciation from her husband and friends and when they did not respond with enough gratitude an old wound was aggravated. The more Jessie tried to get what she needed the more helpless her husband and friends felt ever to please her and the angrier she and they became. In therapy Jessie described a childhood filled with four noisy brothers and a sick, demanding mother. When she came to recognize that her husband and friends were triggering her into this long-ago time when her small childish efforts were unappreciated, she was able to take responsibility for her present feelings and to begin to grieve and rage about how her needs were not met as a child.

No one in the present can ever give us what we did not get in the past. Not knowing this really messes up a lot of relationships. For example, many of us have the romantic expectation that our life partner will make us feel good and meet all our needs. The problem occurs when we do not realize that many of these needs are not appropriate. They are our unmet needs from the past erupting into our current relationship.

Until recently we have not known how to help children feel through their traumas. As a result, I have never met anyone who was lucky enough not to have any internal raw wounds stemming from painful childhood experiences. If we are not helped as children to feel through traumas as they occur we will carry these wounds into our adult lives. And these wounds drive us. We may insist that we are okay, that "there's nothing wrong with me"; nevertheless, we may be blindly acting in a destructive way toward others and ourselves. Consider the hockey parent who would risk his life to save his child from a burning building but who regularly humiliates his child with unrealistic expectations and scathing criticism. This parent who loves his child is out of control, driven unconsciously to fix his old sense of worthlessness with his present expectations.

The way out of the deadly trap of hurting the children we love is to begin to understand how our present pain is connected to our past and to take responsibility for our strong feelings or lack of feelings. We will no longer expect someone else to fix us and soothe our pain when we use our natural healing power to feel and integrate our old hurts. Without this healing we will not be free to be exactly who we are, we will not be clear to behave as loving parents and we will not be able to be more whole and in charge of our lives.

Becoming aware

There are many signs that indicate to us that feelings are pressing to be resolved: when we are feeling compulsive or obsessive about anything, when we are responding inappropriately, when our feelings are too big or too little for the current situation, when the same feeling recurs again and again. Irritability, forgetfulness, confusion and the inability to concentrate may indicate something is pressing to be felt. Insomnia, headaches and many other body signs also inform us that time is needed to feel what is going on.

I learned that, for me, confusion often masked anger. I did not want to face my anger, since I had been conditioned to believe it was unacceptable. But once I understood this phenomenon I found I could go through the confusion very quickly to feel what, indeed, I was so mad about. Later I grieved how hurtful my conditioning had been and how it had kept me from knowing my feelings and therefore, myself. Now I no longer need to displace my anger and berate myself for being confused; I recognize that my confusion is a signal and I pay attention.

As we take advantage of our natural power for emotional healing we realize that everything we sense and feel is a possible door to go through. This does not mean that we need constantly to be aware of processing our feelings, but it does mean that we can be conscious of the doors and go through them when we can.

2

ACCESS DENIED
Our Power Subverted

When our natural emotional healing power is subverted we do not complete feelings surrounding trauma and they stay buried within us. They become a reservoir of unfelt pain. *Feelings are not buried dead; they are buried alive.* They come up when we least expect them. They confuse and confound us. We control them in many different, destructive ways.

Losing our real selves

We learn as children, at a time when we are most vulnerable, to cry less than we need to, to be brave though we are fearful, to act as if anger does not exist. Gradually we lose touch with our feelings, and by the time we are adults our sense of who we really are is distorted. In turn, our emotional health and our physical health are at risk.

Consider the subtle influences that tell young Kyle how he *should* be:

Kyle and his mother are in a large urban mall while she searches for some china for a wedding gift. Kyle is occupied making faces at his reflection in a goblet when he notices his mother leaving the china section without him. He makes one last quick face and follows. It takes only a few moments for him to realize that the woman ahead of him is not his mother but a woman who is wearing a similar coat. By this time, Kyle's frantic mother is searching for her son in all the nearby departments.

When mall security finally reunites the mother and child, Kyle is sobbing and shaking with terror. His distraught mother hugs him, strokes his head and clucks soothingly, "There, there, Kyle. Mommy's here now. Don't cry. It's okay. Don't cry any more. Here, you can use my hankie. That's my big boy."

If you had witnessed this scene you would probably be pleased to note that Kyle's mom is a caring mom. You would know the huge warm hug is important for Kyle's well-being, as well as his mother's. The soothing words are ones most thoughtful moms would use to reassure the child that everything is okay now. Yet when Kyle's mom discourages him from crying he is left with no choice but to shut down his need to cry and to shake. Shaking is the body's response to fear and Kyle needs to cry and shake until he does not need to do it any more. His emotions and his body shut down because he gets the message that his mother does not like him doing this. We now know that *children need all kinds of time to discharge their feelings completely.*

Since the control of emotions is valued in our families and in the culture around us it is no wonder that, when it is our turn to be parents, we perpetuate the cycle. Suppressing, restricting and denying emotions seems "right." When Kyle's mother encourages him to dry his tears she is simply following the example of her parents as well as her friends. She genuinely wants Kyle to feel better but she mistakenly believes that if the crying stops, the hurting stops. In fact the crying *is* the healing. Stopping the crying just drives the hurt underground. Kyle will be fine if he is allowed to cry until he no longer needs to. It takes courage for parents to go against public custom and their own learned experience and be with their children while they cry.

As our own wisdom and our true selves become covered with layers and layers of "shoulds" and "shouldn'ts," we lose sight of how we really feel about anything. Over the years many clients have told me in their initial appointment that they have no real sense of self whatsoever. Yet if we do not have ourselves, we do not have our lives.

Original wholeness undermined

An infant is born originally whole and totally authentic. This is not a common belief. As infants we are completely reactive and we respond to life just as it is. We cannot make judgments about what is right or wrong, nor can we wonder if we are important or if we feel good about ourselves. We just feel discomfort and pain if our needs are not met or misery if we are being abused.

As we grow we get more and more messages about how we should be, how we should think, how we should *feel*—messages first from parents, and later reinforced by the society in which we live. Some messages are directed more toward one gender than the other. These messages take us away from ourselves. We learn that it is not safe to be authentic, to be who we are. We forge ourselves to the shape of others' expectations. One way to describe this is as a false and defended self. Under the continuing barrage of limiting messages our authentic self shrinks; sadly our false self gets larger and larger.

Family restrictions on emotional expression are strong. Many clients have told me that their parents controlled them with just a glance. That was all it took from these powerful people to have their little children squelch their feelings and their need. This is not to say that a child be allowed to toss his dinner about the room to act out his anger. Nor is he to be given the newly painted wall for a canvas in order to accommodate his joy. Supporting our child by acknowledging and allowing the release of his feelings supports his emotional health, and is not the same as giving him licence to rule the roost.

Fearing feelings

Children who must control their emotion begin to fear its full expression, and they begin to fear the emotion itself. If we, as children, cannot be fearful of the dark because "only babies are afraid of the dark," what are we to do with our fear? If our mother lifts us to the mirror to show us how ugly we look when we are angry, what are we to do with our anger? We may be warned to "Stop crying, or I'll give you something to cry about!" and our sister may be praised with "You're so pretty when you smile. Mommy loves your happy face." We may be a joyful exuberant little girl who is told to "Sit down and be quiet." These admonitions leave us with no safe place to feel our sorrow or our joy.

As children we are capable of the full range of human emotions, and it is natural for us to completely discharge our feelings. If our parent does not welcome this discharge we have no choice but to shut down. This can be an everyday occurrence resulting from subtle neglect and abuse, or it can be the result of more overt neglect and abuse. Shutting down our feelings is the way we defend ourselves against unbearable pain.

We are all somewhere on the continuum from shut down to fully feeling. We may have some notion of how good it feels when emotions are allowed to move through us; we may have experienced the relief that comes after a good cry or an outburst of anger. Unfortunately, we may have also experienced this sense of relief quickly subverted by other feelings such as shame and guilt. We may have resolved, next time, to choke back our tears and bottle up our anger. As a result of this shutting down many people report that they have a sense of something missing in their lives, some edge or intensity that is absent. They report wanting more. Remember the song "Is That All There Is?" Often we look to others to provide the missing something, which may lead to discontent with our friends, lovers and children. These people cannot possibly provide the answer to a childhood empty of feeling expression.

Because the overt expression of feelings is viewed as "bad" in our culture we easily become uncomfortable with the open expression of feelings in others. I recall one client who was so armoured against his own feelings of fear that he could not tolerate any fear, or even nervousness, in either his wife or his children. We are often unable to respond to a friend or a family member's emotion with support. We would rather try to make their unhappiness go away. We offer the person something to eat or drink, point out to her all the other good things in her life and minimize what has happened to her. This is indeed sad, since if we could simply listen and allow her feelings we would be truly helping her through her pain.

When health care professionals prescribe anti-depressants for every conceivable loss one might suffer, they become part of the problem. This is truly harmful. I have had clients who have had to do their grieving much later because of this immediate subversion of their feelings. The block created by the drug can be so huge that it takes much longer to connect with the pain and complete the grieving than if the person had been encouraged to let her natural power of grieving occur at the time of her loss. It would be doing a great service if the medical professional could encourage more patients to cry all they need to and for as long as they need to. I suppose this does not happen because doctors are just as afraid of their own feelings as anyone else is.

Consciousness

A conscious person is a feeling person, one who is aware of what is going on outside and inside. The more congruent we are, the more our inside matches our outside, the more real and more emotionally fit we are.

Splitting off, becoming unconscious and disconnected

Each time we are unable to feel an experience, tension develops. We split off from our feelings and in doing so become disconnected from them. We become unconscious about their source. We may reach the point when we are more repressed and defended than we are feeling. This means we are more unreal than real, more irrational than rational. It also means we are holding more and more feelings in our body. If we could see our life tapestry it would be full of knots of unfelt feeling, with more knots accumulating all the time. *This process of becoming separated from our experience, that is, not fully feeling what is happening to us, over time results in living a defended, non-integrated life.*

To keep truths hidden, we concoct stories to explain what we do and to defend against our feelings.

Steven insisted that he was working so hard for the good of his family, and that it was not really surprising that he was too tired to do anything but watch TV in the evening.

In therapy Steven came to understand that he worked so hard because he was terrified of not being a success, terrified that he would not get the approval of his father—a father who had been dead for fifteen years.

Once Steven was able to take responsibility for his feelings and grieve and integrate the fact that his father never accepted him as he was, he was able to stop driving himself and hurting his family with his emotional absence. He became more conscious about his work decisions when he no longer had to split off from the source of his pain and defend.

When we repress our feelings we repress what is real, and this is what produces what I call the false and defended self. I have heard many clients say, "I have no idea who I am or what I want." The false self is marching to someone else's tune, following rules that really do not fit, rules we grew up with: "Speak up. Sit up straight. Don't bother me. Don't be so loud."

We can understand something of the magnitude of the split that has occurred in people who perpetrate terrible crimes. These people are so split off from their feelings that they do not have the normal human capacity for empathy. We all split off from our feelings to some degree, but this is a frightening extreme.

Fear of losing control

Emotional fitness often eludes us because we have learned to be afraid of our feelings as well as those of others; we are afraid our emotions will go out of control. Certainly it makes sense that we might be terrified of our own or someone else's inappropriate rage, but we tend to be uncomfortable with *any* open display of feeling. For example, although it is healthy for grown men and women to cry, we are uneasy with their tears and our own. What we have not understood is that when we restrict emotions by suppressing and repressing them they will be acted out unconsciously and will be out of our control.

As little people we are dependent and very susceptible. Our parents' admonitions about our natural responses make us feel that those feelings are wrong and bad and that therefore we are wrong and bad. We become afraid of ourselves. We hold back the unacceptable feelings with all our might. We become convinced that if we let them out they will harm us. We become fearful of losing control because of this. However, shutting down emotions is like putting a lid on a pot boiling on the stove; feelings contained and unexpressed eventually boil over and damage relationships, or they implode and damage our bodies.

Defenses: keeping ourselves from feeling

Defenses are crucial when we are young, vulnerable and fragile. It is especially then that we cannot take assault or neglect. If we are not allowed to cry and reveal to the world how we feel, we shut down. This repression solidifies into an internal defense that prevents us from feeling the impact of neglect or abuse. We develop layers of defenses against continued neglect and abuse throughout all of our childhood. We defend, for example, by rationalizing, denying, projecting our feelings, blaming ourselves and others, fantasizing, dissociating, and harming ourselves physically. These defenses carried into our adult life damage our relationships and keep us from being emotionally fit.

As we become mature and independent we can let go of our defenses if we know how. If we hang on to them, we block our healing and keep ourselves a mystery to ourselves. There is no way to be totally ourselves until we remove these blocks. Our goal is to become more feeling than defended.

When cracks are forced in our defenses by a triggering event we can see this as either a problem or an opportunity. Being defensive is not "bad," it is a defense, and something to be noticed and felt. We can let ourselves understand that there is some truth wanting to push through. However, our defenses are guarding our blind spots so they are not always easy to see. If we are afraid of appearing wrong or stupid, we may react to any criticism with defensiveness because it feels as though our self-worth is at stake.

When a defense is crumbling we will likely have feelings of worthlessness and self-doubt, and we will be afraid. This is an opportunity to feel these feelings and then connect with the original traumas. Unfortunately, when we continue to hide by raising our defensive walls, we repeat our problems again and again. We never seem to learn our lessons and we continue to try to work out our pain in our relationships, work in a bad situation again, or repeat some other self-defeating behaviour over and over.

People who are well defended seem guarded and distant. It is difficult to really connect with them. Many of us have been trained to be this way, in fact, told by our parents to conceal ourselves and not let people know what we are really feeling. We have been trained to be "nice" and "civilized," that is, emotionally dishonest and hidden. Since our defenses are always holding in our feelings, we are always running the risk of allowing others to see how we feel. It takes enormous energy to keep these feelings concealed by keeping our defenses in place. We cannot be clear and be well defended because when we are defended we do not know ourselves and do not trust ourselves. We cannot relax and be spontaneous and open because we need to watch everything we say and do. I have had clients who have felt creative for the first time in their lives after they have begun to feel through their defenses and have opened to themselves. When we are trying to hold everything in place, we bind our creativity, playfulness and movement.

The problem is that we have been taught to act instead of to live. The more we *act* instead of *be,* the more distant we get from ourselves and the more unable we are to hold it all together. It is ironic that, in fact, the more we are able to go to pieces, that is, break into feelings, the more together we can get.

Unravelling what is in most cases a lifetime of defenses is not done easily or quickly. In fact, our defenses need to be respected. They are there for good reason. Sometimes we have an urge to batter our way through our defenses, to break open, to be free and to do it immediately. To act on this compulsion or to allow others to act their need out on us, to have us get through our pain in a hurry, is very dangerous. Dropping our defenses precipitously leaves us without enough time to process the feelings that do and must arise. They simply come to the surface too fast. We are left so vulnerable that we are overwhelmed and therefore unable to connect with the pain of our past. We may become dysfunctional or shut down so hard that we have to work twice as hard to ever open up again.

There are some therapies and programs, unfortunately, that are designed to strip individuals of their defenses quickly in order to get obvious breakdown responses. It is, in fact, not difficult to get individuals into "big" feelings. There are many methods, especially in the context of large groups, that blast people open to these big feelings. For those seeking a way to feel, this process is very seductive. These methods are dangerous. Although they often get fast results in terms of breaking through, they do harm in the long run by replacing a set of known defenses with a whole new set of prepackaged ones that are much harder to recognize and deal with. For example, when we spout pat, learned responses to explain our feelings ("I've done my anger work" or "I've done my grieving") we are split and compartmentalized; we filter our world through this new defense. Ironically, in a headlong desire to become more connected we end up further away from ourselves.

I have learned in my own therapy and in my years as a therapist to respect each individual to deal with their feelings and defenses in a way that allows them to feel what they need to feel without becoming incapacitated. I trust each individual to do this unravelling at a rate they can handle. There are also many nuances of feeling that are important, and dealing simply with the big feelings such as anger and fear leaves too much out. Some of the most difficult feelings to feel, such as deadness, worthlessness and need, must not be dismissed as unimportant.

Our defenses came into place to rescue us from pain that was too great to feel. These defenses are in direct proportion to the extent of the underlying pain and can guide us. Awareness of them can help us focus in on ourselves and provide another door into our past so that we can feel and connect the pain from our early trauma.

Crucial defenses when we are young

Hating ourselves is our major child defense against feeling how inadequate or even monstrous our parents may be. When we are children, as long as we maintain the hope that we can change things by trying harder and behaving better, we do not have to feel the catastrophic feeling that we are actually helpless to change very much of anything. Hating ourselves and blaming ourselves makes us feel as though at least we have some control.

When we do not have explanations for current life difficulties and see our childhood as "normal" we remain stuck in self-blame and denial: "I'm so stupid," "Well, didn't everyone go through that?" "That's just the way it was then." As long as we are unwilling to acknowledge that things were not always rosy for us as children we will remain disconnected from our real experience. Our emotional health is jeopardized when we acknowledge only the things that were good and deny the things that were not. We stay defended, stuck needing our parents to have been okay. Our parents may have done the best they could, but for many of us it was not enough. *As adults we can afford to feel the way things really were.* When we take this risk to feel we can begin to let go of the defense of self-blame that everything is our fault.

It takes courage to acknowledge what it really *felt* like to be the child we were instead of guessing about what our experience meant to us, but it is worth the effort. It is important to remember that *acknowledging and feeling our damage is not the same as blaming.* It is telling ourselves the truth about our experience.

When we cannot feel, we act out

When we deny our feelings we act them out instead of feeling them; the feelings never get resolved, and this keeps the struggle going. For example, if we did not feel loved and wanted as a child we may act out instead of grieving our unmet need. We may make unreasonable demands on our spouse and friends for unconditional love and acceptance. We may demand that our children look after us in various ways, perhaps by being model children who make us look good as a parent. We may drive ourselves incessantly to acquire more and more symbols of achievement because it was only through achievements that we felt valued as a child.

George lived with an alcoholic father who binged most Friday nights and returned in the early hours of the morning to batter his wife. George's father often expressed his opinion that his son was too sensitive and a wimp; he thought George should be more like the bully who lived next door. The one way George found to feel good about himself was to make his mother's life easier. By age eleven, he was working and making money to give to her.

George acted out his need to feel okay in his adult life by being successful in his job. He put in considerable overtime just to please his boss. Eventually his career ended in disillusionment because he was never able to get enough acknowledgment to feel okay. His marriage ended in hurt and bewilderment because both he and his wife were acting out old needs and blaming each other for not being the way they needed the other person to be. George's relationship with his children was strained and unsatisfying because he expected them to look after his feelings—that is, make him feel wanted and feel sorry for him because of his problems.

George entered therapy. As he worked through the enormous pain of his childhood abandonment by his father and his neglect by his ineffective mother, he came to understand how his need had driven him in his adult life. He felt regret for how he had acted out his need on his wife and children and how he had blamed them, and as he became clearer he began building a more satisfying relationship with both of his adult children. He was able to acknowledge and grieve for how he had contributed to his marriage failure.

When we act out as adults we subvert our healing power, keep ourselves frozen in unhealthy patterns, and diminish our lives in denial. As we observe ourselves we can become aware of our recurring problems. The driving force behind these is undoubtedly some unfelt feeling from the past. A person who can never find anything and who is constantly asking his wife "Where's my shirt? Where are my new socks?" is probably acting out a desire to be looked after. A young person with purple hair and a safety pin in her left cheek is likely acting out a need to be seen or trying to make the inside pain visible. A man acting out by being sexually promiscuous probably needs to feel how much he wanted and needed his mother and father to hold him. The act-out may not be harmful or a problem; it could be just a love for long hot baths which may be an acting out of the need for warmth not received as a child. In any case, only we can unravel what our acting out is all about, and the only way we can do that is by feeling what is being obscured by this behaviour.

The turning point

In my experience, the turning point in therapy occurs when we take responsibility and stop denying and minimizing both our real childhood experience and what we are doing in the present to keep ourselves from feeling.

Some clients come presenting an enormous frozen wall of feelings, unable to access themselves. When they begin to acknowledge its size and recognize that it reflects the pain of their childhood precisely, the wall begins to melt and they begin to gain some empathy for themselves and for their pain. Whatever size or shape our defenses take, it is important that we understand that they reflect our pain accurately.

When we are able to stop blaming ourselves and acknowledge that our present difficulties—whatever they may be and however we are dealing with them—are a direct result of our childhood pain, we begin to open to our natural emotional healing power.

3

THE NATURE OF RESPONSIBILITY AND BLAME

A Necessary Understanding

Taking responsibility for our feelings is the major key for emotional fitness in our lives. When we take this responsibility we gain a deep emotional understanding of ourselves. We then have the possibility of having solid, caring and responsive relationships. When we do not take responsibility for our feelings, problems arise.

Although we are responsible for our actions, reactions, thoughts and feelings as adults, *we were not responsible for what happened to us as innocent children*. We get stuck in blame when we do not take responsibility for the fallout from our childhood. It is our responsibility to recuperate from the pain of our past so that we do not act out that old pain in the present.

No matter how difficult or unfortunate the circumstances of our lives, we are responsible for the changes we need to make; there is no one else who can do this for us. We are being responsible when we engage our emotional healing power.

Responsibility

One of the most important distinctions we need to make is that we are responsible for our own feelings but not for the feelings of others. We are responsible *to* others—that is, to treat them decently and to honour our commitments. We are not responsible for how they feel about us and our actions. For example, I am responsible to you, my readers, to talk about emotional fitness in this book.

I am not, however, responsible for how you *feel* about what I am saying. Not understanding this difference leads people to blame others for their unhappiness and to feel guilty when someone else is unhappy.

Blaming others for our unhappiness and feeling guilty when we can't keep someone else happy is rampant in our culture. It begins in childhood when we get the message that we were the cause of our parents' feelings: "You're going to be the death of me," "You're giving me a migraine," "You make me sick," or "I can't stand this any more." It can come about more subtly too; many children learn to be really good boys and girls in order to keep their parents happy. As children we may feel we will not be loved if we are not "good," but the end result is that we feel responsible for our parents' expectations of us.

We may also feel responsible for our parents' moods. As a child I was always trying to get the angry look off my mother's face; I did not know that her anger was not about me. I learned that I was not supposed to "bother" my father; he would become irritable, light a cigarette and hide in a cloud of smoke. I often ask my clients, "What did you see on your mother's face when you were a child?" Most people can connect with the anxiety they felt when their mother was stressed and unhappy. Some report that they learned to be good, or funny, or really competent in order to try to change that look on their parent's face.

Taking responsibility is a twofold task. We take responsibility by owning our feelings and using our natural emotional healing power to feel, connect and integrate experiences into our lives, and by taking risks to make our lives better in the present.

Taking care of ourselves is an important responsibility

There is a lot of denial involved when we do not take care of ourselves; we deny our worthiness. When we do take the responsibility to take care of ourselves we break open this denial and provide access to our blocked feelings. This is scary because it opens us to core feelings, and yet it feels better because we are closer to who we are.

Taking care of ourselves provides us with the opportunity to be responsible for how we feel. As an adult, and the mother of three small children, I struggled with my mother's ongoing criticism. When I kept connecting to how I felt as a child when my mother criticized me, how frightened I was and how it silenced me, I was eventually able to confront her about her criticism in my current life. I told her that her criticism hurt me and made me feel that I did not want to be around her. When she minimized her criticism—"You know I don't really mean it, dear"—I was able to say that whether or not she meant it, it was hurting me. I was lucky, because from that day forward she never criticized me again. If this had not been the case I would have looked after myself by continually reestablishing the boundary or by seeing less of her. There was no going back to the victimization of my youth once I had felt how devastating and harmful the constant criticism was. My mother also benefited from my action because we enjoyed a closer relationship.

Taking care of ourselves is a risk, but well worth it. The more connected we are to our past and the more we feel what it was really like, the more we are able to take care of ourselves in a connected and straightforward way.

We are responsible for all of our relationships and we are one hundred percent responsible for our feelings.

Accountability is not the same as blame

Being accountable means we do not blame anybody, including ourselves. It means taking responsibility for what we have done, that is, acknowledging our actions and reactions, making amends or apologizing, and making restitution when appropriate. It also means treating others with respect and engaging in problem resolution processes to deal with the differences that are causing conflict.

Clients often arrive in my office declaring that they do not intend to get off on blaming their parents because they know their parents did the best they could. I assure these clients that holding their parents accountable is not the same as blaming them. Confronting our parents in the therapy room in their absence is the way we get to our feelings about what *really* happened to us. This is not about confronting them face to face. No matter how empathetic or compassionate we may feel about what our parents went through in their family of origin, we are still entitled to work through our grief and anger about what happened to us when we were in their care.

When we do not want to hold our parents accountable in this way we are still stuck in our child state, when it was too overwhelming for us to see the inadequacies of our parents and the reality of how we were being treated. Because we were incredibly vulnerable and needed to believe our parents were okay, we found it easier to blame ourselves. Giving ourselves permission to feel what did happen to us is the most important thing. This honours our true, authentic self and leads to a more integrated and fully felt life.

Blaming

Blaming ourselves and others is our most pervasive defense. This is so because it was the only thing we could do to protect ourselves as children. This is what makes it so difficult to let go of now and why it requires an ongoing act of courage to take responsibility for it. When we can do this it provides us with a big door to go through to our feelings of hurt. *Our life is transformed when we can stop blaming.*

Blaming ourselves

It is as small children that we learn to beat ourselves up, believing there must be something wrong with us. When we continue self-blame into adulthood—for example, when we apologize for things we are not responsible for—we are not taking responsibility. The alternative is to allow ourselves to feel how inadequate we are feeling, to connect the feeling to its source and to feel this inadequacy until the feeling is integrated. When this integration takes place we find we are not triggered as often and we stop blaming ourselves and feeling responsible for other people's pain. When we realize that we have hurt our child in the past and keep apologetically bringing it up, we are blaming ourselves rather than taking responsibility by feeling our grief and regret. It is our need to apologize, not our child's need to hear it. Avoiding these feelings by obsessive, apologetic self-blame postpones our healing process and further burdens our child with unfair responsibility and guilt.

It is necessary to explore the source of self-deprecating behaviour and to return again and again to feel this pain until we become self-appreciating, with empathy and understanding for the child that we were.

Blaming others

Dumping angry feelings on others is an act of blame and is a way of avoiding responsibility for those feelings. When we put someone down instead of expressing appropriately how his or her actions are affecting us, we are dumping: "You're such a slob. You leave everything on the floor for me to pick up!" "What do you mean you forgot to make the Visa payment? What do you do all day?" These messages are clothed in blame.

We need to recognize that dumping also occurs in less obvious ways. Only seven percent of a message is verbal and the other ninety-three percent comes across in tone and body language: pointing a finger, hands on hips, arms folded across the chest, a sigh. People often deny what the real message is. It is very difficult to take responsibility for the emotions that are being put out by our tone and body language. Because of this we are often not connected to our bodies and the messages we are giving off. We feel caught when someone points it out to us. Nevertheless, this is an opportunity to notice our defensiveness, own it and feel it and take responsibility for the underlying message. When we take this time we give ourselves an opportunity to cooperate with our capacity to feel fully.

Manipulating

When we use words like "always" and "never" we are manipulating and trying to make the other person feel guilty and responsible for our feelings. If we find ourselves using always or never in an attempt to get what we want we can recognize these as signposts of blame. In my experience, when clients express their need in a more open, honest and direct way it puts them up against their fear.

> Greta blamed her sister Hannah, claiming that she "never" took responsibility for their parents' welfare. She struggled with Hannah all the time, telling her that she "always" avoided issues and family conferences regarding the next step in their parents' care. Hannah's response to her sister's harangue was to get angry and withdraw.

> Greta found herself daily churning inside with resentment. Her husband kept telling her that she needed to let go, saying "That's just the way Hannah is. There's nothing you can do about it."

> As Greta told her therapist about her sister she was encouraged to stay with her feelings of "always" and "never." It was not easy, but when held to these feelings Greta began to seethe with anger about how Hannah had been "let off the hook" in their childhood home. Slowly her anger shifted to her parents and their lack of responsibility in accepting Greta as the "helper" without question and not requiring Hannah to be responsible about anything.

Over time as Greta was able to feel her anger at her parents and how much she had been let down by them in their abdication of responsibility, she was able to address the current issues with her sister without blame. Hannah in turn was better able to hear Greta when she dropped the "always" and "never."

Although Greta felt good about this she became aware of how anxious and afraid she was while speaking with her sister. When she brought this to her therapy she connected to how vulnerable she had felt in her home and how driven she was to be "good" so that her parents would love her. She eventually grieved deeply the conditions put on her parents' caring.

Avoiding responsibility for our actions

It takes a real commitment to ourselves to acknowledge that our actions, which in many cases are applauded by our culture, may be harmful to our well-being and that of our family. When we take personal responsibility for our actions we may stir up conflicting feelings. For example, if we leave some things undone at work so that we can spend more time with our family we may bring up our fear of failure, feelings of inadequacy and guilt and feeling out of control. We may also have to face relational problems in our home that we have ignored.

We have to make a commitment to risk feeling uncomfortable feelings if we are to take responsibility for our actions.

Responsibility to ourselves comes first

It is not possible to be really responsible to others without first being responsible to ourselves. When we are not being true to ourselves we are living a lie. It is our responsibility to state what we need and want. It takes courage to work through the barriers that prevent us from doing this and to recognize that we do have rights, even though we may not feel as if we do. Doing things we do not want to do out of unconscious fear or unconscious obligation results in ever-increasing resentment. The real obligation is to come from as clear and as present a place as possible. This means giving ourselves time and space to listen to ourselves in order to make conscious choices. Listening to ourselves is the beginning of a process in which we feel, integrate and connect to the pain that has held us back. Sometimes we may need help—a listening friend or a professional who will support us as we become accustomed to respecting and following our feelings.

Commitment to feel is taking responsibility

There is a popular notion that trying to heal the past is a way of remaining a victim forever. People are often criticized for their self-indulgence when they allow time for their feelings. In fact, taking the time and making the commitment to feel *is* taking responsibility for our lives. We are in danger of being stuck in blame and victimhood when we do not take the responsibility to work through old incomplete feelings. The "Me Generation" criticism does not make the distinction between looking after ourselves and being self-centred. There is a big difference! We are self-centred when we blindly carry our unmet need from our childhood into our adult life as a voracious need for things and attention. Following our feelings and connecting with our past is not about blame and self-indulgence; it is about dealing with the reality of what has happened to us in our life. The opposite of taking this kind of responsibility is the endless attempt to fill ourselves up with all manner of things, or to blame instead of feeling the pain of the real needs that were never met.

Learning to change

A common way to try to take responsibility is to learn to change our behaviour. All sorts of programs have been created to help individuals to be more successful in their personal lives. We appreciate when there is a positive change in behaviour in ourselves or in our partner, however we are often left with an uneasy sense of disconnection. Our changed behaviour may not last, and we may need to keep going back for reinforcement. We may remain locked in a split, being two people, constantly needing to coach ourselves. Learned change locks us in the rules of our lessons and keeps us acting rather than being who we are.

Letting go

Letting go of blame is an ongoing process. Every time we feel our need to blame and own it, we go through doors to our true feelings and activate our natural emotional healing power. Taking this kind of responsibility is what leads to lasting change. We can revolutionize our lives by taking charge of them in a deep emotional way. Even very aware people slip into blame from time to time. However, taking responsibility for our blaming as soon as we can helps us and our relationships. If we are willing to look at how we use blame to protect ourselves and to keep ourselves feeling in the right, we can begin to make a huge difference.

4

A LEAP OF FAITH

Learning to Use Our Natural Emotional Healing Power

I t requires a leap of faith to learn to use our natural emotional healing power, since everything our conditioning teaches us flies in the face of accepting and using this process. We have all been powerfully conditioned to deny and diminish our feelings.

The route to ourselves is through our feelings

We do not need to go to the Himalayas or an ashram in India to find ourselves. We have been right here inside ourselves all along. *The way we come to know ourselves is through our feelings.* Paying attention to all of them, feeling them and coming to accept them is how we come to know and accept ourselves. A simple concept, but not always an easy one. It is, however, a most worthwhile journey. Our natural emotional healing power is what leads us to ourselves.

Healing begins when we can identify our feelings

The first step toward emotional fitness is to learn to identify and acknowledge what we are feeling. This is not easy after a lifetime of limiting, redirecting and extinguishing feelings. We have difficulty identifying our feelings when there was no room given to them in the first place. The more we can acknowledge what we are feeling, the more we really know ourselves. The more often we connect back to painful incidents in our past, the more we relate positively to who we were as children. This is how we truly find ourselves.

Many of my clients have difficulty identifying how they feel now. They also have trouble identifying how they felt as children. When I ask about their childhood they will often simply say it was fine. When I ask how feelings were dealt with in their house they usually describe at least some degree of restriction, and more often considerable restriction. When asked, for example, "Who was allowed to express anger in your house?" it is a rare individual who answers "I was." Most clients readily say "Not me." In many homes parents even put a lid on happiness and exuberance. Looking at our childhood from the perspective of how feelings were dealt with in our house can give us immediate insight into ourselves and the restrictions that shaped our young lives.

No "should" to feelings

There are no "shoulds" to feelings, yet it is not uncommon for me to hear a client say "I don't know how I should feel about that." The real question is "How *do* you feel about that?" When we try to determine from the outside how we should feel we are on a slippery slope away from ourselves. Our disconnection from ourselves by the "shoulds" makes it difficult to listen to ourselves. We can treat the "should" as a red flag—an indicator that is asking us to listen more closely to ourselves in order to be more connected.

For those who are unable to articulate how they are feeling, it sometimes helps to have a list of feeling words to look at:

resentful	abandoned	crushed	shocked
disappointed	intimidated	defeated	lonely
frustrated	anxious	despairing	rejected
hurt	betrayed	helpless	tense
let down	worthless	hopeless	terrified
put down	confused	ignored	threatened
guilty	trapped	frantic	enraged
numb	dead	flat	angry
sad	ashamed	needy	depressed
regretful	joyful	peaceful	frozen
guilty	powerless	scared	panicky

It is a good idea from time to time to turn off the television, radio and computer and to focus on our solar plexus to discover what is going on there. *Feelings reside in us, in our bodies, and we can trust that when we are sensing something there it is important.* When we get into the habit of regularly tuning into ourselves we will become more and more familiar with what we are experiencing. It will take practice, for most of us have not been trained to feel and to share our feelings. If we tune into ourselves on our way home from work, for example, and acknowledge how we are feeling about what happened there, we will be less likely to dump our feelings from work on our family. We will be taking responsibility for our feelings. If they are too big and out of control, taking responsibility means protecting others by taking these feelings away from them. We have choice. Exercising that choice is being responsible.

Feeling through and connecting

As we are more and more able to identify our emotions we come to know ourselves better. What we need then is an opportunity to feel *through* the feelings. In order to do this we need to experience them as thoroughly as possible:

- Notice the feeling.
- Lie down in a darkened room and intensify the feeling. Let it get as big as it can be.
- Pay attention to what you are feeling and what you are sensing in your body.
- Stay inside the feeling, and experience it as deeply as you can.
- Stay with the feeling for as long as you can.
- Keep returning to the original trigger, the incident in the present that precipitated your feeling, in order to keep the feeling going.
- Have an imaginary confrontation with the person or persons involved.
- Speak out loud to these people who are not present. Say things more frankly than you would in real life. Speak from your gut.
- Record in a journal any insight or connections, or simply record a few words to describe the incident and the strong feelings evoked.

If you feel angry, intensify this feeling by looping a towel and hitting the bed, or punching or kicking a pillow, all the while speaking to the person who triggered your feelings. A short length of plastic plumbing pipe is a good thing to have on hand for whacking objects—your mattress, a cardboard box, a punching bag. There is no right or wrong way to do this; whatever works is the right way. People who have been abused physically often cannot hit, for example, but find support for feeling their anger by ripping magazines or phone books. The notion is often raised that giving expression to our anger in this way is harmful and makes the problem worse. Our anger is not an end in itself; rather it is necessary to give expression to held anger if we are to break through to the underlying feelings.

As we process our current feelings in this way we automatically connect with other past incidents when our feelings were similar, those knots of held feelings along the threads of our tapestry. When we feel these experiences we open to the grieving that heals.

From the present to the past

If, for example, we overreact to our child not listening to us, we can take our feelings to a place where he cannot hear us. We can speak out loud to him as if he were there. We can let our anger out. If we are transported back to a time when we were desperately trying to get our parents to listen to us, for example, we can speak out loud to them about their lack of attention. We stay with the feelings for as long as we can. When we do this, eventually we will be able to work through the feelings and connect the current feeling to the past event(s). Sometimes it takes a long while for connections to be made. This is when our faith in the process helps us to stay the course of feeling through our present feelings to the source that makes them so over or undercharged. When we process feelings in this way they lose their intensity, and in due time we notice that our child's inattention is no longer such a big trigger. Then we will likely automatically communicate more effectively with our child and he or she will more likely listen to us.

If we are unable to take this process very far on our own it is important to realize that this inability is related to the origins of our pain and to the lack of support for our feelings. We were alone with our original traumas. The adults around us did not know, and in some cases did not care, that we needed support to feel through our feelings and discharge them completely. They may not have understood at all what we needed to be emotionally healthy. It is crucial to our healing that we acknowledge that whatever we are able to do or not do on our own is related to the extent of the damage we have suffered. Whatever we are able to do is an important step toward being completely in charge of our lives, even if it is just starting to notice and to name our feelings. *Giving a name to feelings is empowering, whereas to deny our feelings is to deny ourselves.*

Self-acceptance and self-esteem

We are often given the advice that we should accept ourselves more; we should work at improving our self-esteem. It is said that we need to love ourselves and accept ourselves before we can love others. These are common bits of wisdom. The real question is, exactly how do we do this? The answer is that we use our natural healing power.

There is no way we can flick a switch and suddenly accept ourselves more or feel better about ourselves. Many have advised affirmations and activities that bring a sense of achievement. Affirmations seem to be, for the most part, a way to push away negative feelings, to keep them at bay. Clearly this runs counter to my suggestion that we go into our negative feelings again and again, with deliberation, until we connect deeply enough with the source of these unfortunate feelings to shift how we feel by integrating our pain.

When we are desperate to keep the old, worthless, not-good-enough feelings away we may try to feel better about ourselves by achieving more. However, the flood of good feelings that any new achievement brings is short-lived, and we then have to find yet another challenge to boost our ego. This can be exhausting and can lead to burnout instead of contentment and a sense of fulfillment. So many clients say "I just want some peace." The peace they are seeking is a sense of being okay inside themselves; they want to feel good enough about themselves so that they can just relax!

We gain true self-acceptance when we have connected enough with ourselves, with all of what makes us who we are, and with the traumas of our past that have been held firmly within us waiting to be felt. "Connected enough" means enough so that we have empathy for the person we are now and for how we became who we are. This is often very difficult for those who learned to hate and despise themselves as children.

Noted author Alice Miller points out that a child in an abusive family is worse off than adult prisoners in a concentration camp, since the child cannot identify her parents as being wrong while at least the prisoners know their abusers are wrong. Some abused children begin to see how "crazy" their parents are as they get into their teens; others go on believing that their parents are only doing what they have to do because they, the children, are so "bad." Young children automatically fix the blame on themselves when their parents do not take responsibility for their own shortcomings.

The idea that children deserve to be hit, yelled at and put down is prevalent in our society. Individuals who themselves have been hit and verbally abused as children and who believe they deserved what they got carry this belief staunchly forward. A new survey has been released in the United States that says ninety percent of parents hit their children. A radio announcer commenting on this said to her colleague on the program, "I was spanked, weren't you? . . . But I deserved it!" A person who has felt his or her own early pain would not believe that a child deserved to be hit for any reason.

As we use our triggers to go back to heal those knots of unfelt feelings in our tapestry, we connect again and again with the young person we were. We begin to understand more and more that whatever we did we were doing the best we could under the circumstances. Continuing to feel what it was really like for us back then is what changes our sense of ourselves. We connect with the magnificent spirit we have that allowed us to survive and that will continue to help us to thrive. It is a major turning point in therapy when we begin to like or admire the child we were. This cannot be forced; it has to come when it comes.

The source of true self-acceptance and steady self-esteem is in the connection to, and understanding of, our younger selves. As well as childhood traumas there are always events later in our lives that we may regret, for example an abortion that has caused us to live for years with self-hatred or a sense of missed opportunities. These later wounds are also healed as we connect with who we were then and where we came from. When we know from the inside what it was really like for us we do not use this as an excuse for whatever we have done; instead we acknowledge it as the truth and set about genuinely grieving, feeling our remorse and regret. This is how we stop blaming ourselves, take responsibility and heal. It is a practised balance between taking responsibility and having empathy for ourselves.

The kind of self-acceptance and self-esteem that follows from doing this work cannot be taken away from us. We come to know and care for ourselves. We may make mistakes in the future because we are human, but these mistakes will not plunge us into the depths of despair and into another cycle of self-doubt and self-hatred. We will really be able to see our mistakes as an opportunity to learn—just as the books say we "should"!

Better the devil we know

Fear of something worse happening to us if we try to make a change may immobilize us. A woman fears her marriage will end if she confronts her husband with how she is feeling; a man fears his son will reject him if he stops accommodating his every wish; a child does not tell his mother about the schoolyard tyrant because he is afraid the bullying will increase; a young woman does not confront her boss's unwelcome touching because she knows there are twelve others who would love her job.

Having the courage to risk focusing on how we really feel starts the cooperation our natural healing power requires. It involves a leap of faith to risk working through our fear and to trust that the process will lead us to ourselves and our best course of action. Risking change is less formidable as we become more centred in ourselves.

Fear of feeling deeply

In their initial therapy session many clients have expressed that they are afraid of what they will discover if they delve into themselves. This is not surprising. Children who have not been allowed the free expression of their feelings come to fear that what they are holding inside is "bad." For example, as little children who cannot show our anger because we are afraid of disapproval, rejection and sometimes physical pain we come to believe that there is something wrong with us and that our feelings are dangerous. Yet the feelings do not disappear; as adults we must hold our breath and tense our body to ensure the feelings do not escape. Others fear that if we try to get in touch with our feelings we may discover there is nothing there at the centre at all, no real self. It takes courage to label this fear and use it to start the process of really feeling.

Going to the deeper levels

It also takes time to touch into the deep well of our held feelings, and to do it again and again until we have freer access to them. It is truly a journey of experience—one that we were previously unable to feel and to integrate safely on our own.

We lie down on our backs with uncrossed legs, breathe deeply and become aware of our bodies and where we are holding. We will likely feel most vulnerable in this position, but we will be most open to our feelings this way. We allow ourselves to let whatever thoughts or memories rise and we stay with them as long as we can. We feel whatever feeling is there and trust that this is what must be felt first. Often we need to let go of preconceived ideas of what we should feel in order to do this. Whatever presents itself to us, whether we like it or not, will take us where we need to go. The more experience we have with this process the more we will trust ourselves and what we are feeling.

We may experience feelings with words or without. Feelings may erupt, giving voice to early childhood sounds. We try to make sounds that match our feelings, no matter how awkward this may feel.

We may experience strong physical sensations, often without feeling at first. We need to trust these sensations and allow ourselves to take any position we want. We stay with these sensations, focusing on them and breathing into them. This is when we often experience a shift to reliving an early pain-filled original trauma. This experience will need to be visited again and again until we have felt and connected with it enough to integrate it. We no longer need to keep it split off from our consciousness.

Fear accompanies us as we go deeper into our past. We may have the strongest sense of wanting to flee as we open to feelings we have been afraid to feel. It is important that we not act on this, but rather allow ourselves to feel the fear and stay with it. Trusting that all our feelings are coming from within, and that they have their roots in the traumas of our early life, gives us the courage to stay with them and to experience them.

It takes time for us to connect with the scenes of childhood in which we had to conceal our feelings, even from ourselves. Our defenses, when trusted, will let go at a pace that allows us to integrate what we are feeling. Sometimes this seems glacially slow. At other times there is a great cleaving as an iceberg of pain releases from the face of holding. When we feel stuck, focusing on how defended we feel and staying with that will release a flood of hurt from our past—and we will move into the very zone we were held back from.

In order to unlock the doors of unconscious behaviour it is necessary to process deeply, to use our natural emotional healing power to reconnect at the most profound level. It is an enormous gift to be able to heal ourselves of such deep trauma. One client of mine repeatedly put his back up against the wall. Eventually he remembered and relived his father holding him against a wall, his father's hands around his neck. One client would scream "mommy mommy" and then abruptly cut off all sound. He was reliving exactly what happened to him when his mother beat him; as a child, he knew the only way to get the beating to stop was to stop showing any response to it.

In my own therapy, I stayed for many sessions with a feeling of discomfort about the new house we were having built. I stayed with the really uncomfortable embarrassment I was feeling when people commented on it. Eventually I broke through to the memory of my mother saying "You don't deserve that, Janice Ross. Shame on you." This connection led to a flood of early feelings and insights about how this early shaming had left me feeling unentitled and how it had affected me all my life. This also explained why I felt so much better using my married name, which was a very different explanation from the one I had given myself before whenever I tried to "figure out" why I disliked hearing my maiden name.

Proceeding at our own speed is very important. If we are pushed where we are not ready to go we will not integrate what we are discovering about ourselves and will most likely shut down against too much pain all at once. What is important is that we keep giving ourselves the opportunity to open up to our pain. If we do this we will eventually connect with its source and gradually feel it through. We will feel free inside and have more clarity to make good choices for ourselves.

I am not saying we *should* be able to do this on our own. What I am saying is that every step we take in this direction will count toward us knowing ourselves better and accepting ourselves more. Almost certainly we will discover whether we need someone we can count on to be there with us while we feel. This may or may not be a professional, but she or he needs to be someone who will simply listen, who will not interfere and with whom we feel safe.

When we realize we are suffering we can consciously choose to move toward emotional well-being. We can use as many opportunities as possible to acknowledge what is going on inside us, to recognize when we are more open, to pay attention to unfinished business that is pressing, and to risk changing. *It is by deliberately setting out to notice our reactions, our body tensions and our feelings that we cooperate with our natural emotional healing power.*

Patti was depressed, overwhelmed with anxiety and feeling suicidal. Her psychiatrist changed her medication and suggested that she practise "thinking positively." This advice drove Patti further into the depths of despair, since she thought she should be able to do this, and tried and tried but could not. Too many people told Patti she had nothing to feel so anxious and bad about, but she knew how she was feeling. She wanted to take a leap of faith and believe that she had the ability to heal.

If it worked in the long run it would be easier to buck ourselves up with inspirational sayings, affirmations and a thought change. However, there is no quick fix. I encouraged Patti to choose the more difficult path: to use her energy to know herself better, work on solving the puzzle of her life, and become a more feeling than defended person.

Insight and cognitive knowing are not enough

Many forms of therapy are based on gaining insight, and this is why so many people have felt that therapy has not really helped them. Understanding why we feel or behave the way we do does feel somewhat better, but this is not enough. Knowing and understanding do not relieve us of uncomfortable feelings, nor do they relieve us of the need to be defended against pain, for we cannot get *over* painful feelings until we get *into* them—an unfamiliar and scary idea for many people. We can feel fully all the experiences that have moulded us. We can feel through the pain until its intensity lessens, until the day we notice that we are no longer triggered by this person or that event. This kind of inside knowing builds on itself and gives us a powerful sense of ourselves.

Opening up and getting clear

One client said, "My life goes by in a blur!" We may live our lives skimming the surface, wondering why we do the things we do and feel the way we do. Becoming more clear is the goal of all work toward emotional fitness; that is, opening to ourselves and feeling what is going on inside.

We can notice the times in our lives when we are naturally opened up, and use these times to help ourselves feel and heal. For women, one of these times is when we are premenstrual. Instead of understanding that the huge feelings that can surface at this time are coming from inside the individual, our culture has turned this time into a syndrome and a disease. It certainly can be a time of dis-ease, but those feelings are not coming from outer space; they are coming from inside us, and they definitely mean something. It is important to listen to what our feelings are telling us at this time. We can plan our lives so that we can take some time when we are premenstrual to give ourselves the gift of going with our feelings. Christiane Northrup in her book *Women's Bodies, Women's Wisdom* tells us how one of her patients "came to see that the emotional crash that she experienced pre-menstrually each month actually was forcing her to peel off the layers of denial in her life."

Very often the birth of our child will open us to our unresolved pain. It may be labelled "post-partum depression" when we depress the feelings that are trying to come up and "post-partum psychosis" when our feelings bubble up out of control. A friend of mine once said that it took having a baby for her to find out what an angry person she was. As fathers we can be triggered into old, disturbing feelings, such as inadequacy and super-responsibility, and we can use these feelings to heal.

Menopause is another phenomenon in women's lives that is often used against us; when "this time in our life" is seen as a syndrome or a disease, it is another way to diminish all women. However, menopause presents another opportunity for us to notice feelings that come up and it gives us a chance to allow these feelings to teach us about ourselves. I have noticed that people who regularly process their feelings do not suffer huge mood swings during their menopausal years.

The approach of a fortieth or fiftieth birthday is a time when both men and women may open more, a time we can use to our advantage if we choose to explore what our feelings are about. Any kind of loss, such as divorce or loss of a job, wrenches us open. The death of a parent or any close person does the same. Just being tired can be a time of opening. No doubt you have heard the well-meaning words, "You're just upset because you're tired." The truth is you are upset because you are upset; you just know it better now because you are tired.

If we know that loss makes us more open we can use this time of grieving to heal the current *and* the earlier losses. It is disturbing that many people are being encouraged to take drugs to avoid their feelings even when it is a normal human loss they have suffered. In this way our natural emotional healing power is subverted. No matter what the loss, it needs to be felt. I recall a client whose husband had died six months previously. Sheila had been told by her general practitioner that she should see a psychiatrist since she still did not seem to be over the death of her life partner. The psychiatrist told her that she would be on antidepressants for life because she had a chemical imbalance. Sheila decided she did not like this life sentence and came to me to start working through her grief. She was ashamed that she had not finished grieving, since so many people seemed to expect that she "should" be.

When someone dies it is not just the immediate loss of this person that must be dealt with; it is also a coming to terms with the whole of this relationship and what it has meant to us. Instead of putting on a brave face and saying the usual platitudes—"Well, at least now he's at rest"—it would be better to go to bed for three days, to really sink into our sorrow. This would be a good start. For no matter how big or how small the loss, it is important to give ourselves room to grieve. Transitions in our children's lives need to be felt when they happen so that when our children leave home we will have been conscious all along of their lives moving on and will not be overcome by inordinate loss.

Many people dismiss their feelings by saying "I shouldn't feel this way; this happens to everyone." What they do not realize is that *everyone* would benefit from allowing their feelings. Divorce means much more than the loss of a partner; we must grieve for the loss of a dream, and the hope and expectation for that relationship. Any losses will remind us of all the other losses we have suffered. The sorrow of each needs to be felt through.

Risk to heal

It is possible to get stuck in our feelings if we do not take risks to change our behaviour. We behave the way we do because that is what has protected us from experiencing uncomfortable feelings; a bully bullies, for example, because she or he has learned to do so in order not to feel vulnerable. We can consciously decide not to bully and instead allow ourselves to feel the vulnerability. If we are the victim, we may decide to stand up to the bully and confront her or him about the way we are being mistreated. This will mean feeling our fear and connecting to earlier fears. *We cannot heal without risking change and risking feeling.*

What feeling is stopping me?

When we find ourselves unable to change we can ask ourselves, "What feeling is stopping me when I do not take the risk I would like to take, when I do not speak with my own voice, when I do not tell someone something I really need to say?" When we connect with the feeling that is stopping us we can start to work it through. Often we will find that this feeling is some form of fear: fear of rejection, fear of the other person's anger, or fear of their withdrawal. These fears are from the past. As soon as we are able to label them we can work with them, feel their intensity and connect them to their source. When we feel them at their source enough so that they become integrated into our conscious knowing, they lose their grip on us. They are part of the history of our life, but they no longer govern it.

It is time to take back what is ours: our ability to use our natural emotional healing power. It is not possible to do this work incorrectly; we just need to give ourselves the room we need.

5

TURNING THE KEY

Supportive Activities That Help Us Engage Our Natural Emotional Healing Power

There are many activities that can help us learn to listen to ourselves, to open to our experience and to process our feelings. These activities are useful because they help us slip by our normal censors to access feelings that we are keeping hidden from ourselves.

Journal writing

Writing feelings in a journal can help enormously. There are many ways to do this, and each of us needs to find what works best for us. Some of us find that if we write about how we are feeling as a stream of consciousness, without censoring or even stopping to dot the i's, it really moves us along in the healing process. Others keep a log of feeling phrases, particularly ones that we repeat, until we really notice them (for example, "How could I be so stupid," "What's wrong with me," "What an idiot").

When we write in our journal it is helpful to express all our feelings. If we feel embarrassed or ashamed of what we have written, we write that too. We write about our judgment of ourselves, even our anger that we have been asked to do this writing. This exercise is for us, and it is important that we honour ourselves by starting exactly where we are, no matter where that may be.

When we reread our journal we will identify patterns. This is helpful for seeing how we avoid our feelings and get stuck in our defenses. For example, we may see how we are beating ourselves up all the time or that we are constantly finding fault globally, blaming "them."

Writing in a journal is similar to having a good listening friend: we can pour everything out without fear of judgment, interfering advice or dampening reassurance. However, because we are not censoring it is important that we feel safe about our journal and know that no one else is going to see it. We need to find a very secure place for it—if necessary, a metal box with a key or a computer with a fail-safe password.

There is a potential trap in journal writing. We may use it as another means of "getting our feelings off," without risking being honest with ourselves. We may stay stuck in blame or self-blame. For example, if we use our journal only to "bitch" and "gripe" about others or continually put ourselves down, then we stay stuck. If we are stuck in this way we can recognize our need to blame or self-blame and write about this. We can acknowledge that this is our defense. We can become more aware of it in our lives, and we can begin to explore and feel the threat that is driving the blame. We become open to the feelings that are being obscured, protecting us from our hurt.

Collages, clay modelling, painting, crayoning

Any expressive activity that helps us connect with our feelings can be very useful. I have known people who have made a colouring book of their early years and others who have depicted their feelings in a drawing journal. Drawing with our non-dominant hand can connect us with our child state and reveal feelings that otherwise are not readily accessible. The very process of expressing ourselves using any of these methods frees feelings normally held in place with rationalizing thoughts. These modalities can be a direct current into ourselves, free from the constrictions of explanations and "knowing." However, we need to keep in mind that although we might reveal our core in our expression, integration happens slowly as we feel and connect.

Developing a time line

Having a clear, chronological picture of our life from birth to the present is very helpful. A personal time line consists of a record of events that have had significance for us, as well as some comments about what we remember of our feelings connected to these events. Clients find that their time line often triggers feelings that can be starting points for many therapy sessions.

Sometimes clients feel badly because they do not remember much. It is impossible to do this exercise incorrectly. Even forgetting is important information—it reveals how much we have of ourselves. I suggest that in creating a time line an equal space be given to each year of your life, even though many of these may remain blank. One client was sure he knew how long he had suffered the bullying of his stepfather before he left home. In doing his time line he was shocked to discover that he had contracted his sense of time. He had always believed that he had been in this situation for only eight years, when the facts revealed that it was twelve.

There may be information that we cannot remember ourselves and want to get from other family members or friends. This in itself is a process, as we sometimes have to feel our way through to being able to ask for it.

Writing an autobiography

Writing an autobiography is a helpful exercise that follows quite naturally from the time line. Writing the story of our life allows us to open up to significant memories and more importantly to the feelings they engender. This can be done in many different ways: we can start with the whole story, writing chronologically from beginning to end; we can write about especially traumatic time periods; we can try writing about a period in our life that we do not remember very well; or we can write about chunks of our life such as our teenage years. We can write about: after-school time, bedtime, mealtime, our birthday, Christmas, Hanukkah, or other celebrations, what we frequently saw on our mother's face, what we frequently saw on our father's face, who was allowed to be angry in our family, when we felt carefree as a child, what happened when we cried, what happened when we were afraid, what happened when we were exuberant, who made the rules and what could not be talked about in our house. We can list the admonitions we remember, and the name-calling, ridiculing and put-downs we endured. We can write about anyone who helped and supported us as a child. We can write about how we felt if a sibling was favoured or abused. We can make a diagram of our extended family and use colours to express how we felt about these people. We can write about our resentments, regrets and our fears. We can write about what we had to give up in order to keep our parents' love.

We do all these things to help us feel how we felt as things happened to us in our lives.

Writing letters that we do not send

Writing letters that we do not send is a superb way to pour out uncensored feelings. When we know no one will be reading the letter we can allow the feelings to be as big as they really are. Even if the person is dead, that need not stop us from writing a much-needed letter. If we feel blocked in the process because of old feelings of fear of confronting this person, we can simply incorporate the feelings of fear in the letter without stopping the writing.

Sometimes we end up sending a letter to the person involved, but that is usually after we have written a number of letters that we have not sent. In this way we have processed through the big feelings and have become very clear about what we actually want and need to say in the present.

I make the following suggestions to clients: write to people whom you still have feelings about—anyone with whom you have unfinished business. Pour out your feelings, give yourself time to cry and rage and do whatever else you need to do to acknowledge and feel the bigness of the feelings. As you write you may become very clear about your need to actually confront someone who has abused you in some way in the past, or you may feel the need to apologize to someone whom you have hurt in some way. There are no rules. It is up to you to decide if this confrontation or this apology is something you need to do to complete things. If this is hard to know, keep listening to yourself and continue working through the feelings. Maybe you will decide you can finish with this matter without the confrontation, as the person in question may not be able to hear it anyway.

Some therapists insist that a confrontation with an abuser is necessary to heal. This insistence is misplaced. The decision is entirely up to the individual—we are our own best experts. When we rush to confront we often cut short the feeling process needed to complete internal integration of what it was like to have suffered as a child. Confrontation before enough processing has been completed will be an act-out of old anger that will keep us stuck in anger and self-righteousness.

Finding like-minded people to be with

It helps to become involved with others who understand the importance of feeling feelings and who know how to listen. This is real support. If our pattern has been to be with people who do not support us or who criticize us just as our parents did, we can risk not seeing them, or we can confront those who fit the old pattern and find out if they have the capacity to change and grow.

As many people do not know or understand what real support is, I have devised a list to help my clients remember how to request it:

> Please just listen to me.
> I do not need you to fix me or solve my problem for me.
> I am my own best problem solver.
> It helps me to process my feelings when you just listen.
> It moves me along toward my own resolution when I feel you are trying to understand what I am feeling.
> You do not need to agree with me.
> I would like you to allow me my feelings.
> My feelings are not right or wrong, they just are.
> If you cannot listen now, please just say so.

Finding support through reading

Reading is one way we know we are not alone. Reading other people's stories, fiction or non-fiction, can help by giving us further permission to feel and process our feelings. *When we are triggered by what we read we can acknowledge that it has some personal meaning for us, and we can give ourselves permission to feel.*

Using our dreams

Our dreams are usually triggered by something that has happened in our very recent past and is plugging us into old feelings. The greater the number of knots of held feelings in our tapestry the more easily we will be triggered. Our natural emotional healing power is at work.

Our dreams, and especially the feelings in our dreams, can be used to create opportunities to heal. If we stay with an image from our dream we will become aware of the underlying feeling. We begin to make sense of the dream by staying with this feeling. We can always trust it to be right because it is coming from our tapestry; it reflects our buried needs and our buried feelings.

We do the same thing at night in our dreams as we do in our waking life; we try to explain away our feelings. We may think that our bizarre, terrible dream made us afraid. It is more likely that our deep and old fear caused us to make up a bizarre story to explain it. Our dreams are recreating our early pain in an attempt to heal it; they allow us to recapture the pain—anxiety, fear, anger, terror and hurt—of the original situation. The dream is giving us a chance for healing through connection and integration.

When we wake up out of a dream we are still in our feelings. The dream can disappear in a flash, but if we do wake up aware of our dream we can learn to stay still and go inside of it, to stay right in the dream, to stay with the feelings as long as we can. If we do not remember that we have even been dreaming it is wise to lie in bed for some time and go inside to see what sensations or feelings we can identify, for example, a knot in our stomach, a tenseness in our limbs, a squeezing in our chest or a sexual sensation. It is helpful to record the feelings from dreams in our journal.

Our dreams act out for us at night and we can become alert to them and feel the feelings that they contain. Symbols in dreams come from repressed or subverted feelings; losing things in a dream, for example, could be the symbol that recreates the feeling of having lost our father at an early age. However, *analyzing dreams will not make the feelings go away, and understanding symbols will not help us fundamentally change our lives; feeling our feelings is what really makes a difference.*

Recurring dreams are of particular significance. Our organism is determined to complete the feelings of our traumas. It keeps presenting them to us in the form of our recurring dream. If we wish to connect and integrate these feelings we can stay with the recurring dream as long as possible. We can take the time to process the feelings that are stirred up in order to make connections to their primary source so that we can integrate them into our lives.

Photographs and memorabilia

Old photographs can help us remember what it felt like to be a child, an adolescent and a younger person. We can notice how people are placed in the photographs, what the expressions are on their faces, what their body language is saying or not saying. Most important, we can note how we feel when we look at these pictures.

It is a good idea to choose pictures from different stages of our life—significant pictures that we are drawn to. We can place these pictures where we can see them on a daily basis. When we are triggered into deep feelings by something in our lives, we can look at these pictures and know that the strength of our feelings stretches all the way back to the little person that we were.

Any memorabilia that we have can also be used to help us get back into that child or younger person we were. Report cards are especially interesting and may trigger strong feelings. We can look at pictures we drew, projects we did, things we made—all these things can bring back feelings from long ago.

Former homes

We can visit former homes, schools, churches and districts. We can draw floor plans of places where we lived and use colours to express how we felt in the different rooms. We can pay attention especially to places that we remember as significant. We can notice when we do not remember what our home was like. The idea here is to get into the skin of the younger person we were and to remember how we felt.

Art, drama and music

Any activity may trigger feelings worthy of our attention and it is helpful to allow ourselves as much room as possible for feelings stirred up by a painting, a dramatic moment or a piece of music. Because a poignant film may present an opportunity to open, it is unfortunate that most of us do not feel free to cry at the movies; too often an evocative scene becomes a time to shut down harder because of shame and embarrassment. We would likely feel more comfortable allowing ourselves to get into feelings stirred up by a scene from a video movie at home.

Perhaps we already recognize what music stirs feelings in us and we can take this opportunity to risk following our feelings and allowing them to be as big as they are. We can deliberately play that music.

We can give ourselves permission to allow any feeling response we have to a painting to emerge. We often subdue ourselves in an art gallery rather than respond.

Our body

Anything that helps us open to our body also helps us open to our feelings and ourselves. Yoga or gently exercising to music may provide a means for this process.

Since repressed feelings become locked in our bodies it can be helpful to have therapeutic massage. A massage helps us feel where our body is armoured, where we are holding feelings. It is wise to choose a massage therapist who is quiet, who will not be upset if we cry and who will not interpret our experience for us. The massage may bring up feelings, so it is important to allow some time afterwards to stay with any feelings that may have emerged. If we do not give ourselves this time there is a danger that we may unconsciously push down harder to control any feelings dislodged by the massage. It would be unwise to continue to have our feelings triggered if we then continue to shut them down.

There are therapists who work with the body deliberately to dislodge feelings. My concern is that when feelings are pried open in this manner we may not be ready to feel them in a way that allows them to be integrated.

We can acknowledge that body pains—whether they be headaches, back pain, indigestion or a myriad of other symptoms—are connected to held-in feelings. We can use them as doors to go through to our feelings. We can lie quietly and focus on the painful area. We can let ourselves express in words what our pain is saying, for example, "Get off my back," "You're a pain in the neck," "You make me sick." One client said, "I gave myself headaches so I wouldn't feel my heartache."

It is helpful when we are caught going around and around in our heads to deliberately pull our attention down to our body. We can then focus on what feeling messages are coming from within. This takes practice.

Meditation

Meditation that opens us to ourselves is useful; meditation that is used to get control of feelings and suppress them is not. Some leaders of meditation groups take clients to their past, and when feelings come up insufficient attention is paid to them. Some clients may be unsettled for days, not knowing how to deal with what they are feeling. As a general rule I would say that it is better to trust ourselves, to listen to ourselves and to observe our feelings—our overreactions and underreactions—rather than be constrained by some specific time period set by someone else's notion of where we need to go.

There are often groups that form around an activity such as meditation. It is unwise to allow ourselves to bleed off feelings of never having had a loving family by forming a pseudo-family in such a group. Inauthentic hugging and false comfort masquerading as support will, in fact, keep us from feeling what we can feel with real support. When we feel the deprivation from our past we can build authentic relationships in the present.

Prayer

Making a quiet time for prayer allows many people the space to open to themselves and to their experience. It may be a place where pain can be acknowledged.

Language

Many of us perpetuate our disconnection from our feelings by not speaking in the first person. We say things like "When your mother upsets you by being so demanding what are you supposed to do?" When we notice ourselves doing this we can change it to "When my mother upsets me by being so demanding what am I supposed to do?" If we habitually distance ourselves from our feelings by speaking in the second person ("You") we can help ourselves to own our feelings by switching to the first person ("I").

We unconsciously incorporate clues to our pain in our choice of words and metaphors. Language is very close to our feelings. We can help ourselves by becoming conscious of what we are saying. For example, we might incorporate feeding metaphors in our everyday language: "That show just left me hungry for so much more," "This music feeds my soul," "I have a taste for the good life." This kind of awareness can be a door to the underlying nature of our pain. In this example we can feel our hunger and wherever that leads us to in our past.

Noticing our defensive reactions

It is important for us to become good self-observers. We can notice our reactions and can become aware if we are struggling in some way or shutting down. We can make a list in our journal of our common defensive responses and of our common ways of not being honest. We can notice that we are in denial, for example, when we make excuses, when we justify or rationalize what happened to us, when we discount the real impact that events had on us, or when we know what happened but want to believe that it is irrelevant to our life.

Feeling like a child

We can notice and pay close attention to anything that makes us feel like the small child we once were.

All the suggestions in this chapter are to help us engage our natural emotional healing power. They increase our awareness as a step toward feeling and healing. They are not ends in themselves, but rather means to the end of integrating our experience and becoming more emotionally fit. Each of us can find our own best way of listening to ourselves and connecting with our feelings.

Part II
Doors to Go Through

Too often we see our feelings as locked doors, places with no exit. But feelings are in fact doors to go through. We have been conditioned to contain, control, deny and put down feelings. When our feeling doors are wrenched open old held feelings surface rapidly, and we feel "crazy" and terrified not knowing what is happening. When we understand that these are accumulated feelings that are crying to be felt through, we can treat them differently. We can accept them instead of trying to clamp down on them.

Many of us have not known how to learn from our feelings. We have not experienced them as normal and healthy, and because of this we have stunted our natural emotional healing power. When we consciously take back this power and use it to learn to live with our feelings as an essential part of our lives, we increase our personal power and live more fully.

I have chosen the topics that follow because they describe feelings and defenses that need to be attended to in order to become a more integrated person.

It is important to understand that feelings can be used as defenses. For instance, anger can help us defend against grief, hurt or fear, while hurt at other times can help us defend against our anger.

We have a chance to engage our natural emotional healing power when we are willing to acknowledge and face the feelings that our defensive behaviour patterns cover. Repetitively struggling and continually avoiding are examples of such defensive patterns. Our unreal hope constantly energizes these patterns and keeps them locked in our lives. Riding on hope that someone else will change is an example of this.

Honest recognition of our feelings and our defenses is the key to opening doors into ourselves. Only then can we feel and integrate our unfelt experiences so that we do not need to keep them a secret. When we no longer have to keep our feelings disconnected, we no longer have the need to act out what we cannot feel. The more we recognize and then feel a defense, the more opportunity we have to feel what is being defended against—feel it and incorporate it as a conscious thread in the tapestry of our lives.

6

NEED

Unmet Childhood Need, Unconscious Adult Pain

Need is not a word that people use to identify what they are feeling, and yet *unmet need* is the driving force behind our most troublesome, disconnected behaviours. We eat, drink, work, gamble and buy to excess, for example, in order to assuage our old, unmet need.

We experience inappropriate needs as adults if our childhood needs were not met. The acting out of these unmet needs makes it difficult to know, let alone fulfill, our genuine present needs. For example, acting out our need for approval in the present keeps us asking ourselves what we *should* do instead of *what we really need or want to do.*

Unrealistic expectations, arising from our unconscious, unmet needs, damage our relationships when we expect people in our current lives to give us what we should have got from our parents: unconditional love, acceptance, knowing who we are and what we need. In order to take responsibility for our lives and for improving them, it is essential to identify our unrealistic needs, own them as ours, and feel them through to their source. This engages our natural emotional healing power and is an *ongoing* process. It allows us to more readily know what is a healthy, realistic and present need instead of confusing it with the unmet need that is erupting from the past. For example, needing our friend to be available to do things with us all the time, or to be aware and caring about our needs all the time, would be an old need from the past and unrealistic in the present.

It is difficult to acknowledge our need in our culture because we have misconstrued it as a weakness. Many of us are ashamed to ask anyone for help with anything. Because of this it usually takes quite a while for us to be able to use the words "my need" or "I'm feeling needy" to identify openly what we are feeling. Need can make us feel exposed, vulnerable and anxious. We are actually blaming and shaming ourselves for being human when we see need as a sign of inadequacy. Need is a natural part of the human condition and acknowledging it is emotionally healthy.

Children are labelled as misbehaving in our culture when what they are doing is totally reacting, instinctively trying to get their needs met. We would help children a lot if we could see their so-called "misbehaviour" as their bid to have their needs met. It may not be possible to meet our children's needs every time. However, the important need we can meet is to treat them with respect, allow their expression of need and allow any feelings that arise if the need cannot be met at that time. Our children will not have to act out or "misbehave" when we allow them their free expression of need.

Our inability to identify ourselves as needy or as feeling a need strengthens and perpetuates our cultural ignorance about meeting the needs of children. When we cannot feel what it was like to have been a needy child we cannot comprehend the needs of children in general. There is a vicious cycle here; if we are carrying around unmet, unconscious need from our childhood, it is difficult for us to acknowledge and meet our children's needs or subscribe to the idea that children *have* legitimate, enormous needs.

Hating and denying our need and losing ourselves

Dave worked long hours in his job as a plumber. He had long ago surpassed all his goals of having a nice home with a swimming pool in a nice part of town and two up-to-date vehicles in his driveway. He enjoyed being his own boss and was proud of his success. He felt comfortable at work. The part of Dave's life that was not successful was his relationship with his wife and his children. Dave did not really have any close relationships, for that matter. He could banter with his customers, but he could not let anyone get close to him.

When his marriage was in real jeopardy he entered therapy because his wife wanted him to. This was an incredibly scary thing for Dave to do. He had carefully protected himself since childhood by not revealing himself and not needing anyone, but now he was caught between losing his marriage and doing a "wimpy" thing like entering therapy. His marriage won out and he agreed to the first appointment.

He was shocked when he burst into tears after he was asked how it felt to keep himself so distant from his wife and children.

Dave began to realize that he had never been held as a child. He could not remember ever slipping his hand into his dad's or sitting on his mother's knee. He had been humiliated many times at school by bigger boys who called him a suck. When he had been attacked by a bully and came home with a bleeding nose his dad had said "No son of mine will take that from anyone." He was expected to go back and fight, but he could not. Dave became determined to keep to himself and not need anything. As he connected more and more to how he had needed to shut down, he was able to open up more and more to his wife and children.

Our culture abounds with need substitutes. Our need to identify with sports teams and their personalities and our adulation of movie, TV and rock stars are based on our need substitutes. Needs in these areas are considered appropriate, or at least harmless. However, they all keep us from our real selves. *To know our real need is to know who we are. To deny our need is to lose ourselves.*

It is in our childhood that we grow distant from our need and from ourselves. We learn at an early age that what we need is most often very unacceptable. Our need is for time and touching, freedom and curiosity, attention and empathetic understanding, and just plain acceptance of who we are at any given moment. Who we are may have been a hungry, tired, bored, scared or exuberant child. If those upon whom we depended fairly consistently met our needs with acceptance, then we probably felt that it was okay to have our feelings and needs and to be who we were. As adults we then would feel okay in having our feelings and needs, and they would be appropriate. When we do not have this kind of experience on a consistent basis we hide our feelings and needs so that we can continue to gain the approval of our parents. We begin to believe that our feelings are "bad" and that needing our parents' time and attention is unacceptable. We cover up our real needs with demands for substitutes and find unhealthy ways to try to meet them.

> Jim hated his need, but as a teenager he was driven to meet it. He mastur-bated obsessively and ate until he was obese. In his family he was expected to take care of possible business at his stepfather's gas pump and confec-tionery bar—seven days a week from nine in the morning until nine at night—all summer long.

> As a successful professional and the father of two young children Jim found himself experiencing unexplained moments of "blackness." This took him into therapy.

In his therapy Jim connected to the silent hatred he held for his stepfather and how he hated himself for not standing up to this bully. It took a long time, and a lot of feeling, for him to acknowledge that there had been a complete absence of support for him to stand up to his stepfather. In his family any need shown by him was greeted with irritation. He began to feel how he had hated his need; he believed there was something wrong with him for masturbating. He had protected himself by not needing anyone.

Jim began the slow process of accepting who he was and came to the feeling/ understanding that his need was not a "bad" thing and that *he* was not "bad" for needing. He came to re-experience how anxious he had felt each and every day and how he had had to relieve this unbearable anxiety with masturbation.

Jim continued to give himself time to feel his early deprivation again and again, and the blackness abated.

Another way we learn to hate and deny our need occurs when we are called "selfish," when even our wanting is denied.

> Debra said she could not remember ever asking for anything when she was a child. She began to remember how many times she was called "selfish" despite this, and how in her adult life she'd do anything to avoid this label. She got the message as a child that she was not entitled to even ask for what she wanted. Every Christmas she did get to ask for a present, but her parents had more than once played a cruel game of pretending it was not

under the tree and then pulling it out when her devastating sense of disappointment was well underway. She had been bewildered and robbed of joy.

Parents often make their children feel shame for even wanting what is out of their reach to provide. Children do not know that their parents are defending against their own sense of inadequacy when they blame. What children need is their parents' honesty about their circumstances if they cannot afford an item.

Most importantly, children need parental support to feel their disappointment. Feeling disappointment is part of living, and being denied the right to feel this buries the hurt where it festers out of sight. This is how accumulated pain builds, how the reservoir of unmet need gains its size and power.

Disappointment was difficult for me as a child. I learned to defend against even its possibility by telling myself that I wasn't going to get what I wanted. Surprise if I did get it was far better than having to feel disappointment if I did not. I carried this defense into my adulthood and curtailed my ability to ask for anything for many years. Clients have told me that they simply stopped wanting anything, shutting down their need so they would not have to feel disappointment.

Insatiable need

Unconscious, unmet need is often felt as desperation and is insatiable. It is essential that we understand that feelings with this much strength are coming from the past. They will, however, *feel* as if they are about now. Insatiable need feels like the overwrought desperation that we are gripped with when someone we love rejects us or leaves us for somebody else, the kind of desperation we feel when we just have to binge or when we hurt so badly we cannot stand it, the kind of desperation we feel when we cannot get enough of someone or something. Again, the healing process will start when we allow this feeling to be there and to carry us back to a time when we needed to be held, comforted, loved and cared about—a time when we were under two feet tall.

Chuck was devastated when his wife announced she was leaving him. He had been in therapy for some time. To deal with this he booked himself off work, booked some therapy appointments and stayed with his feelings as much as he could at home on his own. He broke through to the heartache

he had never been able to feel when his parents hurt him instead of holding him. He had insight after insight about why he had not been able to
hear the things his wife was saying to him about his behaviour. He came to
feel the true source of his anger and stubbornness that his wife had found
so trying. Chuck had a lot of grieving to do about not being able to see
sooner what he was doing to his wife and children as he acted out his old
anger. He found that as he did this grieving he would go back and forth
between the present and the past.

Trying to get from our life partner, our friends, our children or even our
boss what we did not get from our parents is the way old, unconscious, unmet
need messes up our relationships and keeps us in unhealthy situations. Taking
responsibility for feeling our need in its proper context is what changes the relationship and presents the possibility of greater caring and intimacy.

Julie was beside herself when her husband announced he wanted out of
their marriage. She would not leave him alone, following him from room
to room, phoning him incessantly.

She entered therapy and began to weep as a small child for her father, who
would come home from work and head straight for his bottle of gin without even glancing at Julie.

When Julie felt her insatiable need in the proper context she understood how
she had damaged, and was further damaging, her relationship with her husband.
    The other side of the coin occurs in trying to please a person with this kind
of insatiable need. This is impossible, since no matter what we may do it is
never enough.

Learning to be indirect and dishonest about our need

Children start out being very direct and honest about their wants and needs.
Yet these are frequently dismissed by adults. Even something as simple as a
child saying she is thirsty, and the adult saying "No you're not, you just had
milk with your lunch," becomes enormously confusing. It makes children
doubt themselves and bury their need. When we learn as children that our

needs and wants are unacceptable and ineffectual we become devious about them. This becomes a pattern and we do not even know we are doing it. We carry our inability to be direct into our adult relationships.

> Tanya could not understand why her husband kept saying she was manipulative and indirect. These traits of hers were driving him crazy and he told her that she needed to change if they were to stay together. She was totally bewildered. He also said that he could not stand the fact that she was never decisive about what she wanted to do—she always left the restaurant or the movie up to him.

As Tanya unravelled her past she eventually came to understand that it had not been safe for her to ask for anything directly in her family. She was often told she was selfish and ungrateful. She also got the message that it was not "nice" to ask for things she wanted—it was not the "ladylike" thing to do. So Tanya learned to be very indirect when she wanted something: "Would you like to go shopping, Mommy?" As an adult, Tanya did not feel entitled to say what she really liked or wanted, and so she always deferred to her husband. Her buried anger often appeared when she subtly criticized his choice, finding fault with the food or the movie instead of enjoying herself.

The more Tanya felt of how she had been deprived of her right to express her likes and dislikes and her needs and wants, the more direct she was able to become in the present.

Defending against our need

When we are used to being hurt we may be leery of letting our vulnerability and our need show. Of course, this means that we will not be able to have an intimate relationship with anyone. Intimacy depends on open and trusting hearts.

Shutting down on our need and vulnerability and defending against it surfacing comes in many forms. One of the most common defenses is fault-finding.

> Tory looked for help for his faltering marriage when his wife said she could no longer put up with his anger. He took some courses that helped him understand that he had to take responsibility for his behaviour and was able to make some major changes in the way he managed and communi-

cated his anger. Tory stopped the overt fault-finding, but there were still subtle ways in which he persisted in letting his wife know that she did not measure up to what he expected.

He and his wife did get along much better, but there was still no intimacy in their marriage. Although she would share a lot of her feelings with him, she withheld a part of herself because she did not feel safe. Tory could not let himself be vulnerable with her and withheld all but the most superficial of his feelings. The turning point came one night when Tory burst into tears after an exchange with one of his adult children. He found himself waiting to gain control before he went into the room where his wife was.

Tory again sought help. He began to feel his early hurt when his father rejected him and his mother expected him to be big and strong.

As Tory began to feel the pain of his past he became more and more open with his wife and began to risk sharing his feelings. She had always felt drawn to him and most loving when he showed his vulnerability, and so she became more open with him, and their relationship grew in intimacy. She also opened to her fears and began to take responsibility for what she withheld and why she needed to do this.

Acknowledging our vulnerability and our need, and feeling through our experience of not having our needs met in the past, is the way we can find closeness and intimacy in the present.

Inappropriate needs as adults if childhood needs were not met

There are many, many ways that our unmet childhood need pops up in the present inappropriately and destructively. We must not fool ourselves. Our unconscious self attempts to meet our unmet, held, childhood need and reveals itself in a thousand ways. Some of these ways have become socially acceptable, not recognized for what they are—keeping busy, workaholism, staying thin. Others are socially despised—obesity, sexual deviations, invading personal space. More displaced expressions of unmet need may be:

- *Need for approval*—rushing around trying to be helpful, being the martyr, sucking up
- *Unrealistic expectations in adult relationships*:
  You will make me feel loved.
  You will know what I am thinking and how I feel.
  You will want to help and support me at all times.
  You will want to do what I want to do.
  You will agree with me.
  You will know what I want and need if you love me.
  (Actually, you never can do enough but I want you to keep trying.)
- *Unrealistic expectations of our children*—expecting them to meet our needs
- *Self-centredness*—talking incessantly about ourself, never asking about others, making everything about ourself, wrapped in "poor me"
- *Excessive talking*—going on and on
- *Self-righteousness*—needing to be right
- *Excessive food, alcohol, work, sex, material goods*
- *Dependence on drugs*
- *Affairs*
- *Sexual fetishes*

Vanessa was continually disappointed when her husband, Jack, gave her a birthday or Christmas present. It was never what she wanted and she openly showed her irritation with him. Jack was always bewildered and ended up getting angry back, covering his own sense of inadequacy that he just could not please his wife.

When Vanessa began to feel how much her parents had expected her to be exactly as they wanted her to be rather than knowing her and knowing what she wanted, she began to get some insight into why she felt so horrible when Jack did not give her the gifts she wanted. She realized that it made her feel that he really did not know her and that this was a trigger for her. She learned that she needed to express her desires directly instead of hoping her husband could read her mind. As she continued to feel what it was like to be a little girl whose parents did not know her, she took more responsibility for getting her needs met in the present.

Putting our need on our children

There are many ways in which our old unmet need manifests itself in our expectations of our children. Many of us readily understand, for example, that it is not right to try to fulfill our unrequited ambitions through our children and that we should allow them the freedom to choose their own career path. However, many of us do not recognize that when we are tired, having a rough time with our spouse, or have failed at something important to us, expecting our children to understand is wanting far too much from them. Expecting our children to understand us and to make us feel better is trying to get an old need met. Children are capable of understanding a lot, but it is our *need* for their understanding that is the problem. We needed our parents to understand us, to listen to us and to care.

It is very common to discover that we unconsciously want from our children what we did not get from our parents. We want them to listen to us and to care about what we need. *This is not a child's job.* Children need to feel carefree as much as possible. This notion often scares us. We insist that our children be sensitive to our needs, fearing they will grow up to be insensitive, unkind monsters. Like so many other paradoxes, when it comes to how human beings develop, the exact opposite is true. The more carefree our children are and the more their needs are met, the more sensitive and caring they will become.

It is our unconscious and unmet need that blinds us to our children's present needs.

Shelley was determined to finish her degree even though she had two small children at home and a husband who had difficulty getting flexible hours in his job. She wanted straight A's, but found her life crashing down around her when one of her children began to act out. He was out of control—unwilling to go to bed, refusing to eat and generally being difficult. Shelley was beside herself. She found herself wanting to shake her young son, and this scared her a lot.

In her first therapy session Shelley acknowledged what she had wanted to do to her child, and yet she wailed, "What about me?" This is the feeling she stayed with during this first session.

Shelley was held to this feeling for several sessions before she connected to how unimportant and thwarted she had felt as a little girl. It came as a shock to her to feel what it had been like to be ignored and unappreciated in her family. She remembered how hard she had tried to get approval from her deadened and unresponsive parents. She began to feel how exhausting this fruitless endeavour had been as a child.

In one session she became painfully aware of how her little son's needs had not been met. Her tears flowed with wrenching sobs as she felt how her unmet childhood need had blinded her to her son's need that was right in front of her.

The key to knowing when our expectation is coming from an old need occurs when we have a big feeling (overreaction) about it or when we seem to have no feeling (underreaction).

Carol wanted to be the perfect mother. Although she was not conscious of it, she later realized that deep within she had felt this to be her last chance to succeed at something. Her need to be a good mother meant that she could never relax and just be with her kids. She needed them to be happy all the time and felt responsible whenever family squabbles broke out.

Carol constantly underreacted, pushing her feelings down when she was angry. Or she overreacted, being overly solicitous whenever one of her children needed anything. One way or the other she always left herself out of the equation; she could not be real with her kids.

As she opened to her feelings Carol was able to slowly feel how responsible she had always felt for whether or not her mother was happy. She had not wanted her children to feel responsible for her, but in her headlong attempt to do this she had not been able to let them have their feelings. She had been acting out her own need to be "good" on them.

It is our responsibility as parents to examine our own behaviour and use our natural emotional healing power to heal our old wounds so that we do not have unconscious expectations of our children.

Balancing our needs with those of our children

In order for our children to grow up emotionally healthy it is essential that their needs come first most of the time. This does not mean that our needs as a parent are never met. It does mean that we arrange our lives in such a way as to take into consideration whose need is whose. For example, it is not a baby's need to go to the mall. However, we may need to go to the mall. If we understand that this is our need and that it is actually an overstimulating place for babies to be for very long, we will perhaps trade off with another mother of young children, or shop when our partner is at home to look after the baby, or do the shopping in short spurts. The point is to consider our children's needs. We have a cultural tendency to deny our children and rationalize what we do. We say things like "children are resilient" or that "they have to learn that they can't always have their own way." There is, of course, truth in both of these statements, but it does not work to use such notions to excuse ignoring children's needs. It would be so much better for all children if we could, as a society, acknowledge what is best for them and become much more child-supportive.

When our need blinds us it is easy to become self-righteous. This happens when we are determined that we know what our children need despite what they say.

When parent's and child's needs clash we often witness the adult become a four-year-old in a power struggle with a bonafide four-year-old (substitute baby, two, eight, fourteen). When this happens we can become conscious of our natural healing power seeking our attention. We can use the trigger that our child has ignited and allow ourselves to feel back to what it was like for us to be a four-year-old. This is how we get connected to our old, unmet need. Otherwise we can stay stuck in an unfair struggle with our children. We, as adults, have the power to take responsibility for the strength and charge of our feelings and own our history. Children cannot do this and to expect them to be able to is to expect them to be the adult. If we do this we avoid our responsibility.

When there are two parents who understand the necessity of putting their children's needs first and of owning their feelings, they can help each other tremendously, both to meet their children's needs and to get their own appropriate, current needs met.

Single parents have a more difficult time. Our society could help enormously by considering these parents' needs more, and since we do know what children need for healthy development we could, as a society, take far more responsibility for seeing that their needs are met.

Unmet need: acting out "poor me"

Jane constantly let other people know what a terrible life she was having. She made others very uncomfortable by putting her need out in this way— no one knew how to help her; they sensed the insatiability of her need and it frightened them. Jane had been very abused as a child and her pain was never acknowledged in her family. Her need to let other people know how bad her life was in the present was her acting out of a need to be acknowledged, the acknowledgment she did not get as a child. She was compelled to try to get this acknowledgment in the present.

In therapy, as Jane was slowly able to feel the abuse and the lack of acknowledgment she began to grieve deeply. Only then could she stop playing out her old "poor me" script and take responsibility for making her life better in the present. She had never been able to respond with anything but depression to the admonitions she had had from numerous people to "get on with it." As she did her deep grieving and became clearer about her present likes and dislikes she was able to change her life and begin to experience some joy. She came to recognize more and more that no one in the present could make up for her deprived past. She also felt good about the responsibility she was now taking for her own feelings and for the insight she had into herself.

The only way to escape from the endless cycle of feeling sorry for ourselves and from putting "poor me" onto others is to grieve deeply and fully for the hurt we experienced when our needs were not met as children. We may start this grieving when we are triggered by something we want and do not have in the present. The "poor me" feels, for all the world, as though it is about now. It is the extent of early deprivation that keeps it *pasted* on the present, and it often requires an act of faith and courage to acknowledge that the strength of the present feeling is standing on old unfinished pain. Once we have allowed the desperate feelings of "not having" in the present to carry us back to the deprivation of our childhood we begin to know that it is in the past that the strength of the pain resides.

It is not enough to have an insight and know the ways in which we were deprived as children. We need to make the connection again and again by allowing the feelings associated with this deprivation to be as big and real as we can and to stay with them for as long as we can each time they arise. This allows our innate healing power to work. When we have felt enough of the deprivation from our past, connected to it deeply and fully, we begin to be clearer about what we need to do in the present to get our lives the way we want them to be.

As long as we act out the "poor me" and remain unaware that the strength of the feeling is coming from the past, we will continue to set up our current lives to be in line with our old, unconscious feelings. As part of our disabling behaviour we will remain alone, for example, because that is what is familiar. Our present will mirror our past accurately. We will keep ourselves stuck in feeling sorry for ourselves and unable to know and fulfill our genuine present needs.

Blame as a cover for need

Blame covers need when we expect others to be responsible for our happiness. It is from our parents that we needed to receive unconditional love and caring. They were responsible for our happiness when we were children, not anyone in our adult life.

When we blame others for our unhappiness instead of taking responsibility for our feelings, we keep ourselves from feeling what we needed and did not get. When we can notice that we want to blame, we can start acknowledging that it may be covering the pain of our deprivation as a child.

This helps us start to open to our healing process. We lie down and feel what is going on inside, or we write in our journal. We take responsibility for cooperating with our natural emotional healing power in whatever way seems most effective for us. As we "feel" instead of "blame" we become clearer about our current real needs and how to meet them in the present.

Janet was a blamer. She blamed her kids for her headaches, her husband for their lack of a better financial situation, her parents and siblings for making her feel miserable at every family gathering, and her old math teacher for the fact that she kept making mistakes in her job as a cashier. Janet was never at fault for anything; it was always someone else who had misplaced something or who had made the mistake.

In therapy Janet recalled the constant criticism she received as a child. She made a long list of the admonishments that her mother constantly levelled at her: "You're selfish. You're lazy. How could anyone do that that way? Won't you ever learn?" As Janet felt more and more of what it was like to be at the receiving end of this barrage she came to know/feel how inadequate she had felt as a child. She began to feel her anger at this abuse and her grief at the loss of her childhood well-being. Janet became less critical and blameful and was able to connect more readily with her old hurt when she found herself wanting to blame.

Blaming others for not meeting our needs and taking inappropriate responsibility for meeting other people's needs are defenses that cover the same pain.

Early, unmet need turned into powerful sexual need

Early, unmet need may be transformed and managed by acting out sexually. If needing has been blocked because a child has been shamed for needing, he or she may fantasize and masturbate to alleviate the pain of the unmet need. In this way the experience of feeling needy becomes associated with the sexual drive. It becomes compulsive, repetitive and addictive because of its powerful ability to release built-up tension from unmet needs. Jim, from my second example in this chapter, came to realize that there was a theme in his fantasies when he masturbated. They revolved around being touched and being wanted and he was compelled to act out these fantasies through masturbation time and time again. Another client fantasized about being punished as she masturbated and this relieved the tension that had built up because she felt so bad about herself. The more we integrate what happened to us the less compulsive we will be in acting out these unmet needs sexually.

Our sexuality is so powerful that it can absorb the most painful damage from our childhood, and in its transformation it can refigure in behaviours that are destructive to ourselves and others. Rape, as an example, although properly designated as a crime of power, is a crime where the weapon is a sexual organ. The need of the rapist is transformed from powerlessness to power through the sexual act. Our sexualized needs as adults can be so strong that we can even act them out by trampling on the innocence of children. Incest, molestation, voyeurism, exhibitionism and sexual exploitation are extremes of unmet need turned into powerful sexual need.

Penny suffered enormous guilt and remorse remembering how she had more than once inappropriately touched a young boy she was babysitting. She had never felt that she had the right to speak about how she had been molested by her older brother for years as a child. She felt unentitled to her own feelings of anger about what had happened to her because of what she had done to this young boy. Penny had a lot to grieve.

Many of us may act out our unmet need sexually. For example, extramarital affairs are rampant in our culture. When we understand that our unmet need can be sexualized, we can notice our excessive or distorted sexual behaviour as a door to go through. For sexual behaviour is the same as any behaviour: when it is overcharged we can notice it, acknowledge it and feel it to its source.

Exaggerated sexual need threatens intimacy in relationships. Paradoxically, in our urgent rush to fill the emptiness of unmet need we rob ourselves of the opportunity to connect fully and richly in the present. We will not know the emotional truths that lie behind these behaviours until we take responsibility and allow ourselves to feel them. This is how we become clear. When the extra charge dissipates there is a potential for deeper intimacy.

Dwayne was so caught on needing to have sexual intercourse as soon as he went to bed at night that he became impatient with his wife's disinterest. He blamed her for her coldness, and going to bed every night became a tense time for them both. When this finally led to a crisis in his marriage Dwayne found himself thinking a lot about a woman in his office. He was beginning to justify to himself his sexual turn-on around this woman. This put him up against his moral values and he sought help.

Dwayne connected to an aching absence of never having been touched by his parents in a loving way. He remembered poring over "girlie" magazines as a teenager, sexually fantasizing about these women touching and wanting him. He felt guilty about this.

Dwayne stayed with his earlier needs in his therapy sessions for some time before he was able to empathize with himself as a teenager. He was able to recognize and feel how much he wanted to act out this old need in the present with his wife and his co-worker. He stopped blaming his wife for not "wanting him."

Feeling through need in safety

When we are trying to feel our unmet need from the past we need to feel safe enough to do so. Often when working with a therapist our need will be transferred onto him or her. This transference can be used to help us get to our old need, but our therapist must be trustworthy.

> Trudy sought a therapist because she was absolutely distraught when her boyfriend cheated on her and subsequently left her for another woman. She was wide open to her need when she began therapy. Her therapist was very supportive and complimented her often on her intelligence and good looks. Before long he was telling her that he found her exceptionally attractive. Trudy could feel that she was, in turn, powerfully attracted to him.

> When he made sexual advances toward her she felt it was wrong, but he reassured her that this was what she needed to help her feel good about herself and to get over the pain of her recently lost relationship. Besides, he said he was falling in love with her.

This so-called therapy ended in disaster for Trudy. The therapist did not of course leave his wife, and when Trudy became more demanding about their relationship he found a reason to terminate it as well as her therapy.

Many years later when Trudy was once again in therapy, she felt her rage at being seduced when she was in such a vulnerable state by a person whom she should have been able to trust. She was able to use this trigger to get back to how untrustworthy her parents had been and how much this had hurt her. She had a great deal of grieving to do about the abuse by her therapist and by her parents.

Trudy also had the opportunity to feel through the unmet need from her past that had caused her to be so devastated when her boyfriend had left her. She had to grieve and to feel all the losses of her life.

It is enormously important that we be with someone we can trust when we are trying to feel through our old need. We require therapists who are capable of looking after their own need and not using us, their client, to satisfy themselves.

A therapist's need can collide with ours in many subtle ways. Even the need to feel successful as a therapist can cause this to happen. When a therapist needs a client to make "progress," for example, this interferes directly with the client's need to go at their own pace, a pace at which they can thoroughly integrate their experience. Needing to be insightful and clever as a therapist interferes with the client reaching their own truths unimpeded.

I remember many years ago in my therapy when my need was really stuck on my male therapist. I felt infatuated with him but I knew that this was not real; I knew this feeling of infatuation was really my old need. He was aware that I had transferred my need onto him because I was using this trigger in my sessions. It was a pretty all-consuming trigger at the time.

He stayed in his role as therapist, maintaining appropriate boundaries, while I continued for some time to feel it and feel it—this yearning need. In one evening session when he was wearing a dress shirt open at the neck and with his sleeves rolled up, I really broke through to the aching need for my father who often wore such a shirt. After I made this really solid, huge connection, all the yucky, unrequited love feeling for him completely disappeared. It was like a camera lens suddenly bringing things into focus. He was simply my therapist once again. I know from this personal experience the immense value of having a therapist who is clear and who can allow his or her clients to feel through their need.

We may not always feel safe when we are processing through old feelings because feeling unsafe may be part of what happened back then and part of what we have to feel through. We can acknowledge our fear and at the same time take the responsibility to choose carefully with whom we will do this feeling work.

What children need

While there has been a growing awareness of what children need in order to develop properly, the practice lags behind. In fact, because many people still want to deny this knowledge we really have no idea of the extent of our human potential. We do not know what kind of a world we could have, or what human beings could be capable of, if we treated our children as the very vulnerable, needful little people they are. We continue to head in a disastrous direction as we deny instead of embrace the needs of children. As Arthur Janov has said, "We all seem to be off in the wrong direction, racing to head off the results of deprivation, instead of insuring that deprivation ceases."

Unmet need leads to a sense of worthlessness

When our needs are not met as children we are, of course, not aware of it at a cognitive level. Nevertheless, our unmet needs are at the foundation of our unhappiness and are the cause of our most disconnected behaviours. No matter which feelings we have used to gain entry to ourselves we will eventually arrive at the hurt of our unmet need. Grieving this loss is essential if we are to move toward emotional health.

Many clients at first say, "That's just the way it was. I didn't know anything different." This, of course, is our natural defense, shutting down on the feelings because we do not want to feel their full force. Nevertheless, our pain—of not feeling wanted, loved or important to our parents—has accumulated. Unmet need leaves us with a sense of worthlessness residing deep inside.

7

WORTHLESSNESS

A Final Defense Against Unmanageable Pain

Feelings of worthlessness are often hidden from us, although they may be residing at the very core of our being. Many people are disconnected from this source of their driven behaviour and do not articulate it as the basis of their problems. Others might express worthlessness as low self-esteem or a sense of inadequacy without really feeling its depth or its ramifications.

Our culture abounds with self-improvement remedies and this is indication enough that many people do not feel very good about themselves. Also, almost all advertising is based on fuelling the notion that we are inadequate as we are; we need some product or other to make us acceptable. The cultural images that promote ideals work only if we do not feel worthy. All addictions, compulsions, obsessions and self-destructive behaviours are generated by our buried sense of worthlessness.

It is often difficult to make a connection between our feelings of worthlessness that were generated in our childhood and our present self-destructive behaviour. We may remember some of these humiliating circumstances, but until we allow the feeling/knowing of what it was really like for us as children, we will not heal the trauma enough to free ourselves.

Feeling worthless is a central defense that children must erect to protect themselves from overwhelming feelings of vulnerability. *Feeling that things are their fault gives children a sense of control where they actually have no control.* They cannot afford to see their parents as inadequate or uncaring. Instead, they see themselves as inadequate and feel worthless.

Feelings of worthlessness are perpetuated in adulthood because we do not know how to access these early feelings and feel them through. We have internalized our parents' and others' negative messages, which have now become self-sustaining—we put ourselves down and call ourselves names, treating ourselves exactly the same way the significant people in our childhood did.

We spend enormous amounts of energy trying to keep from feeling unworthy; we are driven to pursue a new job, another degree, a new relationship or yet another new outfit in hopes of staving off the feelings once again. When we try to alter our view of ourselves by scrambling away from feelings of worthlessness, we try to improve ourselves in the area of the "false self," the part of ourselves created to meet the needs of others. We may have an important job, the cleanest house in the neighbourhood and the finest perennial beds on the block and yet we may have no sense of who we are or any energy for enjoying our life.

We are caught in a vicious cycle of trying to fix past damage in the present. We avoid connecting with feelings by papering them over with positive affirmations, ego boosters and temporary fixes.

Real worth is experienced only when we connect with our underlying feelings of worthlessness, feel them and integrate them. Worthlessness is then replaced with a solid self-regard, a regard that does not have to be worked at; it simply, quietly, exists.

There are many ways in which children are made to feel unworthy. Each person is unique and the imprint of our pain is as individual as our DNA. How each person defends against these awful feelings and how we act them out in the present is also unique to each of us.

When our needs are not met, we feel worthless

When our needs are not met as children we come to believe there must be something wrong with us. The younger we are when our needs are not met the more widespread the foundation of worthlessness is and the more difficult it is to access. If our needs were not met as babies we carry a pervasive sense of worthlessness at our core. This can be experienced later in life as an amorphous feeling of despair. We may become depressed.

When we have the capacity to recognize ourselves as a separate person, we translate the feeling that something is wrong into "there's something wrong with me." Because of our complete dependence on our parents when we are so little, we have no choice but to see ourselves at fault when we suffer their neglect. We cannot afford to feel unloved when our needs are not met, so we defend against that feeling by feeling worthless. If we did not defend against such a catastrophic feeling we might not survive.

> Jacqueline felt unworthy in every aspect of her life. She could never relax and just be. She tried to be a good mother, but always felt she fell short. Even on holidays when things were going well she had a pervading sense that something was wrong or was about to go wrong. Her husband was a kind, open person and Jacqueline knew that it was she who could not connect with him.

Jacqueline came to feel/remember that when she had been sick as a very young child she was left alone in her room with no kindness or comfort from her mother. She could only remember her mother coming in and looking at her. When she connected with this experience feelings of complete worthlessness washed over her. Jacqueline opened to many more occasions when she had been neglected and had felt utterly worthless. She came to realize that it was her sense of not being worthy that kept her from being able to be close to her husband or relaxed with her children.

Feeling this very early deprivation was very difficult for Jacqueline. Yet she kept feeling it, because she was gradually able to be more and more "in herself," as she put it. She recognized that the only way to get this connected feeling was to keep going with the triggers into her worthlessness as they appeared.

Again, feeling worthless is a defense against feeling unloved and uncared for. We can also defend against feeling worthless. This is how our feelings and defenses get layered. As we cooperate with our natural emotional healing power by connecting and integrating we can peel away these layers of defenses.

> Kathryn would be kind and helpful to everyone, often completely ignoring any signals she might have received from her own gut about what she really wanted to do. She believed she was a good person because she never wanted to hurt anyone, and yet all of Kathryn's good deeds could not fill her up and make her feel good about herself. She was often irritable when others did not take her advice or did not appreciate her. Since she had also

learned that it is not "nice" to be angry she stuffed these feelings away—and this continued stress was beginning to make her physically ill.

Kathryn had a hard time trying to find and feel her own need. It had been so camouflaged by "doing for others" that she had not recognized that it was her *need to be needed* that was being acted out. Pleasing her mother had been the only way Kathryn got any attention. When someone whom she had been helping let her down she used the opportunity, with great courage, to go into her disappointment and down through it. She felt anger and then need. She kept finding her need to be cared about and her need to be judged as worthy. What surrounded all these needs was the desperate feeling of worthlessness. As she felt more of what it was like to have been the child she was, she slipped below the worthlessness to the horrible feelings of not being valued for who she was rather than for what she did.

In time Kathryn was able to listen to herself better in the present. When she found herself wanting to meet others' needs she was more able to feel it instead of acting on it. As she listened to herself and stopped accommodating and acquiescing to others she felt a stronger sense of herself and her real, present needs.

Not being heard makes a child feel unworthy

When as children our feelings are not heard we experience them as being denied and we do not feel validated or worthy. Our need to feel accepted is not met. Conversely, when our parents *do* hear the message we are trying to get across we feel that it is okay to feel the way we do—and that means it is okay to be who we are. Our ability to be comfortable with, and to allow, our feelings is closely linked to who we are.

Johnny used to come home from school upset about his teacher. His mother would usually say "What were you doing?" or words to that effect. This made Johnny feel misunderstood and judged. His mother seemed to think the teacher's unfairness and bad mood must be his fault.

There were many other times when Johnny tried to tell his parents something that was important to him and they jumped in with their judgments without really listening to him at all. Soon Johnny stopped trying to tell them much of anything. He buried his need and felt that he was not worthy of being listened to and cared about. This was particularly confusing for him, since his parents both cared so much about how he looked and how he presented himself.

As an adult Johnny felt "crummy" a lot of the time. He always felt that everyone else was right and he must be wrong. He avoided confrontation or gave up really quickly when one came about.

At first Johnny denied that there could be any connection between his childhood and his current problems, since in his estimation he had not been abused or neglected in any way. But when he did a time line and remembered instance after instance where he had felt wrong and not good enough, he began to feel how his parents' lack of regard for what was going on inside of him had made him feel worthless a lot of the time.

Oppressed by negative judgments

We are oppressed as children by constant negative judgment and our sense of self-worth is seriously damaged. Our need to feel accepted, cared about and just plain okay is not met.

> As a child Nicci was used to hearing, "For goodness sake Nicci, what is wrong with you?" When she began to feel what it was like to hear those words that she had always remembered but with no feeling, she began to connect with and feel her rage. She grieved that the question had not been "What's wrong, can I help you?"

> Nicci recognized that all of her life she had been what she now called an "achievement junkie." She could see that she had been covering her deep feelings of worthlessness with one achievement after another. Her sense of well-being as she achieved was short-lived and she always became depressed before long. As she continued to feel the abusive negative judgments levied against her in her family, compounded by teasing and ridiculing whenever she reacted with tears and upset, she gradually appreciated herself more. The recognition of how

she had needed to shut down on these feelings as a child gave her a new outlook on her life. She was now able to feel her feelings and move through them instead of getting depressed. She was able to stop pushing herself and to finally relax more. When Nicci was able to stop fighting with herself to keep her bad feelings away, she felt more of the peace inside that she had always so desperately wanted.

This was not an easy or quick process for Nicci. Her feelings of worthlessness kept appearing as feelings of inadequacy whenever she was around her older brother, who continued to be highly valued in the family. Now Nicci felt in control of her life and knew how to "go into" the depression when it appeared in order to get to the underlying rage, hurt and grief. She felt good about being in charge of her life in this way. It was sad for her to observe her siblings, who continued to act out their feelings of worthlessness on each other and in their own families. They did not want to hear about how Nicci was using her feelings to get to the source of her pain, although they no longer attempted to put her down.

Nicci felt better about herself another way: she no longer accepted verbal abuse in the present because she was continually using her natural emotional healing power to connect with the childhood source of her feelings. She could say to her brother, "Please don't speak to me that way," and when he tried to tell her she was too sensitive, she was able to simply repeat in a very straightforward way, "I will no longer accept you putting me down; please don't speak to me that way."

When children are not wanted

When as children we experience that we are not wanted we carry a devastating burden of feeling worthless at our core. Our need to be cherished and to feel loved and lovable is not met.

Jana was the third girl in her family. She was told as a young child how much her father had wanted a boy instead of her. This was a family story. The desired boy was born when Jana was barely a year old, and another brother less than two years later.

Jana's mother constantly moaned about the burden of her children and all that she could have done if she had just not had so many, if she had not had to follow the dictates of the church. When Jana was pregnant with her first child her mother remarked, "I'm glad it's you and not me."

As an adult Jana needed to feel that she made a difference and so was always getting involved in a worthy cause. She would have tremendous energy as she worked toward some goal, and would feel strong and right. Yet there was always a big letdown when the goal was reached or the event was over. She usually found another good cause pretty quickly, since she could not stand the empty feeling and the depression for long.

Jana did not understand this at all until she began to feel how much she needed to be important, to feel that she was doing something worthwhile and therefore that *she* was worthwhile. She felt the tremendous drive behind this. She connected to how unworthy she had felt in her family and how often she had been devastated when her mother said, "Just who do you think you are?" or "Don't get too big for your britches."

Jana was gradually able to be as big as she really felt—she was a multi-talented person. Whenever she felt empty or depressed, she knew to take some time to feel the feelings that lay under the wound of worthlessness.

Threats of punishment

When as children we live under the threat of punishment, whether it is physical or emotional, we cannot feel good about ourselves. Our need to feel safe and secure is not met. We cannot feel lovable.

Ted had been beaten frequently as a child. It was not until he was sixteen and bigger than his father that he stood up for himself and threatened to kill his father if he ever touched him again.

Ted appeared to be a very successful adult. He was very good at his job and made a lot of money. Unfortunately he was estranged from his adult children, whom he could no longer understand at all.

Ted scoffed at the notion that his self-esteem was not very good. When his wife told him that she could see this he recounted his many achievements and pointed out all the wonderful material things and exotic vacations they had as proof there was nothing wrong with his self-esteem. On the contrary, he thought there was probably something seriously wrong "mentally," as he put it, with his wife. She could not be happy no matter how successful he was. He suggested she go to therapy and get herself fixed. In fact, she did seek help.

As Ted's wife slowly regained herself she began to stand up to him. She no longer accepted his put-downs and other forms of verbal abuse. She enjoyed a good relationship with her adult children, which was getting better all the time as she became more honest and straightforward with them.

Eventually Ted fell apart when one of his business deals went sour and he lost a lot of money. He became depressed—and found himself sitting alone in his den crying with his glass of scotch in his hand. Ted felt desperate and asked his wife to make an appointment for him with her therapist. She gave him the therapist's number.

As Ted connected with the severe physical abuse of his childhood he became aware of how worthless he had felt when his mother emotionally withdrew from him. Sometimes when she disapproved of something he had said or done she would not speak to him for weeks. Ted realized that he had had to put away the feelings of worthlessness he felt then and instead concentrate on achieving at school, where he got quite a lot of recognition for his efforts. As he felt his worthlessness he began to feel an enormous sense of betrayal that his mother had never protected him from his father and had even colluded by often threatening, "Wait till your father gets home." Ted could feel how worthless this betrayal had made him feel.

Ted had always thought he had been a good father because he had consciously decided never to hit his children as he had been hit. He had thought they were ungrateful for the things he had been able to give them. But as he felt his grief about his parents not being there for him he realized that he had not been there for his own children. He grieved deeply and for a long time before he was able to connect with his children and acknowledge to them how emotionally abusive he had been. Ted began to see clearly how his blind, inappropriate expectations had been crippling for his oldest son and how he had not been able to value any of his children and really be with them—really know them.

When our sense of worth is undermined by parental rigidity

When our parents are rigid we feel tense and unloved and most often we translate this into self-blame. Our need to feel accepted just as we are goes unmet.

Norman came from a "nice" middle-class family. Everyone really liked his mother and father. The other kids thought they were great and far more with it than any of their parents. Norman never understood why he felt down and blue so much of the time, and thought there must be something wrong with him.

There was a great deal that Norman did not have to figure out because his parents' rigid rules made it clear what was expected. By the time Norman was six he knew exactly how to behave to avoid their grim-lipped looks. He had trouble, however, trying to figure out how to make himself into a better person so that he would be noticed more in his family. Whenever there was conversation between Norman and his parents it was never about how he felt about anything; it was always an admonition about the way things should be and what he should do. It was particularly painful for him to watch his parents listen with apparent interest to his friends.

Norman entered therapy when his isolation and loneliness as an adult became too much for him.

Norman opened to his feelings of unworthiness as he began to feel how bleak and barren his childhood had been and how neglected and ignored he had felt as a person in his house. He recognized that he acted out his unworthiness as an adult by behaving as though he were not entitled to anything. He could not have a successful relationship because he felt so bad about himself; he would terminate it before the other person got a chance to.

An unhappy inheritance: modelling worthlessness for our children

Laura's mother continually put herself down. She could never accept a compliment by just saying thank you, and would instead make some self-

8

SHAME

The Silent Killer of the Human Spirit

S hame is a silent killer because it prevents us from revealing to the world who we really are. When we hold onto our shame as an adult it can be totally debilitating. Like worthlessness, shame becomes a devastating defense because it keeps us stuck.

It takes great courage to face our shame and feel it. It is an enormous key because when we can feel our shame we loosen underlying feelings that are fundamentally destructive to our well-being. In doing so, we free feelings that have been bound by our shame and that are essential to living a healthy, vibrant life.

Our feelings become shame-bound if it was unacceptable for us to express them. When we have to hide how we feel, we come to believe that we are "bad" to have those very feelings and we are ashamed. Cultural directives also bind many families by leading them to believe that some feelings are less acceptable if we are male and others less acceptable if we are female. For example, it has been taboo for males to show that they are feeling weak, vulnerable or out of control with sad feelings. Females have had to hide their anger or risk being labelled unfeminine. When we are ashamed of our feelings we are ashamed of ourselves.

Fear is bound with shame because it was terrifying for us to jeopardize our relationship with our parents by having feelings that were unacceptable. We are bound, as children, not only by having the shameful feelings but having to control ourselves so we will not reveal them. This then leads to many feelings, such as guilt, anxiety, numbness and loneliness.

When we feel inherently shameful, even disgusting, we anaesthetize these feelings in many different ways. We may become addicted to substances such as alcohol, chemicals or food; to addictive processes such as gambling, work or sex; or we may have a relationship addiction. Even though the addiction functions as an escape from the shame, the addictive process is compulsive, repetitive and also *adds* to our shame since we feel humiliated and defeated because of our powerlessness over it. We hate our lack of inner strength.

Addictions may also serve to fill up the emptiness we are left with when our childhood needs were not met. We feel shame about these needs if we were led to believe that we were not entitled to them.

When we are compelled to deal with our needy feelings with addictive substances or processes, we guarantee that we will reactivate the original shame about our neediness. When we binge on food to quell our shameful longing (need), the bingeing intensifies our shame. If we also purge by vomiting, we are filled with self-contempt and self-disgust. The act-out, if intense enough, matches our inner shame and we get temporary relief.

The addiction to alcohol adds another component, since alcohol opens us to our feelings and may be used to release our inhibitions or suppressed feelings that have built up. This relief is paid for the morning after when we become seized with great shame and remorse. On the other hand, some alcoholics defend their shame with bravado and blaming, or they go numb.

Children must bury their feelings of shame when their parents overtly show them that they are not wanted or that they are very unimportant to them. Children feel essentially unwanted when they have to hide who they really are in order to be acceptable. These buried feelings manifest themselves as anxiousness and nervousness in our children.

Many adults who are allowing their natural emotional healing power to work get to their feelings of shame through the door of other more accessible feelings, such as hurt, anger, guilt, anxiety and grief. For others, shame is such a lid on their right to feel that, when they break through and connections are made to the sources of their shame, underlying feelings emerge big and whole.

Releasing ourselves from the grip of shame requires determination. It means we have to face the absolute worst that we feel about ourselves. It is a killer of the human spirit to stay stuck in shame and it deprives us and those around us of who we are.

Origins of shame

Shaming a child is emotional abuse. We, as children, are shamed for everything from bodily functions to feeling good about ourselves. The following harmful phrases are but a few from a lengthy list that I have heard my clients painfully remember:

> You should be ashamed of yourself.
> You don't deserve ...
> You're just like your dad (aunt, grandfather, etc.)
> All you ever think about is yourself.
> I'm so disappointed in you.
> You'll be sorry some day.
> You enjoy being miserable.
> There are a lot of people worse off than you.

Shaming without words

We are shamed without words when our parents or caretakers look at us with disgust, anger, disappointment and disapproval and sometimes even with hatred. We are shamed when our parent sighs and we know this display of exasperation is because of us. We are devastated, humiliated and shamed when our parent punishes us by withdrawing emotionally and not speaking. These are the most difficult shaming experiences to recuperate from since they engender such enormous anxiety and self-loathing in us and are difficult for us to label and defend against.

> Andrew lived his life into his late forties terrified of his mother's emotional withdrawal and rejection. This was a technique she had used liberally when Andrew was very young to keep her little son under control. This made Andrew feel terrible: he felt "bad" and "wrong." His mother's need for control was extreme and Andrew had no support or help from his father, who was a kind man but completely intimidated by his wife and unable to stand up to her.

Andrew went into a deep depression when his mother died. He could not physically tolerate the antidepressants his doctor put him on, and decided to enter therapy instead.

As Andrew felt more and more of the humiliation and shame he had suffered and repressed as a child he was able to feel the other emotions that had been so bound up with the shame. His mother had ridiculed him when he cried as a child, withdrawing from him until he stopped. In therapy when Andrew was finally able to cry his tears came in a flood.

It took a long time and a lot of grieving before Andrew was able to connect and feel his anger. He had been a self-effacing "nice" guy and had always felt great shame whenever his anger began to surface. When Andrew started to notice how he used sarcasm to dump some of his anger he took the risk of expressing it in a more straightforward way.

Andrew felt that his whole life had been a lie because he had had so little of himself and had believed he should sacrifice himself for others. As he slowly regained himself and took the risks he needed to take he uncovered more and more of the old shameful feelings. As he felt these feelings through he began to admire the child he had been and was amazed at how he had even survived in such an emotionally destructive home. He no longer despised himself for his need.

When children have to hide their feelings

Having to hide our feelings in order to have our parents' love and approval is one of the greatest burdens that can be inflicted upon us. When we have to hide our feelings we become fearful that we will not be able to do so, and this becomes an added burden.

Valerie learned early in her life that she could not be who she really was. Whenever she expressed the truth she saw with her child's eyes she was told to keep quiet about it. As well, when she brought home her excellent report cards her parents mostly ignored her, as though good grades were expected of her and were no big deal. Since her sister did not do well at school Valerie unconsciously felt she had to subdue herself and minimize her academic successes.

Valerie's mother taught her that nice girls do not get angry and big girls do not cry. Valerie shut down her feelings and withdrew into herself more and more. In her teen years she spent long hours lying on her bed with headphones on listening to music.

As a parent herself she recognized through her reading of parenting books that she needed to let her children have their feelings. This was not always easy because their sadness and anger often triggered her old repressed feelings and she had to shut down even harder to stay in control. The feelings of deadness within her and in her relationship with her husband brought Valerie into therapy.

Valerie opened to the overwhelming shame she felt any time she experienced an emotion. As she did this she was eventually able to feel more and become more alive. It took her a long time to unravel her pain.

Humiliation and ridicule

As children we feel shame when we are humiliated in front of our friends or in public. Parents often correct children in a humiliating way, no matter where they are or who is around. We see this so often in the mall or at the grocery store. It makes us feel painfully self-conscious. Children are small and defenseless. As children there is no way to protect ourselves against such an assault except to shut down and bury the hurt.

Barbara was constantly humiliated as a child. She would go off to her room to cry, and when she was forced to appear for dinner her brothers would ridicule her and call her "beet face." This treatment was unbearable for Barbara, and so she shut down on any unacceptable feelings and scrambled to survive by being as sweet and helpful as possible.

As an adult it was impossible for Barbara to allow herself to make any mistakes. When someone even implied a criticism she would retreat to her room and her bed as soon as possible, just as she had as a child. She would go over and over in her mind what had been said and what her fault must have been.

Barbara got scared when she had an angry outburst at work. She felt completely out of control. She blamed herself relentlessly for being so stupid and minimized the very legitimate problem that had brought up this overreaction on her part. She decided she needed help.

Barbara entered therapy and began to read the books in her therapist's library voraciously. She came to understand that she should not have been treated the way she had been as a child. However, her sense of worthlessness and shame was so great that it took some time before she could empathize with herself as a child rather than hate herself for being so needy and inept. She had to feel time and time again the humiliation inflicted upon her and how she had blamed herself unendingly. As she felt this she became more open to her needs that were not met and began to grieve deeply for their loss. Barbara became more accepting of herself.

Indifference is a killer that generates shame

Parents are often indifferent unintentionally, but it leaves us feeling unimportant and uncared about nevertheless. When we suffer indifference as children it makes us feel worthless and ashamed of our need.

> Helena felt inadequate too often. Whenever company was coming she was uptight about her house and unsure of herself. This created tension in her home and she knew she became too demanding of her husband and her children.

> When Helena found out that her husband was having an affair she was overcome with shame, feeling that it must be her fault. She was not good enough!

> Helena remembered her confusion around her dad, a jolly, friendly man who treated her affectionately but could not remember her age or what grade she was in when anyone asked. She remembered how embarrassed, hurt and then ashamed she felt when he did not even pronounce her name properly.

> Helena felt the pain of her father's indifference. She grieved for how little he had known her and how she had turned these feelings against herself. She felt her anger at having her need to be cared about turn into shame and recognized how she had carried these feelings of unworthiness into her marriage.

Lack of respect for a child's privacy breeds shame

When our privacy is invaded as children we feel utterly betrayed and exposed. We readily acknowledge that adults have a right to privacy, but as parents many of us erroneously feel we have the right of ownership over our children and whatever they are saying, thinking and doing. When we invade their privacy we trample on their right to not reveal themselves as they test things out.

Invading their privacy is like opening them with a crowbar and their only defense is shame. When we overstep this boundary with our children we often justify it by declaring that our right to know is supported by our desire to protect them. The unfortunate result is that our children are forced to hide more and become more secretive. What is worse is that they may be deprived of a valuable outlet for their feelings.

> Vicki had a lot of problems after she found and read her fourteen-year-old daughter's journal. Jody became extremely rebellious, would not cooperate at home and then refused to speak to her mother at all. She started staying out late and not telling her parents where she was. Vicki was beside herself with her daughter's behaviour and tried to get Jody to see a counsellor. When Jody refused, Vicki sought help herself to see what she could do about Jody.

Vicki was encouraged to stay with what it would feel like to have her privacy invaded. She kept defending by justifying her actions as a caring, responsible, parental deed. In response to the question "What was it like for you when you were fourteen?" Vicki was taken aback as she remembered how she had acted out as a teenager by being promiscuous and using alcohol and drugs. This was a part of her life that she had not even shared with her husband.

As she felt the shame and secrecy of her teenage life Vicki realized how exposed and ashamed her daughter must have felt when she discovered that her mother had read her journal. She wept with grief and remorse and felt a flood of empathy for her daughter.

Being different, feeling different

As a child we may feel different because of how we are, how our family is or how we feel. We may be incredibly embarrassed by the inappropriate behaviour of our parent, our chaotic, dirty house or our unacceptable sexual orientation. We feel shame for real, small, exaggerated or imagined differences.

When a child feels different from his or her peers the only thing that will help is an understanding, listening ear. If we do not feel accepted and understood when we feel different, we feel shame instead. *We are all different and unique; what makes this difficult is lack of acceptance.*

Picking up our parents' shame

Shame is transferred from our parents to us when our parents themselves feel shame. My mother used to say that she wished she could crawl in a hole and pull the hole in after her. Although I did not understand what she meant I felt that something must be terribly wrong and that maybe it was my fault. I felt hopeless and helpless that I could not help my mother. I felt ashamed. As well, often our parents' shame about their sexuality is transferred to us when they cannot be comfortable with their exposed bodies, when they cannot talk freely about normal bodily functions such as menstruation and when they cannot name genital parts correctly or do so with tension and precision.

Becoming aware

These feelings, defenses and behaviours result from shaming:
- We have such a core sense of worthlessness that we feel things will never change or be different—we feel hopeless.
- We fear being exposed as unworthy, flawed or inferior and therefore avoid real commitment and intimacy. We hide from ourselves and others.
- We defend against feeling shame by pretending, pleasing and trying to be perfect.
- We become addicted to substances or obsessive or compulsive behaviours in order to avoid feeling.
- We defend against shame by going over and over what was said and how in order to be sure we are not at fault.
- We constantly feel judged by others. We attribute negative judgments where there are none. We become paranoid.
- We defend by isolating ourselves emotionally and/or physically.
- We are unable to be honest with ourselves and with others.
- We become separate from ourselves and excruciatingly self-conscious, which leads to emotional paralysis.
- We victimize others by holding them responsible for our shame.

- We are unable to honour ourselves. We become either selfless or self-aggrandizing, either passive or aggressive.
- We are unable to express feelings, or we are explosive and aggressive.
- We suffer from severe anxiety and depression.
- We lack self-control. We are completely reactive to others and cannot be autonomous and listen to and rely on ourselves because of our need for others' approval.
- We become blamers, unable to take responsibility for mistakes.
- We suffer embarrassment.
- Minor criticism evokes feelings of humiliation and defensiveness.
- We take responsibility for other people's feelings and behaviour and try to fix other people's problems.
- We apologize constantly and inappropriately.
- We feel grandiose, either better or worse than everyone else.
- We continue the cycle of shame by shaming others, particularly children.
- We become controlling.
- We deny and minimize.
- We become hyper-vigilant, expecting humiliation at every turn.

The preceding list can help increase our awareness that our current feelings and behaviours may indicate that we suffer from shame. Becoming aware is the first step we take to change our lives for the better and to become more emotionally healthy.

Unlike cognitive-behavioural approaches to change which advocate that clients consciously *learn* to change self-defeating behaviours, I am suggesting that we can use our awareness to help us take the risk of allowing the old, held feelings to surface so that we can access our natural emotional healing power. It is important that we do not repress our feelings further in order to behave differently. This is a trick on ourselves—just looking good in a new way. Fixing the outside of ourselves while ignoring our inner, real self is not emotionally healthy. We continue to live a lie.

Once we have begun to feel the full impact of the childhood experiences that made us feel such shame we will automatically begin to drop the defenses that are so debilitating in our present life. As we feel what really happened to us we can *risk change consciously.* It is important that when we make changes we stay open to our feelings. Changes need to be integrated so that they become part of us and reflect who we really are.

9

GUILT

A Straitjacket for Feeling

We all experience guilt, rational and irrational. Most people are able to tell if they are feeling guilty, unlike shame, which is much more difficult to access. We often, however, do not distinguish between rational and irrational guilt. Rational guilt is at the centre of being accountable and responsible. It is irrational guilt that causes us problems because it blinds us to our true, underlying feelings. This keeps us on an unending treadmill of self-blame.

Unresolved, irrational guilt drives unconscious and self-destructive behaviour. We can use it as an entry point to our authentic, true self.

Rational guilt

Rational guilt stems from what we have learned throughout our lives to be right and wrong ways of behaving. We experience rational guilt when we go against our own code of ethics, our own values. We experience rational guilt when we subvert our own integrity. When we can feel our rational guilt it alerts us and functions as a useful guide to keeping our integrity intact. When we live with integrity we are true to ourselves.

When we notice and respond to our rational guilt we are authentically evaluating our actions and taking responsibility for them. We acknowledge that we would rather behave in a different way and determine that we will make a better choice in the future. We acknowledge the consequences of our actions and *genuinely* apologize to anyone whom we may have hurt.

Rational guilt is an alarm system for personal responsibility and is emotionally healthy. It is irrational guilt that causes us so much trouble.

Irrational guilt

Irrational guilt is an internal smokescreen that keeps us from knowing ourselves. It is self-blame and self-reproach. Holding irrational guilt is a defense against feeling anger, fear, need, hurt and other emotions that we would rather hide from ourselves. When we remain stuck in irrational guilt we prevent ourselves from experiencing these underlying feelings. We are stopped from seeing any alternatives and doing anything effective to change the situation.

Like all defenses, irrational guilt gives us a sense of control when we do not really have any; we avoid our overwhelming feelings of powerlessness by blaming ourselves. For example, when something tragic occurs that is out of our control we diminish our sense of impotency by protecting ourselves with irrational guilt. As children this was our only option. When we are emotionally fit adults we allow ourselves to feel the rawness of our powerlessness and devastation. This is real and will pass into the tapestry of our lives as an integrated experience.

When we take on the responsibility for events that we have no control over, we can be sure this sense of irrational responsibility is held in place by our childhood pain. For example, when we have been brought up with a lot of "shoulds" we will be very angry. If we were made to feel that our anger was a bad thing then we will not allow ourselves to know that we are angry and we will feel guilty instead. We will turn our anger against ourselves. This is what irrational guilt is. Remember that as children we had no choice but to blame ourselves when we did not measure up.

When we have critical and judgmental parents we fear their disapproval. This fear is too much for us to feel and we turn it into self-punishing guilt. Again, taking the judgments on ourselves gives us a sense that we have some control: "Why didn't I do better?" "What's wrong with me?" "I always mess up," or "I'm no good."

Guilt becomes a very familiar feeling.

When we wrap ourselves in chronic guilt we are fooling ourselves that we are taking responsibility. In fact, feeling guilty all the time is a way we avoid responsibility. Using guilt to make ourselves feel okay does not really work.

The more irrational guilt we suffer, the more our feelings are driven underground and the less emotionally fit we are. When as an adult we understand that guilt is a defense that we are using to protect ourselves from feeling pain, we can choose to notice it, work with it, feel/know ourselves better and become freer to be who we are.

Danielle pleased her father by achieving academically. She even learned to engage with him at the family dinner table by discussing world events. Her oldest brother, who was a failure in his father's eyes, was unable to do the same.

Years later Danielle found herself consumed with guilt because her life was so much better than this brother's. She was unable to enjoy her own accomplishments and good fortune. She found herself irrationally angry at this brother and then overwhelmed with self-berating guilt. When Danielle realized how much she was beating herself up and how conflicted she was, she sought help.

In time Danielle realized what an impossible situation she had been placed in as a child and how much effect it had had on her life. She got to the feeling of being torn between her need for her father's love and approval and her compassion and empathy for her brother. She felt how angry she was at her father for treating her brother as he had and for locking her into a lifetime of guilt.

Danielle felt relief from her pervasive guilt when she continued to make these connections. Now she was able to be responsive and empathetic without feeling responsible for her brother's difficulties.

Sources of guilt in our childhood

When we as parents are unable to take responsibility for our feelings, thoughts and actions it gets deflected onto our children. "You make me so angry I could scream," "Look what you made me do," and "If you don't stop that you'll be the death of me" all place the responsibility of our actions on our children. These are examples of the blatant use of guilt to control our children.

When this happens to us as children we carry this burden of responsibility and guilt into our adulthood. Our unconscious belief that "there must be something wrong with me" and "it must be my fault" will keep us feeling responsible—caught on the notion that, if only we could do something better, if only we could be different, we would gain our parents' approval. We end up with the unconscious belief that we are responsible for other people's feelings and happiness. This produces irrational guilt and we act out by taking responsibility that does not belong to us.

"Shoulds" and "shouldn'ts" trigger guilt. When we feel our parents' overt need for us to do well, look good and be good and we are unable to live up to their wishes we may be weighted down with guilt. We are very sensitive to the nuances of our parents' behaviour; we experience their subtle disapproval and have no way of dealing with it but to feel a disconnected sense of responsibility.

Guilt perpetuated in our culture

Advertising fosters shame. It also fosters our discontent and guilt. The more we have suffered guilt about our shortcomings as children, the more we feel dissatisfaction with ourselves now and the more susceptible we are to advertising. In other words, the greater the guilt we carry from our childhood the more easily we are manipulated. Guilt prevents us from listening to ourselves and our real needs — we become susceptible to what advertising tells us.

Women who have been subjected to and used by advertising in our culture often feel guilty no matter what they do. One of my clients once remarked that she even felt guilty about feeling guilty!

Feeling through irrational guilt

When we feel our way through the confines of irrational guilt we gain the freedom of self-acceptance. We no longer need to suffer self-destructive thoughts, feelings and behaviours. *When we become more honest about our feelings we give up the need to feel irrationally guilty.*

This is a process based on our own power to heal ourselves emotionally and it is lasting. Let me say again that this is different from trying to change our thoughts in order to change our feelings, or affirming positive thoughts in order to banish the negative.

Guilt is an easily recognized feeling, and as soon as we become aware of it we can check out if it is rational guilt alerting us to some present problem or if it is irrational guilt. If it is irrational guilt we can ask ourselves the question "If I didn't feel guilty what would I have to feel?" The answer will come from inside ourselves. Feelings that arise may be anxiety, unbearable sadness, anger, rage, powerlessness. . . .

Often we walk around for some time just acknowledging guilty feelings before we break through to the feeling that lies underneath. Once we have experienced this shift, we are more readily able to access the underlying feelings when our guilt arises.

Stretched to the limit

The more we allow ourselves to feel guilt, the more we will be able to tolerate it and not be driven by it. When our behaviour is unconsciously driven by our need to avoid feeling guilty we can end up stretched to our limit and completely out of touch with what we really need and who we really are. We may spend time on things that do not really interest us. We may extend ourselves beyond normal endurance and we may not be able to ask for help. No matter how much we do we never feel good enough. Avoiding our feelings of guilt drives us to be permissive with our children instead of responsive. We can become so used to the stress and pressure of avoiding feeling guilty that we believe the feeling-state of exhaustion that we live in is normal. If we continue like this, sooner or later we will hit a wall and discover one morning that we cannot get out of bed.

Guilt as a signal

Again, it is important to acknowledge that our feelings of guilt are a signal. Either we are feeling rational guilt because we have breached our own integrity or we are feeling irrational guilt disconnected from our childhood pain.

Sometimes it is difficult to know that we are feeling guilty. When we justify, defend or make excuses we may be feeling guilty. These can act as red flags for us so that we can become aware of when we are feeling guilty and when we are behaving as if we are guilty. We can notice if we feel guilty when we do not get the approval of someone else. We can notice when we are talking to ourselves in a negative way. This usually heralds that we are feeling guilty about something.

Rather than trying to change our negative self-talk by sheer force of will, we can notice it and allow ourselves to identify what we are feeling.

> Connie nervously explained that she felt guilty all the time. She remembered feeling guilty as a child and now as an adult she was aware that her life was being controlled by her guilt. She sincerely wanted to change this because she noticed she was running herself ragged trying to please her three children and that no matter what she did for her widowed father it was never enough. On top of all this she was holding down a very responsible part-time job as a bookkeeper for a small family business and hosting her husband's frequent business parties in their elegant, five-bedroom home.

> Connie took her therapy very seriously and began immediately to compose her time line, look up family pictures and visit her old school grounds. She had trouble getting into her feelings however, which made her feel guilty. When she was asked to stay with this feeling and she sank down into it, she began to sob. Over time she realized how little she had had of her own life. This was the beginning of her healing.

Guilt as a smokescreen for fear

We can learn to admit to our fears once we know that guilt often covers fear. We can replace self-recrimination by self-observation and ask ourselves such questions as "What did I really want to say?" "Why did I do that?" "What would I prefer to do?" and "What am I afraid of?"

Connie, in the example above, connected to the many times she had felt guilty as a child. When she acted "silly" her mother would often say things like "What will the neighbours think?" Connie began to feel how afraid she was as a child that she would not be loved if she did not perform. It is catastrophic for children to feel that they might lose their parents' love.

As we allow ourselves to revisit our past through our natural emotional healing power, we become connected with how fearful we were as children and how this fear got bound with guilt.

A guilt-ridden child becomes a guilt-ridden adult.

Guilt as a smokescreen for anger

When we become aware that guilt often covers anger we can consciously ask ourselves what we may be angry about. When we agree to visit our demanding mother when we do not want to, it is because we do not want to feel guilty. The price we pay for this dishonesty is suffering our submerged, disconnected anger. We are not being true to our feelings and our own needs. We hurt ourselves rather than risk being honest. When we can feel our way through our guilt and our fear of anger we can begin to make choices that are more congruent and honest. If we feel guilty more often than we feel angry it is probable that we would rather feel guilty than face our anger. When we risk telling ourselves and then others the truth about our anger, we remove the smokescreen of guilt. This helps reveal the knots of held anger stretching back in our tapestry.

One of my clients once said, "My guilt makes me do things I don't really want to do with people I don't enjoy much." This client discovered that she was a much less angry person when she started to look after herself better and not do things she did not really want to do. She began to let her anger surface when others called her "selfish." This anger took her to scenes in her childhood when her simple needs were characterized as being selfish by her angry mother. As she looked after herself better and gained a stronger sense of herself she was paradoxically better able to really be there for others, notably her children.

As Connie connected to and felt her fear as a child she became angry. As she worked through the anger at her parents for being so demanding and rigid she became clearer and clearer about how she wanted to behave in the present. She took the risk of telling her father what she was willing to do for him and what she was not and negotiated different arrangements with her husband for his business events so that she no longer carried the responsibility for them. Connie didn't make big, sudden changes, but really gave herself credit for every small step she took along the way to being honest with herself and feeling her guilt instead of letting it drive her.

Guilt obscures the opportunity to live by our own values

When we recognize the necessity of taking care of ourselves in order to live with integrity and therefore emotional health, we can accept the challenge to look after ourselves better. This can be particularly difficult if we are at the bottom of our own list or do not put ourselves in the equation at all.

It is common to believe something but not live in accordance with that belief. This occurs when the adult part of us knows, for example, that we deserve help with the household chores, but our childhood feelings leave us feeling too guilty to ask. When we allow our natural emotional healing power to work and feel back to the child that we were we can get our gut in line with our head. We can feel okay with what we know to be true and can act in accordance with our authentic, true selves.

The more we do this, the more we will have of ourselves. It becomes a positive cycle: the more often we risk looking after ourselves and feeling through the guilt, the better we feel and the more we are able to look after ourselves.

Irrational guilt keeps us stuck

Irrational guilt keeps us stuck because we do things we do not want to do in order to avoid feeling guilty, *or* we feel guilty and this allows us to continue to do things that are not in our best interest or in the best interest of our relationships. It is a terrible defense in which to be trapped.

> Gord was feeling uncomfortably guilty. For over a year he had been having an affair with a woman he worked with. He felt guilty because he was hurting her by not leaving his wife and because he was deceiving his wife every day.

> When Gord sought help he was very distressed; he did not know what to do.

The guilt Gord was feeling allowed him to believe that he was a very caring person who had "unfortunately" fallen "inadvertently" into this trap. He had no real complaint about his marriage and this was why he felt he could not leave. He could even acknowledge how much he cared for his wife.

Gord was willing to explore his past, although he could not see how it was connected to his present dilemma. So he was surprised to find himself crying as he told me how he had finally been able to please his father when he excelled at basketball in high school. His dad had died when Gord was only nineteen, and the only time he could remember his dad paying much attention to him was when he came to watch him play basketball. Gord began to open up more and more to the hurt and deprivation of his young life. When he was able to feel his need that had propelled him into the affair, he was able to make a decision. He ended the affair. Gord decided to risk feeling his enormous need instead of remaining stuck and living with guilt.

I have had other clients who have been unwilling to let go of the guilt and take the responsibility to end their affairs, to be honest with their partners and to begin to feel instead of defend with guilt. I have had some clients who have wanted to come to therapy because doing so made them feel as though they were doing something about their situation and thus assuaged their guilt. Needless to say, it is not good therapy to collude in helping clients fool themselves. It is essential to help such people acknowledge that their guilt is keeping them stuck.

The greatest gift we can give those around us is to be as complete and whole a person as we can possibly be. We will be this when we can own and express our feelings, look after ourselves, know what we need and want and be able to ask for it and receive it instead of being driven by guilt.

10

ANXIETY, FEAR AND PANIC
Dangerous if Denied

Anxious and fearful children become adults who are anxious and fearful. Anxious and fearful adults find the roots of these feelings in their childhood.

We, as children, hide our fear if we suffer indifference or ridicule because of it. Obvious indications of our hidden fear are nervousness, anxiety and tension, which often reveal themselves in such behaviours as nail-biting, thumb-sucking and masturbating. These in turn are often met with displeasure and disapproval, which drives our anxiety to inaccessible places. We are robbed of our feelings and are forced to be less emotionally responsive. These feelings are driven so deeply that, as adults, we may suffer unattached anxiety and panic attacks that come as a complete surprise.

Limited, overtly fearful experiences, such as a car accident, may be easier to deal with than the constant, unrelieved anxiety provoked in us as children because we live in an unsafe place where our needs are not being met day by day. We become adults who have trouble connecting our adult anxiety and panic to our childhood experiences.

As children our need is to be carefree. For us to thrive we need to grow and develop without anxiety. I often ask clients, "Do you remember ever feeling carefree as a child?" We all grow up somewhere on the continuum from riddled with anxiety, fear and tension to being appropriately carefree.

Some of us look as though we are not afraid of anything. We may take pride in our apparent courage, while being intolerant and even scornful of fear and anxiety in our spouse and children. Many of us carry low-grade anxiety as a constant companion, unable to live our lives fully. Some of us manage to contain our anxiety with rituals, addictions, obsessions, paranoias and phobias, or we are caught as our anxiety breaks free into a full-blown panic attack and we fear for our lives.

Panic attacks occur when we respond with "fight or flight" to disconnected feelings of great fear that, at their essence, feel life-threatening. It is difficult for us to understand that *panic attacks are actually our emotional system trying to correct itself by discharging pent-up, withheld, unidentified crisis feelings.* Once we suffer a panic attack, we become anxious about having another one, and this adds to the overall anxiety quotient. We try to control our anxiety and panic instead of understanding that this is an opportunity to cooperate with our natural healing power to feel the source of these feelings. When we do this, instead of merely coping with anxiety, we face our fears and understand them as a message, not as a weakness to be overcome.

Fear as an appropriate signal

Both anxiety and fear are appropriate reactions to life's threatening situations. They become a problem when they are disconnected from their source. We may or may not be able to articulate what our anxiety or fear is about. What we need to do is pay attention to either feeling when we first encounter it. Anxiety and fear are both signals that something is wrong and we ignore them at our peril.

Anxiety is often a signal that our defenses are crumbling. In fact, panic attacks often follow after a loss, such as the death of a parent or grandparent or the end of a relationship. This makes sense, since any life trauma can open us up to feelings that we have buried. This is an opportunity and instead of closing the door we can open it and follow our feelings.

Signs of anxiety

We feel anxious when we experience demanding, commanding and pressuring messages from inside ourselves; we use such phrases as "I have to," "I must," "I always," "I should," or "You never." We are anxious when we feel out of control, sense impending doom or experience apprehension and dread.

Signs of anxiety include racing or repetitive thoughts, forgetfulness, hanging on to some real or imagined slight, dwelling on the same incident over and over, worrying, headaches, irritable bowel, sweating without exertion, muscle tension, feeling like something is eating at us, trembling, stomach discomfort, itching, nail-biting, tapping fingers or toes, trouble swallowing, heart pounding and difficulty breathing. When we notice these signs we can become conscious of our anxiety and then begin to feel it through. It is really helpful to label our anxiety or fear. We can ask ourselves, "What's making me so anxious? What am I afraid of?" The answers may not be immediately obvious. Again, we can wait to hear them from down in our bodies. Our feelings reside in our bodies and we can trust what we hear from our feelings.

The sooner we face our anxiety and fear the less likely it will develop into full-blown panic.

Sources of anxiety, fear and panic in childhood

1) *Babies suffer anxiety when their needs are not met.* Yet the significance of infants' needs and pain has been too often denied in our culture. This denial is central to our confusion about the source of adult anxiety. In fact, adult anxiety is connected to earlier, terrorizing childhood fear that has been repressed because it was too overwhelming to feel.

> Phong woke every morning with the same anxiety, apprehension and dread and the same tense musculature. She obsessed about the list of things she had to do and often had great difficulty forcing herself to get out of bed and get going.

> Phong had a very demanding and critical mother who never appreciated anything she did and constantly peppered her with admonitions about how she "should" be and what she "should" do. This had been going on since Phong was a small child and had followed her into her early thirties.

> Phong felt like a "bad" person a lot of the time and most of the triggers she brought from her current life to her therapy sessions took her straight back to this feeling.

> Even though Phong knew she must have had a very distressful time as an infant she had great difficulty connecting to this time until she started having flashbacks that were unmistakable.

It was very difficult for Phong to allow that she nearly died as a young child in a refugee camp. She had been very ill because of the inadequate food and facilities, and her mother had been distraught with her circumstance and unable to relate to her sick baby. Phong was able to confirm some of her perceptions with an elderly person who had been in the camp and this helped her to trust the flashbacks she was experiencing. The more she felt, the more she was able to connect with the very real terror of the first few years of life. She also could feel how her mother's emotional absence and abuse had compounded this in the years that followed.

2)   *When a child's anxiety and fears are not heard, the child is left alone with them.* As parents we silence our children: "Don't be silly," "You're okay," "Stop crying." As children we must bury our fear when there is no place for us to go for reassurance and comfort. Many years later we may say "But I didn't feel afraid as a child," but in truth the fear was repressed because it was too painful to feel alone. We may remember some of our childhood fears, but minimize their effects. Denial and minimization are two defenses we use to avoid feeling our pain.

> As a seven-year-old, Neil would awaken terrified in the night. He could remember crawling to his parents' bedroom door and sleeping there. He was not allowed to wake his parents no matter how afraid he was. They were intolerant of his fear and told him he was silly.

> Neil could also remember running to get his mother's medication as a child whenever she became distraught. It was not until he was in therapy that he realized his mother had been having panic attacks.

Neil was quite amazed and full of rage when he realized his mother had been having panic attacks all through his young life and in fact still suffered from them. He was angry because not only had his mother never acknowledged her panic as such, but she had also put him down when he told her he was entering therapy because of his own panic attacks.

Neil's attacks ceased as soon as he entered therapy. He attributed this to the fact that just telling someone who was empathetic about them had relieved some of the pressure. He still feared their recurrence however and avoided eating in restaurants, where he might not be able to swallow—this had previously triggered attacks.

Neil was amazed to realize how frightened he had been as a child, and not just when he woke up at night. He had been afraid all the time of not measuring up to his parents' high standards and of what was happening to his mother when he had to run for her medication. As Neil felt again and again how anxious he had been he began to connect his panic attacks to this enormous reservoir of fear. He was able to experience what he felt in his body when he woke terrified as a child in his bed. He was shocked as he recognized the identical feeling that he suffered in his adult panic attacks.

We can easily imagine the anxiety, fear and panic that children who are overtly neglected and abused must feel. What we do not give enough credence to are the more subtle forms of emotional abuse and neglect. Children who are never allowed to make decisions or have choices appropriate to their level of development suffer the anxiety that comes from never feeling in control of their own lives.

Children whose parents are simply "not there" for them—that is, emotionally absent—suffer the anxiety of feeling all alone and responsible for themselves in a very scary world. When a parent is frequently emotionally absent this becomes one of the precursors of adult panic attacks. This emotional abuse is less easily acknowledged in our culture and this makes it more difficult for us to recognize and identify.

3) *Many parents intentionally use fear as a means to control their children.* When this happens we carry anxiety into our adulthood.

4) *When we as children are required to take on responsibility beyond our years we become candidates for anxiety.* I have had many clients who wanted to jettison their responsibilities as adults because they had far too many responsibilities as children. They felt the weight of these young responsibilities and did not realize that this feeling of weight was coming from the past. As one of my clients began to recognize why she felt such a burden of responsibility as an adult, she was fond of saying, "I was forty when I was four and now at forty I want to be four."

Parental expectation beyond a child's level of development, ability and control is anxiety-producing for that child. There are many overt ways in which children are asked to take responsibility beyond their years. We may have been required to look after younger siblings and do household chores that should have been our parents' tasks. This is not to say that we, as children, cannot be asked to cooperate at our own level of development, but when we are asked to go beyond this it is a detriment to us and *we will be anxious.*

5)   *We suffer our own anxiety when our parents are anxious.* We are caught in a web of anxiety when we are required to participate in family secrets and be silent.

> Jasmine came to this country with her family when she was only five. Neither of her parents could speak English as well as she soon could. Jasmine's mother was very ashamed at the way they had to live in this new country and constantly reminded her two small daughters that they were not as good as those who had lived here all their lives.
>
> When Jasmine was thirteen she was raped by a man who lived in their building. She never told her mother or father because she was afraid they would blame her. She was afraid that it was her fault. Many years later her mother asked her if that man had ever done anything to her. Jasmine was paralyzed and could not speak: she realized that even though her mother must have always suspected that she might have been this man's victim, she had never raised the subject with her before. Even now when Jasmine finally answered yes her mother dismissed the matter, saying that it had happened a long time ago. Jasmine entered therapy.

Jasmine opened slowly to her feelings. She had suffered the aftermath of the sexual assault all alone and had carefully put the incident away, telling herself that it was over and would have no effect on her. Her mother's suspicion and apparent indifference, demonstrated by her silence, shocked Jasmine. As she felt how terrified and alone she had been, she began to realize how her mother's many fears had affected her. Jasmine had learned to tell her mother only the things her mother wanted to hear and kept her own anxieties and fears to herself. She came to realize that the stomachaches she had had as a child were due to her anxiety. They had either been ignored or she had been told she was not eating properly and it was her own fault if she had a stomachache.

Jasmine felt that her mother's anxiety about living in this new country had been transferred to her. She had been berated even as a young child when she had to make phone calls and fill out forms for her parents; she remembered how frantic they were and how frantic this had made her feel.

Jasmine resolved to be more open in her relationship with her own son and daughter. She was sick of the silence and secrets.

Hyper-vigilance

Children become hyper-vigilant when they do not feel essentially safe with their parents. This happens if they have excessive expectations placed on them or if they are terrorized by their parents, family members, neighbours, babysitters, coaches or bullies. Many adults relate to the notion of being on red-alert through much of their childhood. It is as though our internal antenna that we use to sense danger rotates constantly to protect us. It is tragic for us to be afraid of the very people whom we should have been able to rely on in any and all circumstances.

Anxiety, fear and panic locked in our bodies

Most of us feel anxiety in our bodies, usually in our gut or in our shoulders. We experience a sense of dread that seems to be hanging over us. Fear is often described as being felt in the chest. We may shake and tremble as the fear escalates. We all have our own way to describe feelings of anxiety: we are uptight, we are antsy, or our nerves are on edge.

When situations are overwhelming, even life threatening, it is an automatic response to shut down. We need this ability to shut down emotionally. Sometimes our systems cannot take in all at once what has happened, or we need to put our emotions aside temporarily in order to deal with an event. If the threat is severe and ongoing, then our *bodies* get utilized to contain the fear. As Arthur Janov notes, the body wall is used to *bind* anxiety and this results in tension. The containment of fear may be so severe that we may suffer a lifetime of shallow breathing, back problems, sexual dysfunction, obsessive body rituals, ulcers, elevated heart rates, elevated blood pressure, migraines, psoriasis and muscular pain. It takes enormous energy to keep feelings contained in our bodies, and so we will frequently feel exhausted and not know why.

We can use our natural emotional healing power to bring the feelings that lie behind these body pains to the surface in order to be felt.

When we lock our anxiety and fear in our bodies we are attempting to disown them. This means that we must first take the responsibility to acknowledge that the pain in our body is our repressed voice, and that it is telling us something important. *When we pay attention to our body states and acknowledge that they mean something, there is a chance for the underlying feelings that are holding us in that pain to surface and be felt.*

In order to defend against our body's messages we often split off from our bodies by speaking of them as separate entities: "My body hurts" rather than "I hurt." When we say "My body is betraying me" we are participating in a defense. We would be closer to our feelings if we could say "I am feeling betrayed."

Norma was locked in her body pain. She felt no connection to the fear embedded in her childhood and spent enormous amounts of money and time trying to deal with the debilitating muscle pain in her back, neck and shoulders.

When she had been in therapy for some time Norma began to feel all that her depression had been holding down: rage, both at how her father had treated her sister and at how ineffectual her mother had been in the face of this abuse. Norma began to acknowledge that although she had been the "golden-haired girl" and her sister had been the "devil," she had not escaped unscathed. Hearing her sister cruelly punished, restricted and put down had affected her severely.

Norma learned that if she began to feel depressed she needed to give herself time to feel what she was trying to depress. She was relieved to finally have the depression lift and to feel that she knew what it was all about and how to keep it from recurring.

It took Norma much longer to deal with the pain she had bound in her musculature.

Norma sometimes got discouraged by how long it was taking her to feel what she needed to feel, again and again, in order to connect with and heal the muscular pain in her body. Yet at the same time she felt lucky that she no longer suffered from depression. Her life had changed dramatically and she felt really good, especially about her close relationship with her children and husband and the new work she was doing that challenged and fulfilled her. Norma often said that she felt she had been given a key to life when she came to understand that she could process through her feelings and complete them whenever she noticed their troublesome appearance. She felt empowered because she knew how to deal with depression and no longer feared slipping into that black hole.

There are many examples of anxiety, fear and panic being locked in our bodies.

Jennifer feared being "wrong" and "bad." It did not take much of a trigger to put her into terrible anxiety about what she might have done that might have been misconstrued as a transgression. She suffered frequently from lower back pain.

As Jennifer connected to her anxiety-ridden childhood, she was able to be much more aware of when her old feelings of fear were being triggered. As she felt more and more of what it was really like for her to have been this frightened little girl, she had less difficulty with her back.

Randy had trouble in the area of his neck and shoulders.

This problem was alleviated when he remembered and felt through the terror he had experienced when his father held him up against a wall and threatened him with his hands around his throat.

Bob was severely restricted in his executive position because of his irritable bowel problem. When he entered therapy he cried for the first six months throughout every session. He was reliving the anxiety he had felt and how he had had to hide it as a small boy who was expected to keep everyone in the family happy, including his parents and three older brothers.

Even though he had to feel through a lot of shame about his crying, Bob was inspired to keep coming to therapy because his irritable bowel improved after a few sessions.

Once we understand that our bodies and our emotions are inseparable, we can use our aches and pains to take us to the knots in our tapestry—we can heal both body and soul.

Talking ourselves out of our feelings of anxiousness

Because anxiety and fear are often bound up with shame we have a great deal of trouble acknowledging that we are feeling them. We often try to talk ourselves out of them in the moment by talking to ourselves—a kind of self-coaching. We may, for example, invoke a ritual of trying to change how we feel by speaking affirmations over and over: "I can do it, I can do it."

> Lorraine became aware that she never did anything without coaching herself as she went. On her way to work she would talk to herself in the car: "You'll be okay; you know how to do this work . . . Sandra has said more than once that you are really very good at relating to the families of the residents."
>
> On the way home Lorraine would most often be thinking of her twelve-year-old son, with whom she always felt uncomfortable. She figured it was because there were no boys in her family of origin and that her father had disappeared when she was two. She would say to herself, "Now just be yourself, just be natural with Jake. Don't worry so much, everything will be okay. He really is such a great kid."
>
> When she had a family celebration coming up with her in-laws, she would go over for days in advance how she would behave. She would talk to herself and would reassure herself that she was as good as they were.
>
> No matter what Lorraine told herself, or how often, nothing changed. She never felt any different or better. However, she was compelled to continue this coping mechanism.
>
> Lorraine connected with, and felt, how abandoned she had been as a child. She remembered that no matter how hard she had tried to please her mother, all she saw on her mother's face was disapproval and often disgust. Lorraine realized that as a result she had never lived inside herself. She was always observing

herself and coaching herself, trying to make herself perform satisfactorily and trying to make herself feel okay.

We cannot talk ourselves out of our feelings; to try to do so is a defense. The only way to reduce the intensity of our anxiety and eventually begin to live free of it is to connect with its source and feel the impact of the fears from our past. I have witnessed many courageous individuals freeing themselves from anxiety by facing the fears of the child they were. It never ceases to impress me how the human spirit can survive such early trauma, and how we can go on to free that same spirit that was responsible for our survival. We can thank our natural emotional healing power for this possibility.

Panic attacks: the end result of held fear

Panic attacks appear to be about things and circumstances over which we have no control. In fact, these things and circumstances are places to put our anxiety unconsciously when we do not really know what our anxiety is all about. We may not be able to drive our car on the highway, stay overnight alone with our children when our husband is out of town or fly in a plane. We may be restricted in a myriad of other ways. We may say we were frightened by a snake as a child and that is why we have an inordinate fear of snakes now. Clearly we did not have the opportunity to feel through our fear to completion about this incident and so its residue has been carried into our adult life. It has been linked unconsciously to other fears that we were not able to label or feel at the time.

Clients are always amazed when they begin to unravel the real sources of their panic. They have never understood before that they could deal with their panic in any way other than to try to desensitize themselves or avoid triggering situations. They have had little notion that their anxiety, fear and panic stretches all the way back to their childhood experiences.

Lauren was afraid of heights. Nevertheless, when her new husband wanted her to ski with him she determined that she would. She said it was painful for anyone to watch her go down the hill because her body posture reflected her terror.

Lauren had several frightening experiences, two of them ending up in the emergency ward of the local hospital. Each time she had been convinced she was having a heart attack. The chest pain and her inability to breathe were pretty convincing; however, the doctor said there was nothing wrong. She sought emotional help.

Lauren got in touch with a childhood full of nervous anxiety any time she attempted any physical activity. Her mother had passed on her own anxieties to Lauren, needing to caution her to be careful with every move she made. The anxiety and fear Lauren carried was much more complex than just this body fear. She was expected to excel at school and always to demonstrate what an extra-special child she was. She had to perform well in everything she did, and dealing with her new marital situation after a failed first marriage was no exception.

As Lauren allowed herself to be that fearful child again and again, she began to relax and look after herself better.

Common fears

We can cooperate with our natural emotional healing power, and avoid reaching the meltdown point of a panic attack, by deliberately looking at, discovering, labelling and of course feeling our fears. A prerequisite for healing is that we become honest with ourselves about what we are feeling and fearing.

We fear being:

controlled	vulnerable	disappointed	discounted
needy	despairing	judged	inadequate
lonely	criticized	out of control	helpless
violated	foolish	afraid	humiliated
a failure	anxious	abandoned	crazy
wrong	rejected	bad	weak
left out	suicidal	hurt	unacceptable
successful	sad	useless	worthless
numb	controlling	lost	angry
expressive	spontaneous	uninhibited	shamed
stupid	sick	separate	different

We may be less aware of it, but we also fear losing ourselves, not knowing who we are or what we want or need. When we do know our wants and needs, we fear putting ourselves forward. Many of us profess to want intimacy, but deep down we fear allowing ourselves to be that vulnerable by letting someone know us that well.

Sex as a vehicle to release anxiety

Excessive masturbation, promiscuity and an excessive need for sex are indications that anxiety is seeking an outlet. Once we open at all to this possibility we begin to unravel another series of knots in our personal tapestry. We label our anxiety and begin to feel it.

The danger of masking fear

When we mask our fear and keep it hidden from ourselves we put ourselves in jeopardy. We may be caught in a vicious cycle of seeking relief through obsessive, compulsive or addictive behaviour and then feeling bad about the behaviour that brought us relief. We may get hooked on wanting to change the behaviour rather than feel what is driving it. Many programs to help those with obsessive-compulsive disorders and addictions are aimed at controlling, managing and changing behaviour instead of feeling, connecting and integrating the pain energizing the disorder or addiction. These programs treat the symptoms, not the causes.

When we are disconnected from our fear we may overcompensate and put ourselves or others in danger. For example, the father who urges his son or daughter to tackle a ski hill far above their expertise ignores the real danger of his children getting physically hurt as well as the invisible real danger that their feelings of fear will be repressed in order to please him. In some cases, we may engage in exercises to conquer our fear that are designed to leave us feeling exhilarated with our accomplishment and feeling that we can now tackle anything in our lives. The danger here is that the forces of repression we need to call on to keep our fear locked away will deaden us more and make us more of a mystery to ourselves. We may be able to be successful at many things, but we will need to keep proving ourselves and will not know why. When we deny our reality—for example that we are actually afraid to shoot whitewater or bungie jump—we become unreal and we do not know ourselves. In being driven to prove that we are okay we limit our real emotional potential by denying our feelings.

When we mask our fear it puts strain on our body; we become exhausted and our health is jeopardized. We may ignore and deny our body signs and symptoms as well and continue to keep ourselves up and away from our feelings with one challenge after another. We often treat our bodies as an opponent, something to be overcome. We keep going no matter what messages we get from our bodies; this denial splits us off from our reality.

When we underreact to what our bodies are telling us we may put off going for medical or alternative help; we do not take suitable action to look after ourselves. We get disconnected from appropriate concern for our well-being.

One of the most unfortunate ramifications of hiding our fear from ourselves is that we pass on our masked fear to our children as anxiety. Often, as parents, we deliberately hide scary things that are going on in our lives from our children because we do not want to frighten them. This never works, since children have radar antennae and pick up on our distress no matter how much we try to hide it. They pick it up without a place to put it.

Fixing the behaviour

When we try to fix our obsessive, compulsive, paranoiac or phobic behaviour we obscure the chance for our natural healing power to work. The danger in desensitizing ourselves to one defense is that another defense will pop up automatically in its place—perhaps one that is even deeper in our bodies and more unseen.

It is not easy to welcome our debilitating obsessive or compulsive behaviour as a signal that our natural emotional healing power is actually at work. However, the sooner we do this and start cooperating with the process the sooner we will get relief and the peace that comes when we stop warring with ourselves. We need to remember that this natural power we possess is not a quick fix and that *the deeper the wound the longer it takes to heal.* If we find ourselves worrying about how long this process is taking us, we can then feel that defense through to the underlying pain.

No shortcuts to freedom: taking the time to feel and integrate fear

Paying attention to the signs and symptoms of anxiety and fear is where we begin. When we notice that we are unable to behave as we really want to we can consciously ask ourselves questions about what is stopping us. It will always be fear of some sort, for example, fear of the other person's reaction, whether it be anger, withdrawal or disapproval.

Learning to identify and label our fear is a big step in the right direction. We feel as if we are taking charge when we do this and the moment we identify or write the fear down it loses some of its power.

Before we engage in an obsessive, compulsive or addictive behaviour, we can try to give ourselves a few moments to feel what we are feeling. Stopping these behaviours cold turkey does not help us process them. Bringing feelings into our awareness gives room for our natural emotional healing power to become active in our recovery.

Anna came into therapy because of her compulsive behaviour around her fears. She needed to check the door lock several times before going to bed. She could not stay at home or at the cottage alone without being so fearful that she could not sleep.

In time she remembered many anxiety-producing incidents from her childhood. She had been anxious when she saw her mother unhappy; she was anxious to keep up with her brothers academically and to be the athlete her father wanted her to be. She had also been hospitalized for five days at fourteen months of age and had been subjected to many invasive test procedures. Her parents had not been allowed to accompany her or stay overnight with her.

Anna kept returning to her fears in her therapy. She noticed her over and underreactions and diligently brought them to her sessions. She became aware that she compulsively cleaned up at parties and was always the one to help and do the work. She was able to connect this to her fear of socializing because she felt so inadequate. Gradually Anna faced the anxiety and fear generated in her childhood. Eventually she no longer suffered the debilitating fear in her current life that had kept her from staying alone. She could let go of her compulsive behaviour, and she became more conscious and relaxed. She was also able to make better choices for herself.

We can help ourselves by noticing our anxiety and fear and taking the time we need to feel it through to integration before it develops into panic. When we break through to a panic state we are usually *forced* to pay attention. If the panic meltdown does occur we can use this as an opportunity to heal rather than beat ourselves up about it. We can cooperate with our natural healing power at any stage.

11

ANGER

A Release and a Prison

———————————————

Anger is a problem when we do not take responsibility for it, when we do not express it and when we express it inappropriately. Children who are allowed to discharge their anger completely as it arises will automatically express their anger appropriately as adults.

If we carry unresolved anger from our past it awaits an opportunity to exit. It does so as an *overreaction;* it may be a little or a big BOOOM as we find the nearest place to dump it. Road rage is one modern example of this. The degree of anger is proportional to the underlying, hidden pain. Our anger may come out directly, but in an aggressive way, or it may come out very crooked, in sarcasm, for example. Our unresolved, old anger may also stay hidden from us in our *underreactions.* We hold it in our body and suffer fatigue, headaches and a variety of other ailments. We will also suffer some degree of depression.

We have great difficulty taking responsibility for our supercharged anger, tenaciously preferring to keep it directed at others rather than feeling what is going on inside us. We also have difficulty owning the pain in our body as a revelation of our anger.

When we understand that our over and underreactions are signals from our natural emotional healing power we can use them to resolve our unfinished anger from the past. When we do this our anger in the present automatically becomes more appropriate. Our overreactive and indirect behaviours and our body symptoms subside.

Cultural taboos and our fear of anger and conflict

We are most likely to be afraid of our own and others' anger if we experienced disconnected, misdirected anger as children. One of my clients, Marnie, said, "I never want to be like my mother; she was a raging maniac." This was a double whammy for her, since her mother not only frequently raged out of control but also did not allow Marnie to express her own anger. This was enough to have Marnie repress and suppress her anger into her fifties.

Although in our culture males are considered more entitled to their anger than females, I have met many men over the years who avoid conflict and carry their repressed anger deep inside. The huge cultural taboo against women being angry or expressing their anger has caused some to bury it so deeply that they do not know what it feels like at all. Some feel their anger and suffer enormous shame.

At an early age we learned that expressions of anger were unacceptable to others and led to such undesirable consequences as punishment, rejection or the withdrawal of affection or approval. We learned to be "nice" and to hide our "bad" feelings. Our expression of anger was stifled by the requirements that we be reasonable, logical, polite, civil and respectful.

Children are not equipped to explain, defend, justify or document their feelings, although they are frequently asked to do so. When we are asked to do so, our right to our anger is diminished.

> Larry remembered many times when he was little and his parents demanded that he explain why he was angry. He would feel increasingly panicked as they cajoled, "Come on now Larry, spit it out. No more tears—why are you feeling this way?" He remembered stifling his tears. He felt what it had been like to withdraw inside and could remember feeling bad when he saw his parents' frustration. He felt caught and there was no exit for his anger nor for his feeling of badness.

> Larry was frequently blamed for being moody and difficult.

When our expression of anger is fraught with fear and shame we have to stifle it in order to protect ourselves, and so we convince ourselves that we are not really angry even when we are. Our capacity for emotional expression is thwarted.

We control our disapproved anger by contracting our muscles, warding off anger's unwelcome expression by binding ourselves in layers of tension. Anger is energy and it stays bound in our musculature if it is not released. Our muscle tension points to our denied anger; our muscles record this unacceptable feeling that we want to banish. We do feel better when we work out physically; however, this alone does not bring us the connection and integration we need. We can become hooked on working out in order to feel better.

Our fear of anger and conflict stemming from our childhood interferes with our ability to appropriately express our anger in the present and solve problems effectively. We do not feel free to be who we are. We do not feel whole.

The damage of disowned anger

When we do not own our anger we blame others and we are not honest in our communication of how we are feeling. This results in destroyed relationships, fearful children, arrested personal development and a lot of personal turmoil and pain.

It is enormously difficult to own our anger when it is bound by shame. It is a long way back to claim it as our own and to feel good about expressing it appropriately.

If we were not allowed to discharge and express our anger as small children, we will now block or invalidate our experience of anger by asking: "Is my anger legitimate? Do I have a right to be angry? What's the use of getting angry? What good will it do?" We would not ask these same questions about our thirst. These questions likely have their roots in how our anger was treated when we were children.

When we are unaware that we are angry we react in unconscious ways. We damage our relationships because our anger *does* get expressed in devious, inappropriate and unowned ways. Anger obstructed is like a wood stove when the chimney is blocked. If the smoke cannot escape by the straight route it will seep out in some destructive way. We can begin to notice all the ways that our anger seeps out and use this as our door to go through to discover more about our hidden anger.

A major problem with being unstraight with our anger is that it keeps us hidden from ourselves—it just plain does not feel good. Our sense of self is diminished.

Signals of our anger

In order to help us become aware of our anger we can notice:

- If we are aggressive with our anger in most of our relationships, boiling over all the time.
- If we are passive, passive, passive and then aggressive—feel shame and return to passivity.
- If we are aggressive with our children, even though we are mostly passive with others.
- When we are griping, gossiping, cynical, nitpicking or fault-finding.
- If we use sarcastic humour to disguise our anger. (Often entire families engage in this dishonest way of dealing with each other.)
- When we convey we are displeased with someone in such an obscure, beating-around-the-bush way that they have little chance to react to our anger.
- When we cite a third party's reaction instead of saying how we feel about what someone is doing or has done. We say that someone else found this behaviour unacceptable or pull in evidence that other people also found fault.
- When we shirk responsibility for our anger by telling someone else about it and expecting them to pass it on to the person we are angry at.
- When we do not go through appropriate channels with a complaint but instead go over the head of the person we actually have the complaint about.
- When we have symptoms in our bodies that may indicate we are holding anger.

Feeling angry signals a problem. Our anger exists for a reason and deserves our attention and respect.

Dawn's doctor could not understand why her blood pressure was lower. She had been having trouble for some time with hypertension and had not wanted to take medication for the condition.

Dawn knew that her blood pressure had probably dropped because of all the anger she was feeling through and releasing in her therapy. She knew that her body felt very different. She was much less uptight and irritable.

Dawn came from a large family. She had been severely neglected and abused as a child. She was not allowed to express herself at all and was treated like a servant in her home.

Dawn had easy access to her anger. She was triggered into it everywhere she turned. When she took responsibility for it, she began to direct it in her therapy sessions to where it belonged. Initially she vented the anger at her very disconnected, controlling and abusive parents. As she allowed herself to do this, frequently sitting up and hitting the floor with a length of plumbing hose, she began to remember scene after scene where she had been ignored and used. She moved from the disconnected venting to the real traumas of her childhood and the devastating feelings they had caused. She would suddenly be that young child again, and along with the rage would come tears of impotence. She would tremble and shake as she spoke to her mother or father.

It is a long way back for those of us who have suffered severe neglect and abuse. People like Dawn are a testament to the healing power we all possess.

What does owning our anger mean?

Having anger is part of being a whole person. Being emotionally fit means being able to experience the whole range of human emotions, anger included.

Our anger is a response to a threat to our being. When our response is appropriate, it matches the size of the threat. It is when the response does not match that we are overreacting or underreacting.

We own our anger when we take responsibility for the extra charge on it that causes overreacting. Acknowledging that we are in overreaction is very difficult and it takes an enormous commitment to owning our feelings to do so. The sooner we take responsibility for the charge on our anger, the less harm it will create. Blaming is the opposite of owning. As soon as we realize that our anger has turned to blame, we can take responsibility for it by feeling what is driving us to keep the feelings glommed onto someone else.

We also own our anger when we take responsibility for the lack of charge on it which causes us to underreact. Acknowledging our underreactions is very difficult, since we have shut down on our anger and hidden it from ourselves and from others. Owning our underreactions means being open to what we hear from others. Instead of denying that we are angry by saying "Nothing" when someone asks us what we are angry about, we can pause and honestly begin to feel what is there.

When we own our anger we can use the triggers that plunge us into over and underreactions to feel, connect and integrate our past experience. In doing so we become clearer about our present situation. We become better able to act appropriately on our own behalf.

When we become aware of blaming, being crooked with our anger and holding in our body, we can view these as doors to go through.

Feeling anger to its source: taking responsibility

The first step in reclaiming our right to our anger and feeling it is to acknowledge that it is in there somewhere. Overreacting and underreacting are, once again, our two big doors into our feelings, in this case, anger.

In order to take responsibility we need to use whatever trigger we notice. If we are at work, for instance, we may not be able to do this on the spot; however, we can go to it as soon as possible.

Ed decided to do something about his angry outbursts when he realized they were happening more frequently. He could no longer blame them on his wife, since she had left him two years before. He also noticed that his consumption of alcohol had increased significantly. One day at work he blew up at his boss and realized how inappropriate he had been.

Ed entered therapy full of rationalizations for why he was so angry. When he did his time line he made it short and sweet, stating that he really had had a very good childhood.

Ed said that he wanted to find a way to "manage" his anger and that he was not interested in delving into his past. In that same session he began to talk about his father. He mentioned that his father was rarely at home when he was a child. Ed said that his father worked very hard to support the family and be a good provider. When I asked what it was like for Ed to see so little of his father when he was young, he said, "I don't know, that was just the way it was!"

He did open further, however, telling me that before his dad had died, Ed had been able to take him on a vacation that had been something his dad had wanted to do all his life. As he talked Ed began to wipe the tears from his eyes.

Ed asked if he could do another time line—and this time the sadness and anger spilled out as he remembered his excruciating loneliness as a child. He quickly realized that "just the way it was" was far from good enough. He *was* angry at his daddy as a little boy but he was not allowed to show this. As Ed began to feel through his anger he felt transformed—he no longer had to worry about uncontrolled outbursts. He did not have to hold himself in any more and *manage* his anger.

It is not easy to take responsibility for our anger, but it is a major key for emotional well-being.

The difference between venting and feeling anger

There is great confusion among "anger experts" about how anger should be dealt with. Most of them focus on managing our anger and keeping it under control. Some believe in catharsis, a purging of our anger, as a way to relieve pressure and reduce pent-up feeling. Others report research indicating that catharsis does not work and may even foster aggression by giving people permission to relax their self-control.

There is a vast difference between hitting a punching bag or kicking a cardboard box in order to get into our feelings of anger and simply venting anger as an end in itself. If we just keep venting without owning and connecting, it amounts to emotional masturbation.

There is a difference between venting anger and feeling anger. Venting is most frequently getting our anger out by ranting to someone else about it. This does not solve the problem because we are not connecting to it in a real way, that is, feeling its source. Venting, indeed, keeps us from going deeper into the feeling and owning it. We stay stuck, unable to feel what needs to be felt and to make the changes that need to be made. Speaking out loud to a person who is not present but who is the trigger for our anger as a way to connect with our feelings is different from venting. This is the way we begin to process our feelings.

It is important to understand that getting into our anger, owning it and therefore taking responsibility for it, is a means to an end. Some of us feel we will lose control if we let out our anger. This fear of going out of control with our anger is a feeling from our childhood that also needs to be felt. When it is felt, it dissipates.

When we allow ourselves to feel our anger we will break through to its source. We need to feel our anger at its source again and again until we move through to our hurt and pain, which is the basis of our anger, and grieve it fully. When we have completed this process we will notice one day that something that would have formerly triggered us does not do so now. When we have been working to get through an intense feeling for some time this often comes as an unexpected, pleasant surprise. We will feel clearer.

How anger masks other emotions

Anger masks other emotions because it becomes a defense against these other feelings that we must keep hidden from ourselves. If our value is threatened in some way we may feel anger instead of the vulnerability and fear that underlies it. If our beliefs, values, needs and wants are threatened we may also fight rather than acknowledge how we are really feeling, that is, afraid that we may be wrong.

> Richard was often angry at his wife, Terry. He did not understand this until he began to ask himself why and then to listen to his gut response. He realized that he was actually quite threatened by Terry. She was doing very well in her career and his was stalling rather badly. This had been going on for quite a while.

> Richard took the risk of sharing how he was really feeling with Terry. Her empathy for and understanding of his position made it easier for Richard to open more to what was happening to him on his career path and to what he wanted to do about it.

Anger frequently covers fear. Many parents dump their fury on their teenagers when they return home later than expected. Our anger comes up quickly to protect us from our fear of losing someone so precious. This will more likely happen if we are ashamed to show our fear. A more accurate message would be "I was worried sick, thinking you had been in an accident."

Anger is bound with shame in this way. Any feeling that we are ashamed of may be defended against with anger. We may not want to show our hurt, inadequacy, helplessness, anxiety, vulnerability and fear.

Brent lost it with his anger most often when he could not get something to work right. More than once he put his fist right through a wall when he was frustrated.

As Brent took responsibility for his anger he began to feel back to the awful feelings he had as a child when he was trying to build something or fix something with his father. His dad could do anything of this sort, but because of his own repressed anger he had no patience with his young and inexperienced son. Even when his dad tried to hide his impatience and frustration it was very evident to Brent, and like all children he took it in as his fault and felt terribly inadequate.

Brent had always remembered how he had felt and knew it was the source of his current problem with his anger. But he realized one day that just knowing about it was not fixing it.

As Brent allowed his anger to be as big as it really was, he deliberately went to the basement to his punching bag instead of hitting the wall. He yelled out loud at his father and often collapsed in tears to grieve as the little boy had needed to do. He felt how inadequate, angry and hurt he had felt and how lonely it had left him when he could not express himself.

We mask other feelings with anger unconsciously. We do not decide that we are going to hide our vulnerability by getting angry. Once we comprehend that our anger is hiding other feelings from us, it is another incentive to notice our anger and cooperate with our natural healing power.

Hiding in collective anger

Getting on the bandwagon when someone is telling us about their anger is a way to get some anger "off" without really owning it or knowing what it is about for us. It is a common occurrence and quite unsatisfying for the person who initially expressed the anger and just wanted to be listened to. When this happens we often feel the other person is taking our anger away from us and running with it for themselves.

Another way to hide in collective anger is to become enraged about an issue and join with others in expressing our outrage. This is not to say there are not issues worth speaking out about. However, if there is a huge feeling connected to any issue we can be sure that we are getting our anger off and not recognizing its true source. Homophobia and misogyny are huge repositories for disconnected anger en masse.

Deirdre expressed many strong, negative opinions in her first few months in therapy. She apparently did not recognize that many of them were blatantly racist. When she pronounced her beliefs I would always ask her how she was feeling. Inevitably she would feel her anger and go to some current slight that had recently happened to her.

It took a long time before Deirdre was able to let the current triggers take her back to her childhood anger. She was amazed each time she connected with its source. She remembered how her mother had always put others down: the neighbours, other ethnic groups and anyone who did not look good in her opinion. When Deirdre connected with her fear of not pleasing her mother and her rage at her mother's judgmental character she wept at how for so many years she had put out the same unconscious attitudes as her mother.

Warning: protecting our children as we feel through our anger

When we are triggered into our anger we must be very aware of what our children are hearing or sensing. It is important to protect our children as we feel through our anger. It is important to yell and hit things someplace where the children cannot hear. If they are aware that we have left in anger they need a clear explanation that it is not about them. They can be told that we are getting our anger out and we can help them by listening to their concerns.

Tools that help us open to ourselves

Many clients come to therapy either so entrenched in their anger or so far from it that in order to help them get to their feelings, I have found that the following tools help them become more aware and more responsible for their anger. These tools open doors for us to our natural emotional healing power.

When we go through these doors we have the possibility of responding freely and appropriately in the present. We are freer to be ourselves. We no longer need to hide behind our anger or our lack of it.

1) *We can notice when we are dumping anger instead of owning it.* This is a major, necessary understanding—if we blame we are dumping our anger out and this will not help our relationship with the other person; it will not help us become more connected and whole. If we do dump, which we undoubtedly will, we can take it as an opportunity to feel, and we then need to apologize. *We are talking about being responsible, not about being perfect.* If we apologize and find ourselves still ruminating about the incident, this alerts us that there are still more feelings from the past for us to feel.

2) *When we can identify what other feeling is linked with our anger, for example, hurt, frustration, resentment or exasperation, we become clearer about what we are feeling.* Identifying the secondary feeling helps us get to what the actual trigger is in the present, which then gives us a better chance of dealing with the problem. We can process the feelings it stirs up. It is only when we know what is causing our anger that we can begin to do something about it and to feel it.

Sandy always felt irritable at work and did not know why.

She began to notice when she was feeling this way and she tried to identify exactly what she was feeling instead of just this amorphous irritability.

Sandy was able to identify that she was frustrated with some of the procedures that were not written down and changed all the time depending on whom she was talking to. She also recognized that she resented being the person who stayed late when there was a crunch of some sort. She felt unacknowledged and unappreciated when she came up with good ideas and was not given credit for them. She felt terribly inadequate when she could not immediately grasp a new computer program, even though there was no provision for training her on these new programs when they were implemented.

When Sandy caught on to labelling her feelings more specifically she began to be proactive in changing some of the circumstances that were so aggravating to her.

Her bosses were fairly receptive when she was clear and direct about what she needed. Although she did not get all she wanted, she felt really good about being able to ask for the things that she needed.

In therapy, Sandy was able to identify what was bothering her and make some immediate, positive changes in her working life. More importantly, by taking these risks Sandy opened to herself more and found that she had more access to all her feelings. She had layered over her frustration, hurt and feelings of being unappreciated from her childhood with widespread irritability. Sandy eventually opened to a floodgate of early feelings of being deprived of her anger over and over again as a child.

3)   *We can become aware of our characteristic way of responding to others, either by being passive, assertive or aggressive.* We can draw a circle, placing ourselves in the centre. Radiating spokes connect us to other circles that represent the other people with whom we interact on a frequent basis. The next step is to decide whether we characteristically behave in a passive, assertive or aggressive way with each of these people.

This growing awareness helps us unravel the feelings that have locked us in unhealthy behaviours.

4)   *We can consider who owns the problem.* We are often irritable and angry when we are trying to solve a problem that is not ours. It is helpful to notice this and consider who really owns the problem. We waste energy trying to solve a problem that is not ours. If we want our relationships to thrive, we will listen

when the other person has a problem and enter into negotiation if their problem affects us. If we cannot listen at the time we can say so and commit to listening when we are able.

5) *We can notice if we say yes when we want to say no.* Often we say yes because we cannot stand the guilty feeling we will have if we say no. We cannot help but feel angry when we go against ourselves and we then often hide our anger in resentment. Resentment eats at us and kills love.

6) *We can examine the intent of what we are saying.* Others will often say "It's not what you say, it's your tone that I don't like." This can be an opportunity for us to examine and own what we were really trying to convey. The more defensive we feel, the more likely there was some anger there that we were unable to admit to. Only seven percent of a message is verbal and the rest is body language and tone, so there is a lot of room to fool ourselves about the intent of our message. Owning what we intended to say can be an important growth step toward emotional health and better relationships.

7) *Speak in "I" language.* "I think," "I feel," "I fear" and "I want" statements all say something about us; they keep the focus on us and our feelings. This helps us become more responsible for the charge on our reactions.

Be aware that we can bury blame in "I" statements with our tone, words and emphasis. This is where we need to examine our intent. When we make the shift to using "I" statements we can open to identifying and owning our feelings.

8) *It is important to recognize that we are adults and no one is going to read our mind about what we want.* We need to make specific requests instead of wanting or expecting the other person to anticipate our needs or do things we have not requested. This may be very difficult until we have connected enough with the child we were. We needed parents who could anticipate our needs. When we have felt enough of our deprivation and our anger because of it, we will not suffer anger generated by unrealistic expectations in the present.

9) *We can take responsibility for recognizing our part in the patterns that evoke our anger.* For example, although we may want our partner or children to help

us more we may be reluctant to let go of controlling and criticizing exactly how things are done.

10) *We can write "I resent . . ." and find as many endings for this sentence as we can.* This exercise helps us dig out buried resentments and unfinished business. It alerts us to feelings we have not processed enough. It provides us with an opportunity to use our natural emotional healing power to complete and integrate the feelings held from these past situations.

The above tools are useful, but there is a danger that we will remain stuck in managing our lives with what we know rather than feeling. This will keep us in our heads, needing to keep trying to make things right, instead of being in tune with ourselves and comfortable with our lives.

Awareness is a first step, but it is not enough. Confronting issues in the present is healthy, but it is not enough. Neither of these things is enough to give us the peace we are seeking. It is important that all of these suggestions not become an end in themselves but be used on the road to becoming an integrated and feeling person.

12

POWERLESSNESS

A Trap for Victim and Abuser

———————————

The more powerless we were as children, the more likely we will be *a victim or an abuser as an adult.* We either set ourselves to feel the familiar powerlessness as a victim, or we keep the feelings of powerlessness at bay by abusing through power and control. Power over others and "controlling" behaviour is not the same as having personal power and being in charge of our lives.

Control of our lives is essential in order to have a sense of well-being.

The more personal power we have, the less we need to be controlling of ourselves and others. There are only two ways to become personally powerful as an adult: to have experienced appropriate power, control and responsibility as a child or to feel through our powerlessness to its source in order to integrate it consciously. Inability and refusal to do this is to remain locked behind the doors of blame and/or victimization.

It is particularly difficult for both victims and abusers to take responsibility for their feelings and actions. We may be a victim in an abusive relationship, or we may still feel like a victim even though our circumstances are fairly okay. When we are in abusive relationships we are locked in a hopeful struggle. We need to believe that if only we can be different we can change things. We try harder. This is a futile struggle because no matter what we do, the person with whom we are struggling will continue to victimize us if they remain stuck. Once we are out of the abusive situation we may start to connect to the reasons we stayed there so long. The alternative to being a victim, feeling like a victim or behaving like a victim is to feel the dark emptiness of our unmet need that left us feeling powerless as children.

Abusers too are caught in the stranglehold of denied helplessness and continuously act out the compensating power, the power they did not have as children. Our denial as an abuser is often set like concrete, making it very difficult for us to take responsibility. The process that frees an abuser is not different from that which frees a victim. In either case the hopeless, powerless experience of our childhood must be felt through.

The difference between personal power and power-over

Personal power involves living consciously and interacting effectively with others without violating their rights in any way. It stems from knowing and liking who we are. We then feel entitled to ensure that our realistic needs are met and we are willing and able to change situations that are destructive to our well-being. Personal power stands on taking responsibility personally for our feelings, knowing we have a right to them but also knowing that they are ours to be felt and integrated. When we assume personal power we take charge of our part in relationships and own what is fairly on our shoulders.

We live with reality, not illusion and denial. There is a sense of inner energy and lasting strength in this kind of power.

Power-over is a situational power that comes when we abuse our position over another. People have situational power by virtue of their age, experience and accumulated wisdom, wealth, physical stature and even good fortune. Situational power need not be abusive. It is abusive when it involves intimidation and domination. The less personal power those in positions of situational power have, the more likely they will be to exercise and rely on power-over to control others. The more parents, bosses, partners and those in authority rely on control over us to get their needs met, the more likely it is that they have a poor sense of personal power.

In our patriarchal system men have had the political and economic power. However, individual men are often quite powerless and both men and women are capable of abusing their situation of power. Generally, aggressiveness has been allowed and even encouraged in male children, while females have been expected to be good, sweet, pretty and ladylike. This conditioning has left many women doubting themselves and afraid of feeling powerful and many men feeling automatically entitled to power. Carol Tavris in her book *The*

Mismeasure of Woman asserts that male/female differences really stem from power differences. People in subordinate positions develop intuition because they need to be able to "read" those in charge. Where there is a status inequity, subordinates learn to persuade and influence, anticipate what others want or need, placate, accommodate, soothe and cultivate cooperation.

Equality means that we all have the right to equal respect and dignity.

Clearly, if we are to address power imbalance as a fundamental issue to be reconciled personally and globally, we need to examine how we understand power. We are all involved in a dance of control. We need to acknowledge the crucial link that feeling powerless as children sets us up for a lifetime of struggle. We may feel like victims of circumstances and of other people and allow ourselves to be taken advantage of, or we may reenact the power-over model that was used on us as children by trying to control others, amass a fortune or be driven to "succeed." In either case we are trapped in unconscious patterns of power. We do not feel personally powerful.

We can look inside to discover the source of our need for power-over and to find what holds us back from claiming our personal power that is our birthright.

Personal power makes us feel creative and enlivened.

Childhood powerlessness

When as children we are not respected as full human beings and our needs are not met, we feel powerless. This is too overwhelming for us to feel, so we shut down on it and struggle to defend against it.

Sonya had been terrified hundreds of times in the back seat of the family car. Her father drove erratically and dangerously, passing other cars where he should not and constantly tailgating. Her mother said nothing and neither did she.

When Sonya, at the age of thirty-five, went out of control, unable to stop being busy and looking after other people, she crashed. Her doctor diagnosed depression.

Sonya was terrified and tried medication. This calmed the internal raciness. She stopped doing anything except what was essential. She felt confused and could not stop thinking about why she was in such a mess.

Six months later Sonya decided to go off the medication because she was not happy with her life. She knew something was wrong. She began looking for something in the community that could help her. An assertiveness course provided insight into her lack of self-esteem, something she would never have guessed was a problem. She was a very competent person.

Sonya entered therapy and in her first session began to sob uncontrollably for the loss of her father who had died three years before.

It was powerful for Sonya when her therapist accepted her crying and validated her need to grieve. She recognized that the medication had interfered with her grieving, as had all the well-meaning people who had told her how strong she was.

Eventually Sonya connected with the helpless, hopeless powerlessness of being in that car, over and over again, at her father's mercy. She had no voice in her family and no power to react honestly and complain. Her mother modelled passive compliance.

As Sonya continued to feel and connect to many other times when she had felt powerless she no longer needed to stay as split off from herself. She recognized that her goodness and competence had kept her distant from her underlying feelings of fear and hurt. She came to feel and grieve the many situations where she had been tolerant and had not even known she had the right to complain. She found her voice and her personal power began to surface as she courageously faced what had really happened to her.

Abuse engenders powerlessness

There are many kinds of physical, emotional and sexual abuses that leave children feeling terrorized, helpless and powerless. Even if we are not the objects of overt abuse, the fact that we witness it is emotionally abusive to us. Physical and sexual abuse includes any way in which children's bodies are violated or their boundaries invaded. This runs the gamut, from not respecting their need for privacy or not stopping tickling when they ask us to, all the way to incest or molestation.

It can be sexually abusing to a child when a parent is repressing his or her disconnected sexualized need, even if the parent never touches the child inappropriately. Our child radar picks up this sexualized need and we react to it with great discomfort and a sense of powerlessness. Sexualized need in our parents that makes us uneasy manifests itself in different ways: our parent coming on to an outside adult in front of us, strutting naked through the house, being nude in the family sauna while insisting it should be all right, telling sexually suggestive jokes, flirting with our friends or behaving seductively.

Emotional abuse includes minor to major neglect; expecting perfection; controlling everything a child does including thinking and believing; verbal put-downs; screaming; attacking; criticizing; expecting our child to look after us emotionally; indifference to our child's well-being; discouraging independence; demanding loyalty, appreciation and gratitude; expecting our child to be responsible for things we are responsible for; undermining; threatening; trivializing; patronizing; withholding; using scare tactics; denying our child's feelings; abusing things our child values, such as their possessions or pets; isolating our child; harassing; not protecting our children from those who harm them; teasing; scapegoating and using punishment to control.

Any behaviour that falls short of meeting our needs when we are children leaves us feeling powerless.

Abusive behaviour in adulthood keeps us powerless

If we felt powerless as a child we will struggle in our adult relationships. We will either need to feel powerful as a defense against the old powerlessness and will therefore be dominating and controlling, or we will feel like a victim and continually try to get the abuse to stop and get the love we are missing.

> When Joan entered therapy she knew she was unhappy but did not really know why. When she began to describe her marriage it was obvious that she lived with a very domineering and controlling man.

> Joan did not describe her marriage as abusive. She thought it would be better if she knew how to get through to her husband. Every time she tried to tell him how she was feeling about an issue she would end up feeling as though she was the problem. She was always sorry when she made him so angry that he would not speak to her for several days. She could not stand his coldness and would scurry around trying to do things that would please him. She felt inadequate and powerless when he would not tell her what was wrong but would tell her instead to "quit your yakking."

Joan was encouraged to feel what it was like to be on the receiving end of her husband's verbal abuse. She would bring incident after incident to her sessions where she had felt totally done in and unable to respond to him. She began to realize that he had many ways to keep her in her powerless position. All he needed to say was "You're being controlling" or "You blow everything out of proportion" and she would be filled with self-doubt. If she confronted him when he put her down in front of company with a remark that was supposed to be funny, he would discount her reaction by saying, "You're too serious; you can't take a joke." She felt quite crazy when he could not remember having promised her something or denied ever having said such a thing.

I kept asking Joan, "What was that like for you?" and "How did that feel?" Eventually she could feel the hurt and the powerlessness. She began to connect to how worthless she had felt as a child when her only parent, her mother, had left her alone so much, how frightened she had been as she stood by the window watching for her mother. She realized she had never been given any choices about her own life or control of her own life.

Joan gradually began to realize that her husband needed to have power over her. She could see that he was not interested in solving their problems; he wanted complete control. As she claimed more of her personal power in the relationship he got more and more nasty. She asked him to leave and he did so, telling everyone what a "bitch" she was.

Joan had a lot of grieving to do and she had to struggle through a very upsetting separation procedure. Nevertheless, having more of herself had become very important to her. She felt huge relief that she was no longer so intimidated by his bullying techniques and could now take appropriate action to look after herself.

Taking responsibility for being a victim or an abuser

It takes great courage to take responsibility for being either a victim or an abuser. *Underreacting* is the hallmark of a victim and so it is difficult to even know we are taking abuse. If our child is being abused we will often become aware enough to start standing up for our child and then ourselves. It takes an enormous amount of energy to see our children being abused and not do something about it. Seeing our children abused is frequently the impetus for personal change.

Awareness of our victim position comes in different ways. Many of my clients who were victimized as children and were stuck in their victimization as adults entered therapy because they read a particular book, heard someone speak about self-esteem or were confronted by a friend. This has helped them to see that what they are tolerating is not right. Sometimes they have made enormous changes on their own and have come for therapy when they have rocked the boat of their relationship to such an extent that they are afraid it might end. In his book *Bradshaw On: The Family,* John Bradshaw observes that families are like mobiles and when one person changes it throws everyone off balance. Often everyone else in the family will behave in such a way as to try to get the person who has become more assertive back to being the way they were. When the newly assertive person persists in looking after themselves, the spouse either adjusts or leaves the relationship. When one person takes responsibility for the fallout from their childhood and begins to recuperate there is often a very positive ripple effect on the rest of the family. Others may open to their feelings and this makes the relationships much more real and authentic.

Victims

Once we see that the way we are being treated is not right we can start noticing our underreactions and use them to get to our underlying pain. We can closely observe what our bodies are telling us when we defer to others—perhaps we grind our teeth or clench our fists or just feel sick inside. We begin to feel how we hurt ourselves when we do not honour ourselves.

Believing we have no choice really keeps us stuck. When we feel we have no choice about our course of action we can take responsibility by acknowledging this as a feeling that needs to be felt and processed to its source. At the same time we can take the risk of reminding ourselves that we do have choice and that we are responsible for our choices.

Beth believed she had no choice about going back to work after her baby was born. Her husband insisted they needed her income. He said that he did not intend to be the only one working.

Beth agonized over leaving her infant. She could not concentrate at work because she missed him so much and was so worried about him. She made an appointment with a therapist so that she could get a professional opinion on what she should do.

When Beth realized that she had to take responsibility both for her choice to return to work and for the way she was feeling, the floodgates opened. She told her husband that they would have to manage on his income for some time because she wanted to stay home with their baby. She also told him that she was going to therapy and that she wanted them to get some help together too.

Beth's husband was more than startled to hear her assert herself in this way. Although he was taken off guard by what she had to say, he sensed that she was very determined. He tried to reason with her but Beth had realized that she wanted to be with her baby and would not budge. She continued to connect with her lack of power and choice as a child. One day in a therapy session, Beth focused on the heavy feeling in her chest. She was encouraged to breathe deeply again and again and to stay with the heaviness. The pain got worse. She was able to stay with it and was overcome with a feeling of despair. She rolled back and forth as though in agony. She began to cry like a baby. Beth cried for a while and then was quiet for a long time before saying anything at all. She had re-experienced being left alone in her crib as a baby for hours at a time. These hours had seemed unending to her as an infant. The feeling was excruciating and all-consuming. When she made this connection to herself as a baby, she realized why she had had such a strong feeling for her own baby and why she was so determined to be with him. In order for Beth to be clear about the difference between her need and her baby's needs she continued to connect and feel her own childhood pain.

Beth now had a more integrated chunk of herself to bring to her child and her marriage. Her husband became aware that his marriage had actually improved a lot because his wife was no longer so stressed and unhappy.

I have had clients who have come for help after many years of knowingly being controlled by their partners. They have had to grieve not only their loss of self in this relationship and in their childhood but also their collusion in not meeting the needs of their children even when they knew they were not being met. Not everyone is as fortunate as Beth. She was able to listen to her instinct and uncover pain which otherwise might have driven her to go against herself and leave her baby.

If we are victims we can deliberately take risks, as Beth did, to look after ourselves better. The opportunity to do this will present itself more clearly once we are more aware. When we take the risks, we open the doors to our feelings from our past. When we do this, feel our pain, connect it and integrate it into our lives, we are better able to decide what we are willing to do and what we are not willing to do based on what is best for us. This does not mean we never stretch ourselves for someone else; it does mean that we do this more consciously. Our sense of self grows as we use our triggers to take us to our childhood feelings and as we take risks to honour ourselves in the present.

Abusers

Abusers are often jolted into recognizing their abusive behaviour. They may be about to be left by their life partner, their adult child may confront them, or they may even be charged by the police. Whatever way it happens, it is a courageous act when we start to take responsibility for the way we are.

Having control over others can keep our helpless, useless, powerless, worthless feelings at bay. When we focus on controlling others, we assume that we are the only ones who know how things should be. We engage in rigid right/wrong thinking.

As abusers we can start to notice our overreactions and take responsibility for them. We can use our triggers and go with our feelings. We will open up to our own past abuse.

We can all notice when we blame or want to blame. It is easier to clobber those close at hand than to feel the overwhelming powerlessness embedded in our unhappy past. Blaming is fairly easy to identify but difficult to stop doing. The transformation that can happen in these instances is quite impressive since there is dramatic change as soon as we take responsibility for our actions, thoughts and feelings.

Noah crashed into immense pain when his wife threatened to leave their marriage imminently. He entered therapy and was able to stay with these feelings with the help of his therapist. He rapidly found himself raging at his father for his abusive treatment of his mother. Noah was horrified when he realized that in his attitude toward his wife he had become his father. He had always known he would not physically abuse a woman the way his father had, but missed the fact that he had become a rageaholic and very emotionally abusive.

Noah eventually remembered and felt through the humiliation he himself had suffered at the hands of his father. He was in agony when he realized that he had transferred his rage at his father to his wife. She had become the trigger for his humiliation and shame and he had acted it all out on her.

As soon as Noah started to take responsibility for his feelings and his behaviour his wife was willing to give him some time to work things out in their marriage. Once Noah started to feel he quickly grasped what it must have been like for his wife to be treated like a second-class citizen. He had gained empathy for himself as a boy and now was able to have empathy for his wife. Noah was able to let go of his blaming and controlling as he felt more of his vulnerability. He stayed in therapy until the need for his tough facade had faded and he felt much more self-acceptance.

Allowing more and feeling more

When we understand that our children need to have their own power and control in the form of choices that are appropriate to their stage of development, we can start to allow this to happen. When we allow our children more freedom of choice, they will begin to take it and make choices that may run right up against old barriers inside us. This gives us the opportunity to feel more and to cooperate with our natural emotional healing power. For example, we can use the triggers inflamed by our children's new freedom to feel more of our old powerlessness.

Stan took a parenting course with his wife, at her suggestion. He began to realize that he used fear to control his children. He did not yell at them or hit them, but he unconsciously used his very size and demeanour to intimidate them. He felt awful that his children were afraid of him.

Stan made a huge effort to change the way he dealt with his children, seeking therapy to help him do this. He connected again and again with the tough boy he had had to be. During his school years, "Don't mess with Stan the man" was part of his personal mythology.

Stan re-experienced his terror when his own father had raged at him and felt how he had survived these assaults by enclosing himself in a strong, unfeeling armour. Later he started to feel how much he had needed his father to be soft and welcoming.

As Stan went through the layers and layers of held feelings from his past he became more and more open to his children. He realized that he had continued to use his silent, intimidating demeanour in his adult life, especially in his business and with his children. His desire to change this and his willingness to process his feelings changed Stan's life in a very positive way.

Many of us are unfortunately locked inside our powerlessness, terrorized or numbed by our victimhood. Or we are locked outside our powerlessness, terrorizing and numbing those close by with our blaming and abuse.

When we use our natural emotional healing power to feel and integrate our powerlessness, we choose, as frightening and risky as it is, to move toward emotional well-being that is lasting. Our personal power then becomes an open door to others inspiring them to chance the expression of their inner strength.

13

HURT, REGRET AND GRIEF
A Key to Healing

Hurt, regret and grief are healthy and necessary responses to difficulties and pain in our lives. They are enormously undervalued, unacknowledged vehicles for moving toward emotional health. Feeling these feelings to their fullest is an example of our natural emotional healing power at work. When we do not allow ourselves to feel these feelings through, when we shove them away, they reside in us as a heaviness that can pull us down into depression.

Anti-feeling admonitions such as "The best thing is to keep busy," "Don't dwell on it," "You're taking things very well" and "Get on with your life" silence us and make processing our feelings more difficult. Our natural process gets stopped. There is a pervasive fear in our culture of the intensity of feelings and of getting lost in them. If we have not experienced trusting our feelings as a child and were not supported to do so, we have difficulty in trusting that we *need* to stay with these feelings until we integrate the experience and until they then lose their intensity. We may stay on the surface of the feelings and deny their legitimacy, not giving ourselves permission to feel their depth. However, these big feelings reside hidden and denied inside of us, and when they reappear we do not connect them to their source. They appear nameless and disconnected and all we can say is that we are depressed.

Grieving heals our hurt

Children with unhealed hurt grow up to be adults with unhealed hurt.

It is not possible to live and not to suffer hurt. If we have not been allowed to experience the losses and the hurt of our childhood, then we will carry these repressed feelings into our adult life. Feeling our childhood hurt and grieving our losses is what this book is all about because this is the way we become emotionally fit.

We have seen many examples so far that demonstrate that when we continue to use the defenses we needed as children in our adult life, we distort our thinking and we live with illusion. We do not live as fully as we might.

The foundation layer of our repressed feelings is hurt. When we use our feelings to transport us back to being the child we were, we finally come to the sobbing, gut-wrenching hurt that we had to put away because it was too much for us to feel then.

If as children we were not allowed to take the time we needed to discharge our hurt completely, we will not know how to allow ourselves the time we need to grieve completely as adults

Some of us will not allow grief at all. Because of the denial of our feelings in our society and the denial of feelings in our families, many of us cut off our grieving before it is complete. How long we need to grieve is unique to each of us. This needs to be respected and we need to trust our own process. This is really difficult to do when others are battering at us to get on with our lives.

Grieving is a deep process of feeling our loss and an integrating process that heals our pain.

Hurt is a feeling that all but the most shut-down individuals can relate to. What it seems we do not know is that if we allow ourselves to grieve enough we can *heal* our hurt. If we shut down on our hurt before we have allowed ourselves to grieve enough, we get *stuck* in our hurt. It reverberates in our system and we keep feeling it for years. It pops up when we least expect it, at inconvenient times, and we often do not know what it is about. I knew that I was feeling sad about the loss of my brother, but until I got into therapy I did not know how to complete the feelings or even that it was possible to complete them. I have had many clients who know they are plunged into huge sadness when they hear of a loss, such as when Diana, Princess of Wales, died, or when they attend the funeral of someone they hardly know. They have not known, however, that these feelings are connected to losses of their own.

Defending against hurt: feeling depressed

There are many ways that we defend against feeling hurt. We may withdraw deep inside to protect ourselves, just as we did as children. We may lash out in anger because we feel ashamed of feeling hurt, and we refuse to be vulnerable and let our hurt be seen. We may cry, but cut off our tears too soon because we are ashamed of them. We may defend against feeling the full force of our loss and hurt by beating ourselves up, which adds to our suffering. Some of us may hurt ourselves physically, as an outward, unconscious display of our inner distress.

Too many of us have not known that we need to feel deeply enough to complete our grieving. One result of cutting the process short is depression, an extensive problem in our culture. When we suppress the depth and intensity of our grieving those feelings spread to cover our whole life with a blanket of despair. It is then that we *experience* depression, which is our feelings disconnected from their source but attached to all aspects of our life. Depression is an example of underreacting and as such is a major defense.

A depressed person may be crying a lot. I have had clients who have come for help because they are crying all the time and do not know why. This kind of disconnected crying keeps us on the surface of our pain. We feel miserable and out of control but we cannot get our sadness connected.

When we understand that our depression exists because we are holding our feelings, we can make conscious attempts to direct these feelings to the original trauma that occurred in our young lives. When we are crying we can think about times in our lives when sad things happened to us and when we were hurt. When we do this we will drop down deeper into the pain and connect with those repressed experiences and relive them with all the feeling they actually hold. This is completely different from crying, not knowing why, and beating ourselves up for doing so. It is much more than crying and feeling sad about remembered incidents. Feeling sad about our past is not a connecting, integrating experience, although it can be an opening. Connecting with a past experience is a whole body/emotional event. It is unmistakable when we make a real connection and feel what we, as children, were unable to feel and complete long ago.

On the other hand, we may be depressed but not feeling or crying at all. We may be caught in a numbness and flatness that stifles ordinary response. We may feel terribly unhappy. Our pain is so widespread that our life can only be described as dark and often not worth living. However, at the base of this dismal state is our hurt, hurt that we were unable to feel as a child, hurt that we now defend against by disabling our very ability to feel anything but an amorphous, globalized depression.

In my experience, when someone is given the support and acceptance that they need to express and feel their despair they connect with the true source of their depression and do not need to act out by committing suicide. Too often our response to suicidal people is to deny and suppress their feelings. If we are not clear as helpers we will need these people to shut down further on their despair instead of feeling it. The most dramatic way we do this is by prescribing medication and electroconvulsive therapy. Unfortunately these solutions make anyone in this situation dependent on outside remedies for relief, which may have serious side effects and most often require ongoing intervention. We act on the despairing person instead of supporting them to be their own authority, supporting them to feel the underlying source of their despair. Some medication may be a helpful bridge but should not be seen as an end in itself. Ultimately, depression is a result of not grieving our hurt. Our depression has meaning, and it is important to respect it as a door to go through to our feelings.

Defending against depression

We may act out by being caught in a frantic busyness that keeps all feelings at bay. This busyness layers over our numbness and flatness, another cover of our depression, and keeps us even further away from the feelings needed to heal. Many of us feel alive only when we are planning and executing project after project. Our well-being is totally dependent on keeping busy. We do not even know we are depressed. When we acknowledge that our busyness is defending against our depression, which in turn is a defense against feeling our hurt, doors open.

Defending against hurt: overreacting and acting out

When we overreact to present hurtful situations it is our natural emotional healing power alerting us to the need to complete old unfinished pain.

Cara felt hurt very easily—it did not take much and she would be in tears. She wanted her boyfriend, Jack, to be more understanding. Jack felt confused and she could sense that he was withdrawing from her.

Cara was encouraged to stay with her feelings as they came up. She would focus on the heavy feeling in her chest, and before long she would be sobbing. As she cleared out the many hurts from her young life and connected to how worthless she had felt as a child, she no longer brimmed over with tears at the slightest provocation.

Cara was able to explain to Jack about her overreactions and their sources that she was uncovering. He was empathetic and understanding when she no longer held him responsible for her feelings.

Cara was able to stop acting out her disconnected hurt.

There are many other ways of acting out. We may bury our hurt in the depths of our bodies and act out to keep it there. We may hide our old hurt and fear of letting it surface with a perfect body that we beat into shape through excessive exercise and rigid eating habits. We may hide our old hurt from ourselves by swallowing it all the time and filling ourselves up with food until we are fat. We may keep ourselves busy and focused on achieving or we may keep our hurt buried in an addictive substance or process.

Acting out is an unconscious act and it is repetitive. This repetitiveness can alert us to our natural emotional healing power which is insisting that we complete old, unfinished feelings as Cara did.

Noticing and becoming conscious that we are hurting

In order to become conscious that we are hurting we need to be very good self-observers and try to catch even the slightest nuance of hurt. Deliberately pulling our attention into our bodies helps; we can notice the heavy feeling in our chest, the catch in our throat, the welling-up of tears. We can notice what brings tears to our eyes when we read a novel or watch a movie. We can notice what movies we avoid. We react the way we do because there is some significance for us. If we feel like weeping for someone else's pain, it is likely that we know about that kind of pain. If we avoid it we are avoiding our own pain.

Krista believed she had a chemical imbalance that was causing her depression. She did not know what was causing the chemical imbalance. She hated being on Prozac and so decided to try psychotherapy.

In her initial sessions Krista related many hurtful incidents from her childhood that were quite horrible. She did this with no feeling. She was stuck being disconnected from the feelings of her experience for many sessions. Eventually Krista went into group sessions and it was on an intensive weekend that she broke through to the incredible hurt she had suffered. She was triggered by hearing the agonizing sound that another client was making and she reacted to the stories of others with tears.

Once Krista connected with the child she had been and felt some of the hurt she had held away from her feeling self, she opened up to what her life had really been like. She started to watch herself closely for any clues that she was hurting.

As Krista became more aware of these clues she automatically started to have feelings about them. This was different for her; she was thrilled to be feeling. Krista noticed when she was no longer mired in depression. She once left her session with a wry "Thanks a lot for the pain." She remarked that it was weird to be paying someone for helping her feel pain. Underlying this humour was an acknowledgment that feeling the pain was helpful.

There are those of us who are so armoured against our pain that we will do anything not to expose our hurt and vulnerability.

Staying stuck in regrets or moving on and grieving them

Regrets are an inevitable part of the wholeness of life. They become a problem when we are unable to feel and complete them and instead get stuck in them. We can only get stuck if we do not go through them; if we do not know that we must grieve.

Regrets take many forms: we regret how we have treated someone, the opportunities we have missed, the loss of our personal potential, the loss of our self for so much of our lives, our unconscious acting out at the expense of our children, and on and on.

We often regret when we have put our old anger on the people in our lives who we want to be closest to, our life partners and our children. Sometimes we put these feelings on our parents if they are still around, and so we continue to act out, perpetuating a useless struggle without having taken the responsibility to feel our anger and hurt through to its completion. I personally regret that I did not spend more time alone with each of my children. Those precious years passed so quickly and there were many times when we were together but I was not really there for them. I was preoccupied with trying to alleviate the pain of my old, unmet need.

I have always been grateful for the parenting skills I learned thanks to Thomas Gordon and his book *Parent Effectiveness Training*, but recuperating from a childhood that left me needy and angry was what I needed to do the most. The only way to be truly present as a parent is to clear out the old unfinished business so that there are fewer ghosts in the way of our relationship with our children.

It can be painful to look back as a parent. I look back and regret and grieve about the mistakes I made. However, I do not beat myself up. I know that I was who I was at that time. I have been able to connect with myself then and grieve for how I felt, what I was going through, how I behaved and how I wished I could have been.

I know that my responsibility *now* is to have the best possible relationship I can have with my adult children and to delve into any continuing destructive patterns that may be lingering. I know that I need to grieve my regrets as I become aware of them.

We are freer to have a present relationship with our children if we are not blocking our regrets. We are better able to listen to them if they need to tell us something that is bothering them. We will be free to apologize appropriately when we have released the blocks by grieving.

We know we are stuck in regret when we keep ruminating, "If only ... If only ... If only ...." Returning again and again to the same thoughts, going over the same incident endlessly, all point to being stuck in regret. The regret, of course, is a defense against the deeper feelings of inadequacy, hurt and the pain of not being cared about. We can deliberately think about people and events that still cause a bodily response when they pop into our consciousness. We probably know what some of our unfinished business is with old friends, acquaintances, bosses, peers, siblings and parents if we stop to think about it. We can consciously go to these incidents to bring up the old, unfinished business that we are still caught on. Writing a letter that we do not intend to send is an excellent way to start feeling.

The calmer and freer sense of self that comes from cooperating with our natural emotional healing power encourages us to continue with the process. We do not need convincing; it is no longer a leap of faith once we have experienced it for ourselves.

Grieving as we go

Grieving is at the core of our healing. It is important to grieve all the small as well as the large losses of our life. If we have had many admonitions to be big and get on with it throughout our lives, we will not know to give ourselves time to do the grieving we need to do. We might very well be greeted with, "Well everyone goes through that!" What we do not understand when we make this kind of remark is that while everyone faces these losses in life, the only way to truly go through them is to feel them.

All deaths are difficult. Sudden deaths are often more difficult because we have not had any warning and therefore no opportunity to do some of the grieving when we know someone is going to be leaving us. No matter how difficult it is we have to grieve. Of course there are those who stay in denial even when they know that death is an inevitable outcome. I have had many clients who have felt deep regret and grief in the therapy room because they and their loved one had played a game of pretence to the very end. It is really tragic when we cannot use our natural healing power to give us the release we need and to face the reality that is before us.

Jessica wanted to visit the hospital every day when her dad was dying. When she came home upset her husband would say, "Why are you doing this to yourself?" She would try her best to shape up because she did not want to stop going to the hospital and she bought the notion that if she was feeling so upset she must be doing something "wrong."

It is common for us to feel guilty about being upset, which usually means crying or being on the verge of crying, trying to hold back our tears. Jessica carried her incomplete grief for her father for many years before she went down into it and felt the many unfinished feelings she had around that relationship.

Grieving the smaller losses means giving ourselves time to feel when our child goes off to kindergarten or high school, or leaves home for higher education, to travel, to work and live elsewhere or to get married. I am not talking about being defended, mired in a self-centred self-pity about these events. What we need to do is feel what is *happening* in our lives. Any of these events would be a mixture of loss for us but also excitement for our child. If we keep so busy that we do not let ourselves feel anything about these passages we may convert the feelings into self-pity and depression instead. Our self-awareness will be dulled; we may not notice that we are putting too much responsibility on our children for our happiness when we pine for them after they have left and continually ask them when they are coming home.

No place to feel

I have had many clients, both male and female, who have had difficulty experiencing the release of crying and the physiological benefit of this natural healing activity. *When crying is bound with shame it is thwarted.* Some of us could cry when we had a place to go to hide our tears. Some of us had no safe place, no privacy, while others of us were locked inside ourselves unable to cry at all, held back by fear and our excruciating sense of shame.

We need to encourage our tears whenever we can. I ask people if there is anything they notice that touches them and brings tears to their eyes. Usually there is a song, some particular piece of classical music, a particular movie, books about the holocaust, pictures of starving, staring children, a picture from their own childhood, singing the national anthem or something else they can say moves them. These are cracks in our armour and we can use them to help us regain our ability to cry, to process our feelings, to grieve our hurt.

Fear of getting stuck in grief

We are afraid of getting stuck in grief when we have not completed the earlier grieving we needed to do. We are actually fearful of something we are already in. The fear of getting stuck is really a defense against going deeper into our grief. When we understand that we need to allow ourselves all of our grief, we can feel our way through the layers of fear and shame to the core of hurt. These are keys to unlocking our grief.

Time goes on forever when we are children and we do not know that anything is ever going to change. When we feel sadness or fear it feels like forever; it feels so all-encompassing. When we feel this as adults we are locked in the defense and protection that we needed as children in order to survive. Now we can afford to feel how fearful it was to be caught in horrible feelings that seemed to go on forever.

Reclaiming ourselves

We limit our experience of joy if we are holding hurt, regret and grief. When we are able to grieve deeply and heal our wounds from our past we reclaim our authentic, true selves. We can then continue to feel as we travel through our lives. We will face the painful truths instead of needing to deny them and we will grieve our hurts and losses when they happen. We gain emotional well-being.

14

LONELINESS
A Self-fulfilling Prophecy

Many of us believe there is nothing we can do about our loneliness. In fact, we can feel our way to the past through our loneliness instead of assuming that the strength of the feeling is all in the present.

When we assume our loneliness is all about the present we are in danger of staying stuck in it. It is only when we allow the feeling to carry us back to other times that we can become clear about what we need to do about our present loneliness. There is a danger when we do not understand that loneliness can be felt deeply and that it does have its roots in our past. *The danger is that we may arrange our present to keep ourselves lonely.*

Children cannot begin to feel their loneliness without help. In the absence of enough help we do our best to look after ourselves, whether it be learning to soldier on, creating imaginary friends, sexually fantasizing, acting out or withdrawing deep inside, just to name a few coping strategies. These strategies are defenses, and when we carry them into our adulthood they keep us stuck. When we start to undo the bindings that hold these strategies in place we discover the real feelings of our lonely, hurting childhood.

Evelyn was a martyr. Her husband had died in his early fifties, and her only daughter had been accidentally killed many years before. Evelyn held herself back from engaging in extended family functions and presented a stiff upper lip whenever she had to get through socializing with anyone.

She believed that she must keep suffering her tragedy and that loneliness was her lot in life.

Her doctor sent her for counselling when she developed severe muscle spasms in her back. Evelyn could not see what good it would do her. She viewed her back problems as just one more thing she would have to bear.

Evelyn cried in her first session and in her second. She kept trying to stop her crying and pull herself together even though she was encouraged to stay with her tears. In time, Evelyn connected to what it had been like for her as a child, stifling and burying her pain, being expected to carry on no matter what. As she did this she opened to the grief she held about the loss of her daughter and husband. She was able to be closer to her extended family.

Loneliness is culturally acceptable; being alone is not

In our culture loneliness is seen as part of life. Our friends and relatives who care about us may want to come to our aid if we express or they notice our loneliness. In fact, our culture is loaded with examples of our need to rush in and fix loneliness. Romance books and many movies, television dramas and popular songs have as their theme the "achey-breaky" notion that we must avoid being alone at all cost. They suggest we can fix our loneliness if we just have someone in our life who will love us. "I'd Rather Die Young Than Grow Old Without You" was a dandy example of this from my younger days. Billion-dollar businesses rest on this romanticization of loneliness.

The rush to fix loneliness has made it appear culturally unacceptable for us to be alone; perhaps we are flawed in some way if we are alone, perhaps there is something wrong with us if no one wants to be with us. For many, being alone feels shameful; women have been brainwashed to believe they are nobody without a man. However, in reality, *being alone and being lonely are two distinct phenomena.*

Many of us know the feeling of being lonely even when we are with others; conversely, many of us know the pleasures of time alone not feeling lonely at all. Loneliness is not an intrinsic part of being an adult human being and it is not about being alone as an adult. The pervasiveness of loneliness in our culture is linked to our suffering as children.

The nature of loneliness

Feeling lonely has to do with how we connect to ourselves and others.

We feel lonely when we are disconnected from ourselves. We feel disconnected from ourselves when we do not know who we are and we live our lives taking direction from others. We do not feel essentially good about ourselves, centred in ourselves, grounded. We are always looking outside ourselves for our answers. We will feel this disconnection from ourselves if we were neglected or abused as children and if our feelings were not heard and accepted. As children our disconnection gets exacerbated every time our feelings are denied—our loneliness increases.

When we do not connect in a *real* way to others, we may feel lonely. *If we did not have real connections to our parents as we grew up we will feel lonely in the present.* We will stay feeling lonely until we grieve this hurt fully. When we hold onto it as a defense we will act out dramas of loneliness. We might erect a wall that makes it difficult for friends to be close, or we might flood our friends with our need, driving them away.

If we do not allow ourselves the opportunity to feel what our loneliness is all about we may let it drive us into, or keep us in, unhealthy relationships. We may become dependent on our partner to keep us from feeling lonely.

Kristen was constantly struggling with her husband, Joel. She resented his buddies and his interest in spending a lot of time with them—time she felt he should have wanted to spend with her.

Kristen had originally come for therapy because she suffered debilitating anxiety and fear that kept her dependent on Joel to drive her everywhere. As she focused on her solar plexus, where she said she could feel the anxiety in her body, she was encouraged to breathe in to this spot. As she stayed with the feeling she became aware of an ache in her chest and a feeling of deep loneliness.

Kristen said the feeling felt very familiar. As she stayed with the feeling I asked her to remember other times in her life when she had felt like this. She immediately remembered being alone in her room listening to her parents party with their friends downstairs. She could feel how alone and afraid she had felt.

Kristen was encouraged to continue to notice the ache in her body as she went about her daily life. She would lie down on her bed as often as she could when she noticed the ache. She brought many memories that came up for her at these times to her therapy sessions.

She had been an only child and her parents both drank a lot, and frequently. Kristen connected to enormous discomfort and anxiety when some of the men they had over would pick her up and tell her how cute she was. She remembered the sickening smell of the alcohol and how unsafe and alone she felt as her parents ignored her plight.

Kristen had been blaming Joel for her feelings of loneliness. It was tempting for her to keep blaming him but the more she connected to the loneliness of her childhood, the less she needed to explain her feelings of loneliness in the present as having to do with Joel. When she stopped haranguing him they were able to talk about their individual needs and work their schedules out in a more satisfactory way. Kristen continued to feel, connect and integrate many feelings resulting from the neglect in her childhood.

Some couples seem glued together, neither of them able to face their loneliness.

Pam and Frank were together all the time. Their dependence on each other became a real problem when their first child was born.

Pam came for help when she got really frightened about Frank's depression. Eventually he agreed that he was depressed and did not know why, and he too entered therapy.

Frank felt terribly guilty that he was depressed when he had a beautiful baby son and his life seemed to be going so well. As he got "into" the black feelings and stayed with them for session after session, he felt the depression lift slightly. He knew that he must have suffered when his father died in an accident when he was eleven years old, but he could feel nothing about it and could not say that he had ever missed his father. He talked to both his mother and his sister about his childhood because he had a lot of blanks that bothered him. His mother told him how withdrawn he had been after his father died. She had worried about him but said that she had been depressed for six years following her husband's death and knew that she had been no help to him. His sister, who was five years older, said that she had immersed herself in her friends and had paid little attention to him in those years.

Frank brought this information to therapy but still could not make a feeling connection to what it was like for him after his father died. Frank decided he should take more responsibility for the baby's care, something he had not done before because of his depression, and he began to spend more time with his son.

Frank was able to feel in his therapy how amazing his little son was. When he stayed with this feeling he started to cry, which then led him to the deep grief about the loss of his own father. He crashed into how lost he had felt, not only without his father but also without his mother and his sister.

Frank realized that when he met Pam he had felt more complete. His need to be with her to the exclusion of others had been extreme. As he began to feel his loneliness in its proper context he shared with Pam what was happening. Her experience had been very different from his but it had left her with a huge unmet need that she had been trying to fill through her husband. As she felt through what had really happened to her as a child they both became more independent, yet emotionally closer. They were able to be apart from each other without being debilitated by the terror of loneliness.

The underestimation of children's loneliness

We have discounted the loneliness of infants and children. Very young children suffer loneliness when they are not with their parents. We still take newborn infants from their mothers and put them in a nursery. Letting my infant children be taken from me at their birth is one of the greatest regrets of my life. I have needed to grieve about this many times. Times are changing, and recognizing that babies need to be considered as real people is becoming more popular in some segments of our society and in some countries in the world.

As I have said many times, when children's needs are not met they suffer. Not having our needs met leaves us feeling misunderstood. Not being understood feels lonely.

When as children we are alone, feeling needy, worthless, shamed, guilty, anxious, fearful, angry and hurt, we are excruciatingly lonely. When we cannot express our feelings we are left alone with them.

We underestimate how lonely our children feel when we are emotionally unavailable to them. Children become frantic because their fear and loneliness is unbearable. As children, we may know that there is food on our table and a roof over our head, we may have brothers and sisters in our homes, but if we do not feel we have our parents' awareness and caring then we will feel left alone. We will not be able to identify or articulate what we are feeling; we will feel lost and will no doubt believe that there is something wrong with us.

Many of my clients have described tormenting loneliness as teenagers. Some of them have known they were lonely. Others have only discovered that this is what they were feeling when, as adults, they have connected with why they played their music all the time, why they played it so loudly, why they threw themselves into an activity or relationship that was all-consuming, why they acted out the way they did, or why they struggled incessantly with their parents or siblings. It is in our teens, when we are forming a stronger sense of our identity, that we are wracked with emotions we do not understand. Unless we have listening, caring, attentive parents we will have trouble handling the nature and size of our feelings. Carrying a pervasive sense of not being good enough into this stage of development often results in a teenager withdrawing deep inside and shutting down.

As teenagers we are at a vulnerable and volatile stage. Too often we are abandoned by our parents, who get caught up in their own pain when we push for independence and our right to be who we are on any particular day. We get abandoned by parents who feel we can take care of ourselves or who demand we follow rigid rules. We get abandoned to be with other lonely teens. All of this isolates us and exacerbates our loneliness.

Neglect and loneliness is a major problem for children and young people today. Our society has rationalized adult behaviour when it falls short of meeting our children's needs. We say we have no choice but to work as we do, be as stressed as we are and have as little time as we do to really be with our children. When we insist we have no choice we are not taking responsibility. Latchkey kids are lonely kids.

Setting ourselves up to reenact our childhood loneliness in the present

If we do not understand that our loneliness has its roots in our past, even when circumstances of our life may seem to account for it in the present, we will stay stuck in the familiar loneliness. Our unconscious self directs us to feel over and over again what is so familiar from our past. This is our natural emotional healing power trying to get our attention. When we do not take note and respond to it by feeling through to our childhood loneliness, we stay stuck in reenacting our childhood.

> Liz firmly believed she was lonely because her husband had died too young several years before. She continually talked about how she had always thought he would live much longer than sixty-four years. Her daughter urged her to seek some help when she saw her mother becoming reclusive and depressed.
>
> Liz said she really enjoyed coming for therapy. When she was asked to stay with what it felt like to be in a room alone with the attention of an empathetic listener, she sobbed and sobbed. Liz learned to go into her feelings of loneliness in between her therapy sessions. She began to take responsibility for feeling so lonely by connecting more and more to the very lonely little girl she had been. Her parents had been preoccupied with the Depression and then the Second World War. They had little time or empathy for their daughter, whom they believed should be seen and not heard.
>
> When Liz felt more and more of her childhood loneliness she stopped talking about the injustice of her husband dying so young. She began to get

involved in some activities that interested her and reconnected with some old friends, something she had felt unable to do before. Her daughter was thrilled to hear her mother laugh again.

Being caught in the grip of old, unfelt, incomplete feelings of loneliness restricts us and reduces our potential at any stage in our lives. Acknowledging that we are responsible even for our loneliness is the first step out of the trap of reenacting our past. We may try to do this by pushing ourselves to go out more, but this will not change how we feel inside. Really taking responsibility means feeling the roots of our loneliness.

Getting clear using our natural emotional healing power

When we use our loneliness in the present as a trigger to connect with and feel through to the loneliness of our past, we begin a process of getting clearer. We can remember what it was like for us as a child. We can acknowledge that we created imaginary friends or fantasized—we must have been lonely.

It is that leap of faith that gets us started: picking up a pen and starting to write, visiting our old neighbourhood, allowing the tears to come when we feel them filling our eyes, facing the dark feelings within and deliberately entering further into the lonely feeling when it is pressing down on us.

Although this is never easy, the freedom within that it engenders is so rewarding that no one I know who has faced their feelings and their life in this way would ever want to return to the disconnected, lonely way it had been.

The more we go through the doors to our past the more open they remain.

15

NUMBNESS, DEADNESS AND FLATNESS

Formidable Defenses

Numbness, deadness and flatness are enormous defenses that we wrap around ourselves in order to survive. We shut down to protect ourselves from feelings that are too overwhelming to be felt at the time. Unravelling these defenses requires that we identify and feel the numbness, deadness and flatness. These feelings are very difficult to feel and to stay feeling. It often takes a long time before they open to reveal the underlying pain. The strength of this defense, as with any defense, is directly related to the severity of the underlying trauma. People experiencing numbness, deadness and flatness often underreact to the impact of real situations in their present life. This undermines healthy, vigorous relationships.

This deadened state of being is one of the most difficult defenses to experience and feel. It is difficult for any of us to feel through the deadness to its source on our own.

Robbed of our spirit

There is nothing more horrific than to see a child robbed of his or her spirit.

We, as children, are robbed of our spirit when the adults in our lives act out their need on us. This happens when our parent denigrates our grade two painting, asking "What's that supposed to be?" when our teacher yells at us for speaking to our friend or when our coach screams at us for making the wrong move or puts us down for being a "wuss." These adults, in these moments, are dumping their need to be important, right or in control on us. They are dumping their disconnected anger on our child spirit.

Many of my clients have described how they protected a little piece of their spirit by withdrawing far inside themselves. This is the defense we needed as children when our spirits were attacked; we numbed the outside to protect the inside.

There are many ways that our spirits are assaulted as children. What is truly amazing is the power of the human spirit to recuperate from such assaults.

Defending against assault

The major way that we, as children, defend against assault is by shutting down. The more we have to do this the more we will feel numb, dead and flat. As with other defenses, when we carry these into our adult life they put a severe restriction on us, and our ability to live to the fullest and to thrive is diminished. We flee to our heads; we become expert intellectualizers and rationalizers. We find an explanation or an excuse for what is going on in our lives. We cannot use our feelings as guides to understand our world because we have numbed, deadened and flattened them. Others experience us as disconnected people but we cannot feel our own disconnection.

Don came for help when his wife said she could no longer stand how shut down he was and wanted to leave him. Don had always claimed that he did not know what she was talking about. He could always explain "rationally" why he did not feel more when his mother had died, for example, or when his brother had actually cheated him.

When I asked him to talk about his life and then kept asking, "What was that like for you? What did that feel like?" Don realized that he had no feelings. When I asked him to go down into his body and see what he felt there he could find no feeling.

Don stayed with this absence of feeling in his body for many sessions. He became very self-observant at work and at home in order to try to catch even a fleeting feeling. He realized that he often did feel angry at work but never expressed it; he could actually feel how short-lived it was and how quickly he suppressed it. I gave him a long list of feeling words that he looked at to help himself identify anything that he might be able to catch that was going on inside of him.

Don did not know of anything overtly assaultive in his childhood. What he did connect with was how emotionally flat both his parents were; he never saw them very stirred up about anything. His mother did not cry when her mother died or when Don's father died. He could remember a few times when his father "blew his top," but that had happened rarely and had never been talked about or resolved. When I asked Don how his feelings were dealt with he answered, "They weren't."

Don finally felt sadness and cried a little but then decided to leave therapy. He said that he felt he had really opened up a lot and was glad he could feel more. He thought it would be "good" for him to move on since his wife had decided to leave him. He said he did not feel like fighting for his marriage. Although Don had begun to open up and feel more, sadly he was still locked in much of his numbness when he left therapy because he had not had enough experience feeling, connecting and integrating this defense.

Resignation: the precursor to numbness, deadness and flatness

Resignation can be a red flag that we can learn to notice and use to get into our feelings. Resignation is different from coming to genuinely accept a situation or the way someone is. I have found that clients often say they have accepted something when what they really mean is that they have resigned themselves to it. Whenever anyone says to me "That's just the way it is, I've accepted that" or "I've come to terms with it" I ask them what that *feels* like. When we stay with the feelings about a situation that we think we have accepted we can frequently feel the "give up," the resignation.

The more we have been required to resign ourselves to circumstances as a child—"Well life isn't fair, you know"—the more we will feel numb. When our feelings are not heard and accepted we shut them down, we give up, we resign. Resignation becomes a slippery slope into depression, numbness, deadness and flatness. There are different degrees of depression resulting from feeling numb, dead and flat. Many clients describe it as a sort of low-grade depression that they have lived with most of their lives; they have never felt quite alive. Others say they have felt the black bleakness of their lives for as long as they can remember.

Noticing when we feel numb

We can learn to notice when we are not feeling present, when we are "zoning out." We often look back and say "Good grief, I wasn't there!" Early in my therapy I recognized that I was so busy at Christmas it went by in a blur and I did not even experience it with my children. I resolved to change that pattern the next year; I wanted to feel my little daughters sitting on my knee, I wanted to see the fun and excitement as my sons opened their presents.

We have all had times when we have shut down. Many women have told me how frequently they shut down when having sex. Our grandmothers were actually instructed to shut down, to "Lie back and think of England."

Many clients have told me that they know they shut down when they visit their parents, in-laws, their children's school, etc. When we become aware of this shutting down we can use it as a door to go through. We realize our feelings shift and change as we feel them but if we continue to numb them this can last forever.

When we feel numb and underreact to situations we may not recognize at all our lack of feeling or the fact that we are underreacting. If we are open enough we may be able to benefit from what someone else tells us about our lack of responsiveness.

Underreacting followed by overreacting

In people who shut down a lot there is often a pattern of "passive, passive, passive" behaviour followed by an outburst of aggression. We are shut down because being "out there" with our feelings was not acceptable when we were children. When we become aggressive we often feel guilty and quickly return to being passive.

This is a pattern we can become aware of. We can try to follow each and every little feeling no matter how small it may seem. Many clients say "I need to be really angry before I'll say anything." However, we can catch ourselves feeling annoyed, irritated, edgy or grumpy and start to take risks to express these feelings. Sometimes we wear our passivity like a badge of merit until we see the harm it does.

When we take the risk of breaking the "passive, passive, passive, aggressive" cycle we will stir up the feelings from our childhood that entrenched this unhealthy pattern.

Margaret had been taught that it was not ladylike to express her anger. She hated herself when once in a while she went out of control and said things she deeply regretted.

As Margaret took more and more risks to say what she needed to say to her friends in the moment, she began to feel a lot of anxiety and fear. She was afraid she would have no friends left. As these feelings surfaced she connected with the wrath of her mother when she was a very small child, and how she had been made to feel "bad" about most of her childlike behaviour.

As Margaret connected with and felt the forced suppression in her childhood she cried and raged. As she trusted her feelings more and more she felt more and more alive. Although she did lose a few friends, she had the reward of feeling better at having expressed herself and of developing more real, satisfying relationships with others.

Shutting down: a devastating gender design

Terrence Real in his book *I Don't Want to Talk About It* demonstrates that males are socialized in such as way that they are "systematically pushed away from the full exercise of emotional expressiveness and the skills for making and appreciating deep connection." According to Real they would rather act out distress than talk about it. He believes that men suffer from the classic symptoms of depression—hopelessness, helplessness, despair and numbness—but that they attempt to escape depression because they believe it to be "unmanly" and so hide it even from themselves. This attempt to escape is the act-out responsible for many of the problems we think of as typically male: difficulty with intimacy, workaholism, alcoholism, abusive behaviour and rage. Men have difficulty coming for therapy because the "giving in" to the pain they need to experience is viewed as humiliating rather than something that will bring relief. Real says that "the stable ratio of women in therapy and men in prison has something to teach us about the ways in which each sex is taught by our culture to handle pain."

Shutting down on emotional expressiveness has been a devastating gender design for males. It is essential that men overcome their conditioning so that they can acknowledge their early wounds and use their natural emotional healing power to regain their birthright of wholeness.

It is very common to have women coming for therapy because they are upset about their partner's lack of responsiveness. In therapy they often connect with their own numbness, deadness and flatness. They are triggered by their partners back to a time when their parent was reactive rather than appropriately responsive to them. In turn, they had to shut themselves down to cope with their parent's reaction. When we are able to feel how we have had to shut down to survive in our childhood, we are better able to confront our partners appropriately about their lack of responsiveness. We also become more empathetic to their plight.

Our unconscious need to break through the numbness

Our unconscious need to break through the numbness drives us to find templates of experience that fit our deadened fear and hurt. We mistakenly seek experiences that either blast open our numbness to underlying feeling or override it with "exceptional events" that momentarily provide us with a sense of being alive and living in the moment. Both of these extreme exercises require repetition, however, in that we are driven to achieve this event-dependent high again and again in order to be released from our numbness.

We become caught on external stimuli to move us toward feeling. We may become dependent on getting our feeling hype from group encounters, sustaining euphoria with drugs, seeking intense infatuations, needing the gambler's chance of being on a roll and wielding violent, omnipotent control over another person. We get hooked on the high as a counterpoint to our numbness. This high becomes so important that we often disregard our bodies' warnings and in some cases even take pride in dismissing our body pain.

When we act on our unconscious need and fail to acknowledge our drive as a message from our natural healing power, we get locked in "out-of-ourselves" behaviour.

Feeling through our numbness takes us to our true feelings. It is then that we have a chance to process them to completion. We come to know that we can truly live in the moment.

Feeling through numbness, deadness and flatness

When we feel down through our feelings, whatever they may be, wherever they may start, sooner or later we will feel how we had to shut down. Clients will often say "It's gone," referring to the feeling they were just experiencing. Now they must feel exactly how quickly and how thoroughly they had to put this feeling away as a child, how they had to shut down to survive. These clients are encouraged to stay with the shut-down feeling. When we are able to stay with this feeling of shutting down, we will go through it to feel the underlying feelings that are being defended against by the shut-down—terror, unmet need, worthlessness, shame, guilt, anxiety, anger, loneliness, regret and powerlessness—we will feel the incredible hurt from our past that as adults we can now afford to feel; we will grieve.

Those who suffered severe abuse, such as sexual abuse, often feel how they had to dissociate from their body in order to survive the assault. We dissociate to defend against physical pain, powerlessness, terror, confusion, pleasure and shame. It takes great determination to stay with these feelings as long as is needed to connect and integrate them into our lives. Many of us would like to slip away from this process and act out our anger against the perpetrators. This perpetuates our defense.

Those of us who have been sexually abused as children will have dysfunction in our sex lives. For example, deliberately thinking of something else and "getting through" the sex act is a form of dissociating. We do not want sex but we submit to it because we think we should. We go against ourselves. Many women report that they have been doing this for years and have not realized that it means there is something wrong, something to pay attention to. Men who dissociate in order to perform are also locked in obligation and are separated from their real feelings. Many men and women report fantasizing about other people when having sex. This too is a form of dissociation. Dissociating is not a matter of being wrong. Feeling how we dissociate can provide us with an opportunity to feel what happened to us that locked us in this unfortunate dysfunction. Feeling the underlying pain that supports this dysfunction allows us to move toward a more satisfying and intimate sexual relationship.

Unfortunately, sexuality has been such a repressed and taboo subject that many of us cannot speak of it no matter how uncomfortable we are with what is going on in our sex lives.

Once we become aware that we often shut down we can begin to feel what this shut-down costs us. We can use the trigger to feel our way back to why we feel the way we do about sex. It is very common to start a relationship or marriage with lots of "turned on" feelings and lots of sex, and it is confusing to both partners when this changes. What is important is that we take responsibility for how we feel and what has happened to us.

Gertrude didn't know what a "normal" sex life would be like. She often felt guilty because her husband said there was definitely something wrong with her—he called it "frigidity."

Gertrude admitted in her first therapy session that she sometimes enjoyed sex but that for the most part she hated it. She was able to tell me in her second session that she had been sexually abused by her grandfather for three years, from age four to age seven. She had never told anyone about this before and felt great shame that it had ever happened. Gertrude had always believed that she had put this behind her and that it did not affect her life. She realized now that it was affecting her marriage in a very big way.

Gertrude felt stuck for quite a while. She could not feel anything; she was shut down. She was determined to try to get to what she needed to feel, because she thought that otherwise she might lose her marriage. Her husband was not very understanding even when she was able to tell him that she had been severely abused as a child. He wanted the problem fixed.

Her husband's attitude became a big trigger for Gertrude. She was able to go with her anger at his lack of empathy. She knew how much courage it had taken her to tell him and this helped her connect with why she had never told her mother. The little girl had not expected empathy from her mother; she thought her mother would have blamed her.

Gertrude was able to focus on where she felt the anger in her body. She would stay with this in her sessions until she was able to yell, first at her husband and then at her mother and grandfather. Her anger would come in short bursts and then she would feel herself shut down and go numb. As she continued to feel the shut-down and really focus on how it felt in her body, she gradually opened up to remembering more of the details of the assaults. She would alternately weep, rage and shut down. This was a slow process for Gertrude but she stuck with it.

Eventually Gertrude demanded that her husband do some reading about being the partner of someone with severe sexual abuse in his or her past.

When we know that feeling numb, dead and flat is not the way we need to live our lives, when we know that we were neglected and abused as children, when our lives are not going well today or when our partner is telling us that we are unresponsive, we can use this as a doorway through to a fuller life.

Difficult as it is, we can feel our way through numbness, deadness and flatness to be free of its debilitating weight.

Part III
Unlocking Relationships

Acknowledging and using our natural healing power helps us to bring to consciousness the forces that are interfering in our present relationships. When we are unable to free ourselves from the personal binds in our relationships, it is because we are unconsciously gripped by our past experience. Trying to work out old pain in present relationships causes us to reenact our past. We set ourselves up for familiar feelings, a perpetual life rerun fuelled by hope that keeps us stuck.

The more we heal our past, the more we react appropriately in the present, the better we feel about ourselves and the better our relationships are.

Being ourselves in our relationships is our greatest asset. It allows us to stay connected to the other person but to feel separate from their pain and their behaviour. We are better able to listen and have empathy for others because we understand that we are responsible for our thoughts, feelings and actions and the other person is responsible for theirs. We are also able to be direct in our communication. Others can trust that we mean what we say; they need waste no energy guessing.

We also understand that when we are in relationships with others, there is a constant dance of balancing our needs with those of others. We are able to put our wants and needs forward and have others do the same. We are able to negotiate and to work through to fairness. When we unlock our relationships we treat others with equal respect and dignity and we are self-honouring.

Our ability to access our reality means we do not live with illusions or delusions. We do not want to be controlling of others. We consciously ask ourselves, "What is within my control and what is not?" when faced with complex and painful situations. When we are helpless to really make things different for someone we love, we give ourselves time to grieve.

When we are faced with requests from others we can ask ourselves, "What am I willing to do and what am I not willing to do?" "Can I do this without resentment?" This helps us arrive at clarity when we listen to our response from deep inside. We then act without violating ourselves. When we do this, we also honour our relationship with the other person because we do not do things that will cause us to resent them and withdraw from them.

We may face life situations that require us to give to others because of what is happening to them. We can be aware of how much we are stretching ourselves and keep acknowledging this to ourselves. The important thing is that we be conscious.

Becoming conscious is the way we unlock relationships.

16

LIFE PARTNER RELATIONSHIPS

A Place to Grow

———————————

———————————

Taking responsibility for our feelings and therefore ceasing to blame ourselves or others is the most crucial step we can take to enhance our life partner relationship. This is true whether we are in a heterosexual or same-sex relationship, whether we are married or living together and whether we are young, old or somewhere in between. Since we have so much riding on it our life partner relationship is often the most difficult place for us to own our feelings and stop blaming. It is where we pour all our life hopes and play out our unconscious desires and locked expectations.

In this relationship we unconsciously reenact our past, suffer familiar bad feelings and unconsciously hope for a different outcome this time. We struggle to get the love, acceptance and approval that was missing in our childhood. As our partner "disappoints" us we get caught on old feelings that erupt from the past.

Old, disconnected and unmet need from the past is impossible for life partners to fill and it manifests itself as unrealistic expectations in this relationship. We struggle and struggle, unaware that we are locked in trying to get old, unfelt experiences worked out in the present.

Disconnected feelings from the past make it difficult to negotiate differences in the present. What could be a simple problem-solving exercise turns into a merry-go-round of misunderstanding and blame. Excitement and drama generated by repetitive discord may substitute for authentic closeness when we are unable to be open, trusting and vulnerable with our partner.

What may feel even more deadly is when we shut down, become distant and alienated, refusing to engage with one another.

My clients are often startled when I ask them to begin the change process by understanding that each of us is one hundred percent responsible for making our relationship the way we want it to be. We are not, however, one hundred percent responsible for the outcome.

When we want change

It is frequently the case that one member of a life partnership expresses unhappiness and seeks help either for him or herself or for the relationship.

It is important to understand that we cannot change anyone else; the only person we can change is ourselves. This is not a discouraging state of affairs however, since when we change ourselves we automatically change the relationship and our partner is pressed to respond differently. It is not possible to continue to respond in exactly the same way if the other person has changed his or her pattern of reaction and communication. There is of course a risk involved since our partner may not like the way we have changed, may not be able to grow and may therefore leave the relationship. Many of my clients have been amazed to discover that their partners are capable of change when they themselves change their habitual way of approaching problems.

If we have been the one wanting things to be different and we have taken responsibility for changing our dysfunctional patterns, then we will likely accept the eventual dissolution of the relationship if our partner cannot make the shifts he or she needs to make. If we cannot do this without blame, then we have not finished feeling through what we need to feel.

It is unwise to leave a relationship precipitously because we are suddenly completely fed up with the way things are or because we have no feeling at all left for our partner. This is unwise because if we do not take the responsibility for making the changes we need to make in order to have the relationship the way we want it to be, we will simply take our dysfunctional patterns and old pain into our next relationship.

Julia and Ken came for help when the discord in their marriage became unbearable for both of them. They blamed each other for exactly the same things: "You never listen . . . You have to have everything your way . . . You're too controlling, you always think you're right!"

They both began to do individual work, producing time lines about their lives and writing in their journals about how they felt. They also started to read about relationships. They each said they wanted to take responsibility for their feelings.

Julia was able to go with her feelings both at home and in her therapy sessions. She noticed how she was triggered by Ken's absoluteness and realized that she usually gave up when there was any controversy. Julia began to connect with her fear of staying present when there was conflict and how she found it easier to fade away or get confused. She felt how voiceless she had been as a child, how afraid she had been in her alcoholic family. Slowly she began to be able to risk staying and expressing herself more. She realized that she and Ken were very different in some fundamental ways.

Ken had been very hopeful when he started into therapy but soon got discouraged and said that Julia was getting more stubborn not less. He was unable to stop blaming Julia, and as she became truer to herself he got angrier and more discontented. He acknowledged that he was not writing his feelings in his journal but wanted me to know that he was continuing to do quite a bit of reading.

Julia was heartsick when she saw that Ken did not really understand that he was not taking responsibility and that he was continuing to blame her. When she would say "Please don't blame me" he would get angry and say "I'm not blaming you; don't use that psychobabble on me." When she would try to talk to him about problems in their relationship without blaming, he would turn the problem back on her and say that it was all her fault.

After a year of individual and some joint therapy, Julia left Ken. She had become clearer and clearer and he had become more stuck and more blameful. She did a lot of grieving about the loss of her marriage and all the other losses in her life. He left therapy still bewildered about what had happened to him.

Ken was a very shut-down person. All he could really feel was anger, which he felt constantly both at home and at work. He tried to change the way he dealt with Julia and his employees; however, he could not maintain any new way of being. He wanted Julia to appreciate it every time he controlled his anger and he also wanted her to appreciate the flowers he brought her and all the other thoughtful little things he was now doing around the house. Julia felt that she deserved to be spoken to without being blamed and that she was not obliged to "appreciate" him not being abusive. She did not want the things he was doing to try to win her over. She wanted to be able to talk to him and to work through their problems.

Unfortunately Ken was not able to stay with the numbness inside that he felt in his therapy sessions. He could talk about his childhood, but could not feel anything. He wanted to be able to fix things in the present and used the books he was reading to point out to Julia what he perceived she was doing wrong.

He could not cry when Julia finally left; all he could say was that she always needed to have things her way.

Many individuals arrive in my office stating that they have tried everything. They are often pleasantly surprised to realize that there is a fundamental understanding they have been missing. They have not known about taking responsibility for their feelings or about our innate healing ability which alerts us to the need to acknowledge, feel and integrate old held hurt.

Dealing with differences

It is important to have a method for dealing with differences in our life partner relationship. The more whole and emotionally fit each member of the partnership is, the easier it will be to deal with differences. When our partner differs from us and we have a problem with this, we need to own our feelings.

It drove Vivian crazy that Zak wanted to try lots of different things when they made love. She knew what pleased her and wanted to do only that.

Vivian had a lot of trouble talking to Zak about this difference. When she stopped blaming him for needing what he needed and started feeling how uncomfortable and embarrassed she was by his desires, she started to open up. Vivian was able to re-experience what it had been like for her in her family when her parents had been overtly sexual in her presence. She had felt embarrassed and ignored, and she was left alone to cope with how she felt. The only thing she could do was shut down on these feelings. As Vivian worked these old feelings through she was able to reveal to Zak what it was like for her as a child and how this made it difficult for her to be free and easy sexually. He was very understanding and together they began to open more to each other.

When we do not take responsibility for our feelings we are likely to get stuck in the "I'm right, you're wrong" scenario. Needing to be right and needing to blame are both defenses. When this happens problems do not get resolved and around and around we go. We can begin to notice if we are stuck, needing to be right, and we can start feeling that need to its source.

We can put our needs, wants, resentments, discomfort and unhappiness on the table for discussion. We can notice if we cannot openly do this; we can feel what that is all about. We can always choose to feel.

Expectations

Whether they are expressed overtly or not, we all bring expectations to our life partner relationship. Before we commit to each other it is wise to talk thoroughly about our expectations. I have discovered in my work that few people actually do this. Nevertheless, it is a place to return to when there is a pinch in the relationship. When change happens we often experience problems, and we need to express our expectations of how things will be now that this change has taken place. As we get clear about our expectations we can then negotiate agreements to meet both our needs as much as possible.

Expectations are a problem when they are unrealistic. They are unrealistic in our current relationship when we are unconsciously trying to get an old need met. As I described in chapter six, old, unmet need erupting in our present relationship can really mess it up.

Once again, the route out of this mess is to take responsibility for our feelings. We do this by allowing ourselves to feel back to our childhood through the triggers in our present relationship. This is how we get clear about what is realistic, present need. Sometimes we understand this concept but we get trapped trying to figure out what is and is not realistic. We will not be free of our unrealistic need in the present until we feel it to its source and feel and connect enough to integrate it. We cannot think ourselves to emotional fitness.

The protection game

We often rationalize our inability to express who we are in our life partner relationship by saying that our partner really could not take the truth of how we are feeling. It is emotionally unhealthy when we lie to ourselves, rationalizing our inability to express ourselves by telling ourselves that it might hurt the other person.

Tricia always felt great when her husband, Trevor, was out of town on business. She and the kids were much more relaxed around the house and at the dinner table. Tricia realized that she felt happier.

She was horrified when I asked her what it would be like to tell Trevor the truth about this situation. Tricia said she could not possibly do this, since he would be so hurt. I asked her to imagine saying it to him and to stay with the feelings this brought up. She could immediately feel how frightened she would be. As she stayed with her fear, she began to feel like a very fragile little girl and she started to tremble.

Tricia returned to these feelings many times in subsequent sessions. As she realized more and more how anxious and afraid she had been as a child to express herself at all, she began to understand how this connected to her present feelings with her husband.

Tricia came to realize that she herself was subverting the very thing she wanted more of in her marriage: some closeness and a sense that she and her husband were in this together. Her childhood fear was holding her back from standing up to her husband about his rigid demands about how she kept the house and how the children behaved. She acquiesced instead, and only fully enjoyed her home and her children when he was out of town. She had played a protection game by not telling the truth about how she really felt, believing she was protecting him when she really was protecting herself. She had been stuck in her old childhood fear.

Tricia took the risk to feel her fear as she told her husband the truth. She kept feeling her way through this as he reacted to her more assertive behaviour. She was able to assure him that what she wanted was a good relationship with him; she told him this hinged on her feeling free to be herself in the relationship all the time and not just when he was out of town. As Tricia shared with him what she was connecting to about her past, Trevor began to open up more to looking at himself and why he reacted the way he did to a less than perfectly kept house or to noisy, exuberant children.

Any "withhold" usually damages or at least limits our relationship. It is important that we tell ourselves the truth about what we are withholding and why. When we do this, we can start to feel what we are afraid of and we can work our way through our fear.

Attraction to others

Being attracted to others is part of the natural fabric of life. Attractions are unavoidable if we are in any way open to ourselves and our need.

We can, however, become stuck in our attractions, refusing to chance feeling by shutting down on this yearning need and believing in the falsehood that we "should not" feel this way when we are in a life partner relationship. When we shut ourselves down, believing we should not have these feelings, we damage our life partner relationship. When we withhold from ourselves in this way, we withhold from our partner; openness, sharing and real connection are missing. When we shut down on our need and simply put off dealing with ourselves, as surely as the sun rises, we will find ourselves caught again by new attractions and we will have to redouble our efforts to keep ourselves at bay.

On the other hand, we may act out by blindly following our attraction, disregarding our partner and our commitment. In order to do this we must divide ourselves, become dishonest and deceitful and live with secrets. This in fact is part of the attraction: the high that many of us feel as we act out the fantasy of getting something that is prohibited. All this has its roots in unfelt pain from our childhood.

What is certain is that we weaken the bond between our partners and ourselves when we either withhold what is honestly going on inside us or withhold and act out our needs behind our partner's back.

If we can accept that we all feel attractions, we can move toward more honesty in our relationship. There is then an opportunity for each of us to share what is happening inside us. This may trigger feelings such as jealousy in our partner but this too is a feeling that can be acknowledged, felt to its fullest and taken to its root.

This is one of the toughest territories in any life partner relationship. This is because we place most of our life hope in our relationship. When this hope is unrealistic and disconnected from its source we are deeply disappointed when our partner fails to meet our unconscious needs. We then become susceptible to looking elsewhere to have our hope fulfilled. We may overreact, become infatuated with someone who appears to be a perfect match for our unconscious need, and we may act out. The intensity of our infatuation matches the intensity of our early deprivation. As with any other feeling, we have the opportunity to notice our overreaction, take responsibility for it and use it as a door to connect to the underlying need.

Healthy relationships require that we take responsibility for our desperate need to be loved and that we feel it to its source. They require that we trust, difficult though it may be, that each of us has a blueprint of need from our past still at work in us. Sharing our attractions with our partner and working out all the feelings that come up draws us closer. Our fears lessen, intimacy is enhanced and we grow within our relationship and within ourselves, instead of staying stuck, locked in our disappointment.

When we take responsibility for our need by recognizing our attractions as need rooted in our past, we can feel back to what we did not get and connect again and again to it until our unmet need is integrated. Our lives broaden and our connection with our partner deepens when we pursue all our feelings, sharing them as they become incorporated into the revealed tapestry that makes us who we are.

Jealousy

We suffer jealousy when we do not feel good about ourselves. We blame our partner for making us jealous. This lack of ownership of our feelings keeps us on that ever-turning merry-go-round of intense, possessive feelings that we twist to believe are real, caring and responsiblity. We are supported in this belief by our culture's constant theme in story and song of lusting, cheating and using jealousy to manipulate. The intensity of emotion drummed up in this way is an empty substitute for the real thing. Even when we believe we have just cause to feel jealous in the present, we can discover that, as with other intense feelings, the strength of the feeling is coming from the past.

Keri Ann was at first happy with her partner's vivaciousness and obvious easy rapport with others. They had not been together long, however, when Keri Ann began to feel jealous when she saw Alicia talking to other women.

When she confronted Alicia she was told she would have to get used to it because Alicia had no intention of changing who she was. Alicia told Keri Ann that it was her problem but without much empathy or understanding.

Keri Ann believed that Alicia got far too close to other women. She was frustrated that she could not get Alicia to see this.

Keri Ann entered therapy when she realized that this issue was causing a serious rift in their otherwise compatible and caring relationship.

Keri Ann was stuck for a while because she wanted to believe that her feelings were all about now. She did know that she herself did not have very high self-esteem and that this stemmed from a quite unhappy childhood; however, she asked, "Wouldn't anyone feel this way if their partner was practically fooling around right in front of them?"

In one session, as she was held to what it was like to watch this happening, Keri Ann felt a huge pain and heaviness in her chest. As she focused on this feeling and breathed into it, she began to sob deeply. She was back in the house she grew up in, feeling three years old. She was watching her mother feed the new baby as she balanced another child on her lap. Keri Ann could feel herself standing and watching with her thumb in her mouth and her head down. She could feel the immense pain of her need for her mother. When she came out of the feeling many minutes later she quietly said, "I couldn't even cry about it then; she would have been mad."

Once Keri Ann had done considerable grieving about her childhood neglect and had connected to how worthless she had felt, she talked to Alicia again. She shared with her what her connection had been and what a huge root there was to the feelings triggered by Alicia's behaviour. Alicia was able to listen because Keri Ann was talking about herself; she welcomed this closeness. She invited Keri Ann not to hold her feelings back and said that she would become more aware of how she behaved.

When we take responsibility for our feelings there is more likelihood for empathy. When there is empathy there is more opportunity for each person in the relationship to grow.

Trust

If as children we could not trust our parents we will have difficulty trusting in our adult relationships. We may reenact our childhood by finding a life partner who indeed cannot be trusted, or we may be with someone who is entirely trustworthy but we cannot experience this as so.

Sometimes we have to make a conscious decision to trust so that we can own our feelings of not trusting. This is hard to do and we have to call on the reality of the situation to help us make this decision. For example, we have to be able to see rationally that we have no reason not to trust. If we make a decision to trust, then we can allow ourselves to notice our feelings of distrust and we can go deeply into them every chance we get. If we do this they will undoubtedly lead us to the betrayals of our childhood. These we can grieve and integrate.

It is particularly difficult for us to trust ourselves and our instincts when our partner lies to us. When we do not trust ourselves, it is hard to see our way clear. As we connect more and more to the betrayals in our past, grieve our hurt and integrate our experience, we will trust our feelings more in the present and take the action we need in order to honour ourselves.

Commitment

Barry and Paula had been living together for three years. Barry wanted to get married but Paula kept putting him off, saying "Why risk spoiling all this? Why can't we just leave well enough alone?"

Barry was really confused. He did not understand Paula's attitude and asked her to go into counselling with him. She reluctantly agreed.

Paula had trouble talking in the first therapy session because she started to cry and could not stop. She was encouraged to stay with what she was feeling while Barry was encouraged to sit quietly with her and observe how he was feeling.

Paula said she was extremely embarrassed and really wanted to leave. She courageously stayed when she was asked to. I explained how important it was that she allow herself to have her feelings, whatever they might be. I began to ask her questions about the family she came from.

Paula decided to come for individual therapy because she realized that her tears meant something, and as she gave a brief account of her original family she realized why she was so reluctant to commit to Barry.

Paula grieved a lot in the ensuing therapy sessions. She felt how really frightened she had always been as a child when she thought her parents were going to split up. When she was in her early twenties they finally did and Paula was devastated. She had been so angry that she had refused to have much to do with either of them since. She had stuffed her feelings away.

Most often in life partner relationships we are afraid of losing the other person or we are afraid of losing ourselves. It is most difficult to commit to another person for life when we are afraid. Commitment is central to an emotionally healthy relationship and is essential if our partnership is to flourish. Commitment engenders support and creates an atmosphere of trust where we can take risks to reveal who we are.

Rejection

If we have suffered rejection as children we will be afraid of rejection in the present. This will likely manifest itself most in our life partner relationship. Our disconnected fear of rejection can cause us to behave in ways that are detrimental to our current relationship.

Allan became enraged when Cynthia wanted to go out with her friends. To convince her that she was wrong for wanting to do this he would point to many of the couples they knew, saying "None of the other wives just take off like that."

Cynthia said she wished Allan had some friends of his own whom he could enjoy apart from her. She felt she had a right to time with her friends.

In Allan's individual sessions a picture emerged of Allan as a very good boy who always attempted to help his mother and keep her happy while his father drank and womanized. Allan had always been very angry with his father for how he had treated his mother. He said he thought his dad was a real jerk. He began with this anger in his therapy sessions and was surprised to discover that he was also angry with his father on his own behalf. Allan had always thought that he did not care about his dad, that he did not need him. As he felt through his anger he kept touching on the awful, lonely, worthless feelings he had felt as his father rejected him in favour of the bottle or his women.

As Allan grieved for the loss of his father's love he slowly realized that his mother had also rejected him. She had frequently made derogatory comments about men and Allan had felt, of course, that she did not like him either. She had also been so preoccupied with her own pain that she had not given her son the time, caring and attention he so desperately needed.

As Allan worked through the pain of being rejected as a child, the feelings of rejection that had gripped him when Cynthia wanted to go out with her friends lessened. He came to comprehend that when Cynthia wanted time with her friends she was not rejecting him.

We will keep feeling rejected and blame it on our partner until we take responsibility for our feeling and feel it through to connection and completion. We can notice when we feel rejected, deliberately allow the fear to surface, label our fear and perhaps lie down and focus on it. We can feel it for as long as we are able, even if that is only for a few moments.

Becoming aware of defensiveness

Margaret and Jordan Paul in their excellent book *Do I Have to Give Up Me to Be Loved by You?* illustrate that our fear causes us to react protectively; we become closed and defensive instead of open and vulnerable. They suggest that it is helpful to look at every communication to discover what our intention is. Are we closed and defensive, wanting to blame, or are we open, wanting to learn about the other person?

Becoming aware of our intention will help us own our tone and body language and become more truthful with our partner and ourselves.

When we are able to notice that we are defended, behaving defensively, we can use this awareness to label our fear and begin to feel it. As we do this we open to our healing power and give ourselves the opportunity to know ourselves better and to share who we are with our partner.

Kate and Glen decided to try to help each other when either became defensive. They had lived together for two years and before they got married they wanted to iron out a few "glitches," as they put it, in their relationship.

This couple learned a great deal about themselves and each other as they gently confronted each other when either became defensive. Sometimes they would have to take a "time out" because there was too much anger and defensiveness in the air but they promised each other that they would come back to the issue and explore it. They did this faithfully. Sometimes there were tears and real connection to early pain and often there was connection to earlier hurts in their relationship that had not been dealt with and had remained as unfinished business for both of them. When they married they felt they had a very solid grounding; they were not afraid of losing themselves or each other.

Resentment kills love

It is a common occurrence to have a client arrive in my office stating that he or she does not love his or her life partner any more. It does not take long to determine that this person is carrying a lot of resentment and in many cases has been accumulating it for years.

Taking responsibility for harbouring years of resentment is the first step in getting clear about this situation. I ask clients to make a list of all the resentments they can think of, even the ones going back many years. When we take the responsibility to feel and stay with our resentment, we uncover many things about ourselves. Resentment covers fear. We will likely find that we were afraid to stand up for ourselves and instead tolerated a situation and silently blamed our partner. We will likely discover how afraid we were of making our partner angry or of losing him or her. When we stay with the feelings generated by the situations that we resented, we go back to the many times this happened in the relationship and then to times in our childhood that made us too afraid to protest.

We are better able to speak with our own voice in the present when we connect with these times and feel them to completion. When we start to unlock our hearts that have been bolted shut by our resentment, we often begin to feel something for our partner once again. If our partner can hear our pain and understand how we have felt there may be a satisfactory outcome for both of us in the relationship.

If our partner cannot hear or understand what we are saying we may decide to leave the relationship because we no longer wish to struggle to get something that we cannot get. Usually these are important things, such as equal respect, equal dignity, support for being our own, whole person, the willingness to work through differences and the willingness to engage in some degree of intimacy. What is important here is that we feel through our childhood struggle for love and understanding. We do this to be clear that we are leaving our current relationship because our *adult* needs cannot be met and not because we are caught on disconnected, unmet need from the past.

We may decide, on the other hand, that we can accept our partner as he or she is and that we can live with them without resentment. It is not emotionally healthy to continue to live with abuse of any kind.

We stay stuck in resentment when we want our partner to feel responsible for us, when we want him or her to feel "bad" for what has been done. This is staying stuck in victimhood and blame instead of grieving and moving on.

Verbal and emotional abuse

Any kind of name-calling or put-down is easily recognized as verbal abuse. Many people do not acknowledge emotional withdrawal, refusal to talk, refusal to listen, refusal to resolve issues, refusal to admit to angry feelings and blame as emotional abuse. In her book *The Verbally Abusive Relationship* Patricia Evans spells out many more forms of verbal abuse. This book has been a real eye-opener to many of my clients.

When one partner argues with the other's thoughts, feelings, beliefs and perceptions and discounts their experience, it is what I call "crazy-making" behaviour. It is one thing to disagree about an issue; it is something else to imply the other person is "dumb, sick or stupid" for having such an opinion.

> Brian continually told Dana that she was wrong to feel the way she felt. He would argue with her every time she stated an opinion or said how she was feeling about something. Dana would doubt herself and feel really "crazy" when he would follow up with such statements as "You don't know what you're talking about" or "You're looking for a fight."

> Dana entered therapy because she could feel herself obsessed with trying to figure out what she should be doing differently so that she could get through to Brian and so that there would not be so much discord in their home.

It took Dana months to connect with the deep hurt she had felt as a child when her older brother had baited her with facts and figures and told her she was an "idiot" when she did not know some fact or other. He had often told her she was "useless." Dana had a lot to feel around this, including her anger at her parents for not protecting her against this assault. What was worse was that they had had different expectations for her and her brother. She realized that she had not been expected to do very well academically. Her mother had often told her that "You know we'll love you anyway, no matter how well you do at school." For years, in Dana's analysis of her childhood, she had thought this was a kind thing her mother had said. When she relived what it had actually been like, and what it had meant to her, she realized that it had put a huge lid on her potential. Her mother had come from an era when girls were not supposed to stand out and so she had undervalued her daughter's potential and subdued her personal power and capability.

As Dana connected with her anger and hurt and integrated her experience she felt more connected to herself—stronger and less self-doubting. She was able to tell Brian that she would not tolerate his put-downs and his superior stance.

If our partner is judging and critical there will not be intimacy in the relationship. The judging person often denies that this is what they are doing by claiming that they are just trying to be helpful. This is where it is important for us to listen to how we are feeling and trust it. We can insist that we do not want to hear blameful "you" messages, that what we will accept is hearing how our partner is *feeling* about something we are doing without blaming us.

It is often difficult to identify what we are feeling when our partner trivializes what we have said or done. We may end up feeling confused, depressed and frustrated and not know why. We have trouble feeling good about our accomplishments.

Peter arrived home ecstatic about his performance review. Finally, things were really going well for him at his new job. He had been working really hard.

Doreen said, "You could have done just as well at the other company if you had focused on what you needed to do."

Peter spiralled into despair. In the days that followed, he could feel how depressed he was. He realized that his work life was finally going well and that he "shouldn't" be feeling this way.

Peter was scared and decided to call the therapist he had heard about from his co-worker.

Peter was encouraged to feel his fear. He was afraid that he might break down and not be able to work at all. This took him to familiar feelings of anxiety that he might not be good enough to please his parents. Peter realized that in any relationship he had, he was anxious that he might not be good enough. As Peter felt back and forth between his childhood and his home and work life now, he recognized that he was stuck in these old, bad feelings about himself. He kept feeling, and as he did this he worked through the awful feelings of despair repressed from his young life. Eventually he stood up to Doreen and no longer allowed her to put him down or trivialize his accomplishments.

Laura was terrified when Jake said that if she left him, he would see to it that she would not get custody of the children. She believed him, because he pointed to her depression and her inability to function every month when she was premenstrual as probable cause to have the children awarded to him.

Threats are a common form of emotional abuse and are particularly frightening when they involve the children. In Laura's case it was years later in therapy that she grieved long and hard about having given up her life to stay with this man because she was so afraid that he could have taken her children from her. Consulting a lawyer or talking to someone in social services in order to understand our rights is an essential ingredient to being able to deal with this sort of threat.

> Ginny felt undermined whenever she and her husband, Scott, went out with their friends. He would often laugh when she was telling their friends about something she was doing. She could not put her finger on it but it felt like he was making fun of her. She felt terribly inadequate.

> On her friend's urging Ginny entered therapy. This friend had called Scott on his behaviour, telling him that "It makes me really uncomfortable when you laugh at Ginny."

> As Ginny connected with her anger at how she was being treated she also connected to a great deal of childhood abuse. As she felt her way through what had happened to her, she began to stand up to Scott. At first he simply escalated his put-downs and techniques to make Ginny feel bad. When she held her ground and told him in a straightforward manner that she would not put up with it any more, he crumbled.

Fortunately Scott was able to do the emotional work he needed to do to start taking responsibility for why he needed to undermine and put Ginny down. As he felt through his own sense of worthlessness as a child and the monumental hurt that lay under it, he was able to share what he was finding out with Ginny and they grew closer. His need to undermine her evaporated.

When our partner consistently forgets agreements and incidents that are important to us it constitutes denial and a form of abuse. It is common to hear "I don't know what you're talking about" or "You're dreaming, I never said that." Again, this leaves us feeling exasperated and totally helpless. Going with these feelings and getting connected to our past abuse is the way we can gain clarity and enough of ourselves to clearly request and press for change. We press for change when we do not give up and when we are willing to state the consequences if our partner is not willing to work a problem through with us. We will not be taken seriously if we do not honour ourselves enough to insist on a discussion and resolution to a problem that is important to us.

Anita sought help because she could no longer stand how frustrated and unhappy she was. She reported that her husband, Tom, was angry most of the time and refused to discuss any of the things that bothered her about their finances, their children and how they spent their time.

Anita felt that the problems must be her fault. She had believed that if she just kept trying she could make the relationship better. Anita had tried to understand Tom and she had tried to get him to understand her. She had no ability to set limits and express what she would and would not accept.

Anita brought all her current triggers from her relationship with Tom to her therapy sessions. As she went with her anger and frustration, she felt again and again how helpless and powerless her exchanges with him made her feel. As she stayed with these feelings she connected with the helpless and powerless child she had been.

Gradually Anita began to see that the power struggle she was engaged in with Tom was a fruitless one. She realized that he was not interested in solving problems but rather that he needed to dominate and keep her down.

The more she felt and connected with her voicelessness and helplessness as a child the more strength she gained in the present. She realized that she could not stay with Tom if things did not change. She was very upset at the model they were providing for their young children and knew that she could not live with herself if she did not take a stand.

Anita decided to put it in writing for Tom. She asked him to read her letter and react to it away from her. She told him that after he had done this she would speak with him. In the letter she told Tom that if they could not learn to sit down together and resolve the things that were bothering her and the things that were obviously not working in their relationship and in their family, then she wanted them to seek counselling together so that they could learn to do this. If Tom would not agree to this she would not remain in the relationship.

We are underreacting when we tolerate any form of verbal or emotional abuse. We need to listen to ourselves as closely as we can, allow ourselves to see the truth of how we are being treated and go through the doors we can go through to allow our natural healing power to work for us.

When our partner is shut down

Nonresponsiveness in our partner can be frustrating and disappointing. Again, the only person we can change and work on is ourselves.

> Sandra was exasperated that Eric never got worked up about anything. She also felt that there was no passion in their relationship and no real emotional connection. She did not know what to do.
>
> Sandra was surprised to discover two things in her therapy. One was that her feelings in her marriage were familiar to her. She felt what it was like to live with parents whom she could not connect with much at all because of their busyness. They were both well-known professionals and had busy social lives as well as their careers to think about. Sandra and her sister had been looked after by a series of nannies in their early years.
>
> The other thing Sandra was surprised to get in touch with was the fact that she herself was pretty emotionally shut down. She had thought she was the expressive and outgoing one but she connected with how she had developed this facade as a child to please her parents.
>
> As Sandra opened up to herself she was able to talk with Eric about the distance she felt in their relationship. She arranged a long weekend away for just the two of them and got a commitment from him to spend the time addressing how they both felt about each other.

The continuum from alienation to intimacy

We can all locate our life partner relationship somewhere on the continuum from alienation to intimacy. Most of us want to move our relationship toward intimacy. While some of us may say this, we may in fact be very afraid to do so. It helps us move when we understand that we can shift how we feel in the present by employing our healing power to help us finish with the unfinished business from our past that is standing in our way of a close, intimate, satisfying and vibrant relationship with our life partner. When we make the choice and take the risk to move toward intimacy, we can label our fears about becoming open and vulnerable and then begin to confront them.

Stereotyping undone

Believing that women and men are from different planets is a detrimental idea. The belief that we are and forever will be polar opposites is destructive and limiting to both sexes. It is time for us to face the reality that we are all human and that our relationships will improve when we learn to help each other toward authenticity. A "them against us" approach helps to preserve gender stereotypes that are inaccurate generalizations and that are damaging to how we view each other.

It helps us to understand that women and men have been *conditioned* differently, and therefore, in a general way some differences can be identified. What is dangerous is when we believe that this conditioning is something else—some inherent difference that cannot be changed. Pandering to stereotypical differences in order to have better relationships does not work. *Authenticity in relationships is what works.*

When we free ourselves from the prison of gender conditioning, we discover that autonomy, usually seen as a masculine wish, and connection, usually seen as a feminine desire, are both possible and desirable for us all. Whole, emotionally healthy human beings need to be both independent and connected to others at the same time. In fact, it is not possible to be truly connected to another in a healthy way if we are not first our own autonomous person.

Both men and women have the capability to be whole, to experience the whole range of human emotions. We both have a natural emotional healing power to move us toward emotional fitness. This power works in exactly the same way for all of us; we need only take advantage of it.

The stereotyping of marginalized couples such as same-sex or mixed-race partners causes an extra burden of stress in their relationships. Here as well, we can get locked in an immovable "them against us" outlook in reaction to this stereotyping. This can become a rock-solid defense that limits our opportunity to be authentic with each other. When we blame globally, even when we have been victims of blame ourselves, we are not taking responsibility. When we attribute any characteristic to a particular part of our society, we are blaming and not taking responsibility for our feelings. When we notice our "them against us" position, we can begin to take responsibility and to open to what lies under this defense. Only then do we have the opportunity to grow personally and have our life partner relationship thrive.

With the divorce rate being what it is many of us feel discouraged about the potential for our life partner relationship. It makes us fearful of making commitment and being open. However, in this relationship lies the opportunity for a lifetime of growth and expanded potential. When we courageously engage our emotional healing power to unravel the knotted pain from our past, we free ourselves to enjoy a richer relationship.

17

PARENT/CHILD RELATIONSHIPS

Conscious and Responsive Parenting

The main ingredient for our children's emotional health is a good relationship with us, their parents. A good relationship with our children has the same elements that any good relationship has. It requires that we respect them, that we treat them with equal dignity and that we honour them as separate individuals capable of being whole and becoming autonomous. It requires that we engage our natural emotional healing power in order to take responsibility for our feelings and reactions and to be as real with our children as we can be.

Being loved and feeling loved are two different things. Parents may tell their children all the time that they love them but children do not feel loved unless they experience loving behaviour.

The key to healthy parenting is knowing ourselves and taking responsibility for the health of our relationship with our children. Having children gives us an opportunity like none other to expand and to grow emotionally.

When we have children we cannot avoid the fact that we will come face to face with our past; children open us to ourselves. When our children behave in ways that really upset us, on an unconscious level we are forced up against how we once felt. Until we bring these memories into consciousness and feel them through to integration, they will trigger us and we will over or underreact, both of which damage our children's well-being. We may feel that we are being "driven crazy" by our children who are not as repressed as we were, who refuse to do things that we were forced to do or who get what we needed but did not get.

This is the very opportunity that will help us grow. It depends on how open we are to ourselves.

We must recognize that we will pass on to our children what we have not dealt with from our past. This is not frightening or hopeless when we know how to engage our natural emotional healing power to complete our feelings from the past so that we can be more clear and present with our children.

Being a good parent is the ambition most of us have as we hold our newborn in our arms. It is a scary prospect, especially since there is no topic that generates more advice, more heated, unsolicited opinion and more defensiveness than that of how to raise children. It is also scary because our children often open us to feelings we may not have known we have, let alone understand.

When we take responsibility for our overreactions and underreactions and use our natural emotional healing power to connect them to their trauma source in the past, we become more conscious. This is what enables us to be responsive to our children.

Meeting our children's needs is what is important for their emotional health. Our relationship with our children will be good if we are, for the most part, able to meet their needs.

Providing a healthy and responsive environment is an ongoing process. The key is to listen to our children and ourselves in order to meet their and our real needs for emotional connection.

Valuing children

We live in a society that does not value children enough and because of this those who serve children are not valued as they should be. If we as a society acknowledged the importance of meeting children's needs, we would employ the highest calibre of people, the most emotionally healthy people, to be our teachers and daycare providers and we would pay them commensurately and willingly. Our most important criteria for employing them would be their ability to treat the children in their care with respect and equal dignity. They would be skilled in listening, direct communication and problem solving. They would be skilled at helping children express and work through their feelings and would provide ways to help them do this. How children feel about what they are doing and learning would be of prime importance.

Those in charge of children would care as much about their inside, their feelings, as they would about their outside. This would mean that we would have to believe that children are born originally whole and that they are innately good and not evil. We would say "the terrific twos" instead of "the terrible twos," and we would not start dreading the teen years soon after our children are born. We could switch from our controlling, punitive stance toward children to a loving, guiding mode. We would recognize and honour the miracle of life and growth and we would have faith in our children. Research supports the fact that children do better when they are not controlled by fear in their homes or in the institutions they are required to attend. Permissive, laissez-faire approaches are also not what children need. In these instances they are given power and control that is not appropriate and that does not meet their need to feel safe and cared for.

If we could bring up one generation of children whose needs were more fully met we could change the world. Change, however, is based on each of us making choices that are more responsible, not less. If enough of us partake in this personal and parenting affirmation, we will move toward a better world with each and every step.

Meeting our children's needs

It is difficult to meet our children's needs if we have not had our own needs met as children, or if we have not felt through what that was like for us.

We may feel that our children are "driving us crazy" when they seem to *need* twenty-four hours a day and when we feel empty ourselves and have no more to give. This is when it becomes easy to blame them for their very need. I have heard parents say, "He was like that from the day he was born!" They were perhaps referring to a "demanding" child. The truth is that babies are demanding, they do require that their needs be met and they let us know about it loud and clear. If we, as parents, are not prepared for this total need that is a baby, and if we are triggered by it because our needs were not met at this stage, then we may start blaming our child even this early. This becomes a vicious cycle; as our child's real needs are not met and he is treated as demanding and given the impression that he is "bad," he will internalize this deeply and will likely act out and become what he has been labelled to be. The truth is that some children need more attention than others. They will thrive, however, if their needs are met without blame. Our job is to be prepared for our children's differences. No two are alike.

We react to our children's needs when we cannot feel what happened to us—when we are disconnected from our own needs that were not met. When we understand that our reaction to our children's needs is our responsibility, we can start to use it to connect with our past pain and to become connected to what happened to us, rather than staying stuck in a reactive cycle.

When our children do not get what they really need they misplace their unmet need onto things. As a result we have become a consumer society— one that puts enormous pressure on parents as it preys upon our children's unmet need, which has become twisted into desperately wanting what they see on television.

Many parents are quite frantic these days because of their own internal pressure to have a certain standard of living and at the same time to meet the needs of their children. It takes an act of courage and responsibility for parents to design their lives so that they can meet their children's needs and at the same time acknowledge their own.

Eleanor was a stay-at-home mom. She felt really good about this and enjoyed her relationship with her three children, aged seven, nine and twelve. She was concerned about her husband's lack of relationship with them; he often commented on how the kids told her things they had not told him. Eleanor had entered therapy to deal with problems she was having with her mother.

Her mother's unresponsiveness and lack of interest in her grandchildren triggered Eleanor. She had never thought of this as having anything to do with her personally, but as she allowed herself to go with her anger about how her mother was treating her grandchildren, she began to connect with what it had been like for her as a child.

Her mother was a teacher and had always been very busy with her career. Eleanor had looked after the younger children and she realized that she got affection from them but none from her parents. Eleanor felt through to the huge hurt about her mother's disinterest in her, as well as about her father's disconnection from her because of his alcohol abuse.

As Eleanor connected more with the deprivation of her childhood, she began to get even more concerned than she had been about her husband's lack of connection with their children. Eleanor struggled with Ray for some time. She did not care about all of their material wealth and she confronted him about his apparent caring more for this than for their children. Ray loved his wife and children and as Eleanor persisted with her unhappiness about what both her children and her husband were missing, he began to recognize his pain at not being more involved with his children. He began to pare down his workload at the business he owned and spend more time with his family. Eleanor was able to support Ray in making changes without blaming him. Ray's sense of well-being flourished in his home as he became more connected to his children's lives. The children had more of their dad.

Needs are needs and they cannot be rationalized or excused away. When children are able to fully express their needs, they do not grow up feeling badly about having them. When we are unable to meet their needs, we can help them by listening and reflecting back to them what we have heard ("You're really disappointed that you can't come to the party with Mommy and Daddy") so that they know we have understood them. They need us to let them have their disappointment and cry about it until they are ready to stop crying about it. As I have said before, this may be difficult for us if we were not allowed our tears as children. It is essential for our children's emotional health that they be allowed and supported to finish what they have to feel. They do not need us to fix everything for them. They do need, however, our presence and support.

As parents, we need to be able to sort out what is our need and what is our children's need. When we are able to meet our children's real needs, most of the time, we will not have to worry. We can be assured that they will become self-directed, sensitive and responsible adults.

Parental need

We want what is best for our children. If, however, we have a need to be seen as a "good" parent this will keep us concerned about our children's behaviour as a reflection of us instead of an expression of them and their need. We may require them to become hidden so that we will not be found inadequate as a parent. We may require them to put away, for example, any behaviour that may indicate to others that they are insecure. As long as we act on our unexamined need, we will not be able to have a relaxed and authentically connected relationship with our children. When we recognize our need to be seen as a "good" parent we can use our innate healing power to get to the root of this need by feeling and connecting to it so that it stops interfering with our relationship with our children.

Some of us, as parents, are able to break the cycle of overt neglect and abuse. We are able to give our children what we did not get and at least to not hurt them in the way we were hurt. However, we still get caught in our old unconscious pain and act it out on our children even when our intentions are quite the opposite. We may, for example, be unable to bear seeing our children unhappy because of our own unconscious hurt and so we may not be able to be with them while they cry and feel their disappointment. We may buy them things we cannot afford because of this. We are driven to see the delight on their faces in order to fend off our unconscious sorrow or anger. We are trying to give them things to fix up our unfelt deprivation. We are easing our own pain through our children.

We have our natural emotional healing power to help us out of this trap. At first this may seem like a formidable task, especially if we do not have a life partner who can support us and who is also doing his or her emotional healing. Even a small step in the direction of connecting to ourselves is helpful and gives us the energy and encouragement to take the next steps.

It is our unconscious pain that keeps us unable to respond to our children and who *they* really are. Many of my clients have said "My mom and dad never knew who I was." Every time we as parents have an entrenched agenda for our children, it makes it difficult to see them for who they are. We can become more aware by honestly examining our expectations of our children and feeling what this means for us. It takes a large dose of honesty to be an effective parent. Fortunately, it has a double payoff in that, as we experience more of who we really are, our children benefit by feeling free to be more of who they are.

Having a good relationship with our children requires that we be responsive to them. When we become more conscious about the sources of our pain and when we move toward feeling it, connecting it and integrating it, we automatically become more real and authentic and therefore more responsive. Our entry point is to notice the strength of our reactions.

When our children trigger us

We will be triggered by our children most when they are at the stage of development where we suffered most. This is why we find that some of us love infants and others cannot relate until our children are older; some of us have a ball with teenagers and others cannot stand them. Owning our feelings and using the triggers our children present us with is the most emotionally stretching experience we are likely to have.

A wailing infant can evoke rage, fear and feelings of inadequacy in us. We may feel utterly helpless and afraid because we do not know what this tiny creature needs and cannot stop the wailing. Our rage may be a defense against our feelings of vulnerability. We may have been told that we will instinctively know what our infant wants which only adds to our feelings of inadequacy. We may also be carrying a load of pent-up emotions because we were not allowed or supported to cry all that we needed to cry as children. When we are thirty-something and trying hard to feel like a responsible, well-organized person managing our lives, the last thing we want is to feel helpless.

> Donna was frantic because her new little son was crying incessantly. A friend gave her Aletha Solter's book *The Aware Baby*. She was somewhat relieved to read that babies need to cry to discharge their feelings and that the best thing she could do would be to lovingly hold little Ethan and give him her attention as he cried.
>
> This was extremely difficult for Donna to do because she felt so awful to see and hear him in such distress. She did notice that when she could do this he would cry vigorously, sometimes for an "interminable" length of time, and then sleep deeply and waken more settled.
>
> Donna's husband, Ian, could more easily be with Ethan when he cried, so when he was home Donna started going into another room and lying down on the bed as Ethan cried with Ian.
>
> The first few times she did this, she sobbed and felt like a very helpless little child. Her sobbing turned to anger as she remembered her mother's words, "Big girls don't cry." She felt two years old. As she felt all this, her

anger grew and she became furious at her mother for telling her that she should leave Ethan to cry it out *on his own* or she would "spoil" him.

Donna also did some grieving about Ethan's birth. She realized that it had been a difficult one for him and she needed to grieve how sorry she felt about this.

Donna was engaging her natural healing power both to feel and integrate what it had been like for her to be a small defenseless child and to grieve her most recent regrets. The more she did this the more relaxed she became with little Ethan. She began to feel more competent about her ability to mother him and less influenced and confused by what others had to say.

In the twentieth century, in our technological society our babies have become more separated from us than ever before. They have been taken from us at birth and they sleep in a room by themselves once they are home from the hospital. This is not what our babies need. They have been given substitutes for the warmth, closeness and sound of our voices. They have been given night lights, stuffed animals and music boxes. A myriad of sleep-related struggles have developed because of this, with many child-rearing experts giving costly advice about how to get our babies to go to sleep. Some of the repressive methods used may work but a price is paid for this repression; our babies' sense of trust is diminished, they feel helpless and powerless and will no doubt become fearful and anxious. Training our babies to meet our needs greatly diminishes their well-being.

The anxieties generated at this stage show up as problems at later stages of development when our children may have difficulty leaving us to go to school, for example. These early anxieties will follow them in their life until they feel them, connect them and integrate them.

Marcia had been in therapy for some time and was feeling deeply.

As she allowed herself to feel the frantic feeling in her body it was as if she was trying to pull someone toward her. This feeling kept surfacing in her therapy sessions, and although she connected with many other feelings and their source over a period of time, she could not seem to connect with what this frantic pulling was all about.

Marcia came to a session quite sleep-deprived one day. Her three young children had been sick and she had had little sleep for over a week. As she sank into the enormous need of her children that she had been dealing with and how unable she felt to give any more, she began to feel the familiar frantic feeling in her body. As Marcia focused on and stayed with this feeling, she felt how much she had needed to be with her mother and to have her mother's body next to hers.

Marcia was able to continue to feel the anxiety and fearful franticness of herself as a small child, deprived of the warmth and reassurance of her mother's body.

Marcia was very glad to have made this connection and to have been able to keep feeling this feeling every time it arose. She said that she had become much more able to be with her own children and listen to their needs instead of anxiously trying to fix things for them. She noticed too that her youngest child seemed to be able to go to nursery school more easily and wondered if that was because her own anxiety about this separation had lessened.

As we use the feelings our children bring up in us to feel back to our own trauma, we notice that an internal shift happens; we become more free and easy with our children. There is more room for enjoyment as we struggle less.

Mark had been so excited when his son was born and he could not believe what a "little monster" this beautiful baby had turned into. He came to a parenting course because he wanted to know what to do. His wife, Leah, was worried when she saw the strength of Mark's reaction to little Christopher.

Mark entered therapy when he realized, from what he was learning, that he was overreacting to the determined signs of independence in his son. He was afraid he would lose it one day and hit Christopher.

Mark asked his mother what he had been like at age two. She told him that he had at first objected to the playpen but after a while he had settled down and played quietly there while she did her housework.

Leah had insisted they babyproof their house and put anything that Christopher could harm or be harmed by out of his reach. Mark's mother had laughed at this and said they would soon learn that Christopher would have to adjust to their world. She said she was not putting things up when they visited her.

As Mark allowed himself to feel how much he wanted to force Christopher to do his bidding, how enraged he felt when Christopher said "no" to him, he began to feel the rigidity and control that he had experienced as a child. His rage at Christopher turned into rage at his parents for their inability to see him as a person when he was little. He said he felt as though he had been raised in a straitjacket and that it was no wonder he had so many headaches and shoulder and neck pain.

Christopher's growing sense of himself presented many triggers to Mark and he was able to use them to keep connecting to the repressed and controlled nature of his young life. He also used his body pain as an entry point. It was an enormous relief to Mark to be able to feel his anger. He felt that he had been a mystery to himself, and so it was energizing for him to no longer hold his feelings. He was excited about his growing understanding of himself and what that meant for his marriage and his child. After he had done a lot of feeling, connecting and integrating, he was able to tell his mother quite clearly and without rancour that he and Leah had different ideas than she did for dealing with children.

Ainsley became increasingly anxious as her three-year-old daughter insisted on things being a certain way. Kayla would kick up a terrible fuss if she did not get the red cup and the yellow straw and she was adamant about wearing what she wanted to wear.

Ainsley told me that Kayla was turning into an "obsessive compulsive" just like her father. I asked Ainsley to describe how she felt when Kayla was demanding and insisted on definite ways of doing things. Ainsley felt enormously frustrated that her daughter was so precise and insistent, but realized as she felt this that it really was not difficult to let Kayla have what she wanted. What really bothered Ainsley was her fear that Kayla would be like her husband, Kevin, and so her urge was to erase any behaviour that signalled this. When Ainsley stayed with how she felt about Kevin and his compulsive needs she got very angry.

Eventually Ainsley went from her anger and helpless frustration at her husband to the helplessness and fear she had felt as a child. As she worked her way through these feelings, connecting with her powerlessness and integrating how she had had to repress her anger in her family, she began to confront her husband about his obsessive and compulsive needs. He refused to do anything to change, saying "That's just the way I am." Ainsley continued to press for things to be different and Kevin agreed to go for some joint therapy sessions with her.

Although there was still a lot of work for Ainsley and Kevin to do, Ainsley was no longer afraid that Kayla would be like Kevin. She realized that Kayla was her own person and that her insistence on things being a certain way was actually age-appropriate behaviour. She could relax with Kayla and enjoy the knowledge that her daughter was "trying on" being her own self.

It is common to react to traits in our children that remind us of traits we do not like in ourselves, our siblings, our parents or our spouse. *If we remain unconscious about our reactions, we will produce a self-fulfilling prophecy; we will get exactly what we are afraid of.*

Margo felt that she had struggled with her weight forever. She had been a chubby child, and she remembered all her mother's efforts to get her to slim down. She was not allowed to eat ice cream when the other kids did and had been told that she had been put on a skim-milk diet when she was only two years old.

As Margo connected with her pain about being "fat," and the terrible, lonely struggle she had had with this as a child, she got very angry. She realized that her mother had been very embarrassed by her own mother who had been a "fat" person. Margo's mother was a perfect ten even at age sixty-five.

It was a long way back for Margo to keep feeling all the years of agony over her body. She felt a lot of rage at her mother for being so obsessed with Margo's weight, virtually from the time of her birth.

There are periods in young children's lives when they naturally cut back on how much they eat and other times when they are in a growth spurt and eat a lot. Our children's eating patterns often trigger us as parents.

Elizabeth disclosed that she was feeling terribly anxious because Samantha seemed to have lost all interest in eating. She had done everything she could to interest Samantha in food, but to no avail. Samantha simply said she did not want it.

As Elizabeth felt her anger and frustration at Samantha when she would not eat, she began to experience it as a rejection of her. She realized that it had always made her feel good to give her child good nourishment, first with food from her own body, and then with the best she could provide in accordance with what she read children needed. Elizabeth realized that it made her feel as if she was not good enough when Samantha would not eat. Identifying this feeling opened her to a flood of childhood memories and pain.

Elizabeth not only remembered feeling unworthy and inadequate as a child, but also struggling with her own mother over food. She could feel what it had been like to sit at the table long after everyone else had left because she was not allowed to leave until she had eaten what her mother had put in front of her. She felt a lot of anger at both her parents for not allowing her more choice in what, and how much, she ate.

Elizabeth connected to the fact that unconsciously she resented that Samantha had so much choice as a child whereas she had had none.

Elizabeth kept using the triggers from her daughter to feel her way through her childhood distress.

Roger was furious when his four-year-old lied to him. He caught him with a friend's action figure after he picked him up from daycare. Kurt insisted it was his. Roger finally got the truth out of Kurt and marched him over to his friend's house and made him apologize for taking the toy. Kurt cried as his dad lectured him and that made Roger even more angry.

When Roger came for his therapy session he sheepishly told me that he had overreacted to Kurt's lying but that it was one thing that he just could not abide. I asked Roger to stay with this feeling and to try to locate it in his body. He could feel it in his chest and gut; he also had his fists tightly clenched.

As Roger focused on how his body felt and looked at his young son in his mind's eye, he exploded into sobs.

He cried for a long time. When he could finally speak he told me that his father had once insisted on him telling the truth, and when he had his father had whipped him. After Roger told me this, he alternated between sobs and rage at his father. He ended the session weeping about how he had humiliated Kurt.

Once Roger made this connection he realized that he needed to treat Kurt and his other children quite differently if he found they were lying. He decided he needed to try to understand what they might be feeling if they took someone else's property. He thought that next time he would reflect back to them their *wish* to have such an item and then he would listen. He thought he could help them understand that it was wrong to take things that belong to others without making them feel they were bad. He also realized that they lied only because they were too afraid to tell the truth. He resolved to keep feeling what he needed to feel so that he could help his children instead of hurting them.

Tony thought his son was turning into a "wimp." Ryan was nine years old and he was afraid of a lot of things. It did not matter to Tony that his wife, Ellen, said she had heard that nine was an age where children often have fears coming up.

Tony would often humiliate Ryan in front of his siblings and others by pushing him to do things he was afraid to do and putting him down when he said he was afraid.

Ellen finally put her foot down and insisted that Tony stop treating Ryan this way. Tony wanted Ellen to stay out of it; he thought she "coddled" Ryan too much. Ellen had been in therapy for some time and she had felt enough of her own abuse as a child that she was determined not to let her own child suffer alone with no one to defend him. Tony was pressed to stop his scapegoating of Ryan but he refused to explore why he needed to behave this way toward his son.

It is unfortunate when we do not take responsibility for our feelings that our children trigger in us. By not taking this responsibility we continue to put the blame on our children, and this blame seeps into deep crevices within them making it increasingly hard for them to be able to access how they feel and why. Unhappily, they become a mystery to themselves and so the sad cycle continues.

Changing our outward behaviour toward our children simply to appease our partner will not enhance our relationship with our children. It can only breed resentment in the long run, which will show its ugly head when we are most under the pressure of stress. Our "good" behaviour will rupture and we will overreact, hurting our children with our sudden, unfair blowout.

Blaming teenagers is rampant in our culture and recent studies have shown that teenagers are an enormously stressed group in our society. It is easy for us to feel rejected when our teenagers are testing out their own values and wondering how much they want to be like us or not. If we are not secure in ourselves, unable to be our own person and not feeling in charge of our lives, then we will not be able to be there for them. Even though these young people may not seem to want to have much to do with us, they need to know we are there and that we love them. If we cannot do this, it behooves us to explore why.

Lorna was feeling desperate because Kim had started to get "lippy" with her. It felt to Lorna as though thirteen-year-old Kim had changed overnight. All of a sudden Kim seemed to be constantly finding fault with her mother. It was really hard for Lorna to hear this and she became defensive and vigorously fought back.

In her therapy sessions, Lorna was encouraged to stay with her defensive feelings when it felt like Kim was attacking her. As she yelled at Kim in the therapy room, she began to see her own mother and remember how much she had wanted her to shut up. Lorna remembered how controlling her mother had become in Lorna's teen years. She cried as she remembered how close they had been when she was younger and then how it was as though she could do nothing right when she became a teen.

As Lorna worked through how her mother had tried to hold on to her and control everything from the way she dressed to the friends she had, from the books she read to the music she listened to and the courses she chose at school, she felt angry over and over again. She realized that, although she would never have wanted Kim to go through what she did, Kim was probably feeling much as she had as a teenager. Lorna now understood that she was feeling rejected and criticized by Kim just as she had been by her mother and that the strength of the feelings was coming from that long ago time.

As Lorna made these connections and felt her feelings as a teenager again and again, she became less defensive with Kim. As she was able to listen to what Kim was actually saying, she could agree or disagree with Kim's observations without the huge charge that had previously been there. She thought Kim was really right about one thing: she should be thinking about what she wanted to do with her life now that her last child was entering high school. She was thrilled to feel that she had been able to re-establish a closeness with Kim and also to give her daughter the room she needed to establish who she was apart from her mother.

Carlo simply could not understand his middle son, Dean, who was eighteen. He had a ring in his tongue and had recently acquired a tattoo on his upper chest and arm. Carlo barely communicated with him any more at all, and in fact rarely saw him since he had separated from Dean's mother. He had never felt that he really understood Dean. His other two sons seemed to be doing fine but Dean was always doing something "weird and unpredictable."

Carlo did not take responsibility for how he felt about his son and how he viewed him. He stayed stuck in his negative and unsupporting view and the gap between them remained. Taking responsibility is not an easy thing to do when we are locked in our own pain, prisoners of our past. Carlo's rigidity continued to deprive him of participating in his son's life.

Our children need our trust, our faith in their ability to grow and change positively, and they need us to enjoy who they are. It is our responsibility as parents to examine why we cannot trust, have faith or enjoy if this is the case.

We can use our observation of our inability as a door to go through. We can learn to be responsible for our feelings, our over and underreactions and our lack of ability to be responsive.

We, as parents, want to feel confident that we can provide what our children need to become self-reliant, fully functioning, feeling adults who are capable of living meaningful lives. We gain this confidence as we engage our natural emotional healing power to heal our old trauma and to clear our vision in the present.

I have heard many times from clients, "I swore I'd never be like my mother/father and then I hear myself and I'm horrified." It helps when we understand that it is what lies beyond our everyday reach in our unconscious that can wreak havoc with our most carefully laid plans. We can then address the conflict between how we want to be and how we are able to be. We can bring more and more of our unconscious pain to consciousness so that it does not continue to defeat our present intentions. We can call upon our natural emotional healing power to effect change. We then become less reactive and more responsive.

Helping our children complete their feelings

"Children should be seen and not *hurt*" and "Children should be seen and *heard*" are two positive twists on the old damaging adage. One of the greatest burdens a child can have is feeling all alone with emotions that seem unacceptable to adults. "Children should be seen and *not heard*" was what many of us experienced as we grew up. We have the power to change this.

We can be the best support and we can help our children the most if we can get clear enough of our own old pain. Then we can listen to them, accept their feelings and be present for them as they feel all they need to feel to discharge their feelings as completely as possible. Thomas Gordon's book *Parent Effectiveness Training* contains a clear description of how to "active listen" to children in order to demonstrate to them that we accept how they are feeling and that we hear them. We cannot use this as merely a technique, however; we need to be clear enough that we really *want* and *intend* to hear our children.

If our children are allowed to express their full range of feelings they will not have to develop a whole range of unacceptable behaviours in order to try to be heard. When we label our children's attempts to get their needs met as "misbehaviour" instead of seeing it for what it is, we foster more of the same behaviour. Acknowledged feelings go away sooner and more completely than feelings that are denied. Our "whining" child will stop whining sooner if he or she gets the attention needed. It is likely that when our children whine they need some loving attention so that they can cry hard and finish with whatever is bothering them. When they really need to cry they will find something to cry about. This something may seem trivial to us but we need to trust that they are doing what they need to do. Most often when our children are allowed to cry all they need to cry, they finish and become sunny for the rest of the day.

We as parents have had difficulty understanding the difference between expressing a feeling and acting on it. We are not as afraid of our children's feelings as we become more familiar with our own. We come to know that pent-up feelings are more dangerous by far than expressed ones. We are less likely to act on a feeling if we are able to express it. Our children need to be able to say "I hate my sister" and to understand that their anger is okay but hurting their sister is not.

It is a relief to most of us when we understand that the best way to help our children is to listen to them and support them to feel what they need to feel. This relieves us of the false responsibility that results in trying to "fix" or "rescue" our children. It also means that we can help our children no matter what trauma they may suffer or no matter what our circumstances are.

We want our children to be alert, aware and open to learning. When unacceptable feelings must be repressed then the ability to experience excitement, interest and curiosity is also shut down. It is impossible for our children to pay attention and learn if they are harbouring feelings they experience as dangerous and bad. If they are full of conflict and pain and no one is helping them, they may become hyperactive, unable to concentrate and to learn.

We help our children with the reality of their lives by listening to them instead of denying their feelings. When our children are not listened to and helped with their feelings, they tell themselves stories so they can survive. One of the stories I told myself was that my daddy must really love me since he was always away at work making money. My mother always told me how much my dad loved me even though he was not around much. Finally as an adult, in my own therapy, I had to feel the truth. My dad did not want to spend much time with me. My mother could have helped me with this when I asked where he was and when he was coming home. She could have said, "It must be really hard for you when Daddy isn't here." Then I could have felt sad, and felt that it was okay to feel sad, instead of twisting myself like a pretzel to try to make sense of a lie.

When we become more conscious, as parents, we no longer spend endless amounts of energy trying to control things that are not within our control. We talk *with* our children, not *to* them, and we are not afraid to tell them how we feel. We trust our children rather than attempting to control them. We are open to their experience; we are close.

The best thing for any child is to have parents who are glad to be alive, who love and support them and who are willing to engage their natural emotional healing power to make this so.

18

OTHER RELATIONSHIPS

Adult Children and Older Parents, Adult Siblings, In-laws, Friends, Peers, Employers and Employees

---

Τhe backbone for a healthy relationship is respect and empathy for ourselves and others. *Acknowledging that our current relationships are influenced by unconscious, unresolved pain from our past is the major key to understanding the dynamics of human relationships.* We are one hundred percent responsible for ourselves in relation to others; we are responsible for our thoughts, feelings and actions. Viable and healthy relationships require that people take this kind of responsibility. The resulting clarity allows us to accept the limitations of relationships that we might wish could be more.

We often try to create the family we needed as a child and did not have. Because of this we may make damaging decisions and cling to neurotic hope. We may act out old needs in any of our adult relationships.

Adult children

We often continue as adult children to be stuck in our childhood behaviours, avoiding confrontation or struggling by grinding away at our parents to get them to change. Using our natural healing power can be particularly difficult because our parents of today are the people who hurt us when we were children. The most important thing for us to do is to feel the pain of our avoidance and struggles and process it so that we live internally free of the ties that have bound us to our old hurt. We then see ourselves and our parents more clearly.

We do not need to be stuck acting out being our parents' little child throughout our adulthood if we know how to process our feelings. We can get free of this restriction. There are many indications that we may be stuck and it is helpful to become aware of them. We can ask ourselves:

- Can I say no to my parent(s)?
- Do I feel resentment toward my parent(s)?
- Do I tell my mother or father only what they want to hear?
- Do I need their approval when I make a decision?
- Am I afraid to disagree with them?
- Do I feel responsible for how my mom or dad feels?
- Do I feel that no matter what I do it is never enough?
- Do I keep hoping that my mother or father will change?
- Do I have things I need to say to my parent(s) but do not?
- Do I get angry and rage at my parent(s)?

As we must in any relationship, we can watch for our under and overreactions as signals that we are being triggered. If we have not felt and processed our damage we will be triggered.

As we relive what it was like to be their little child and feel, connect and integrate our experience, we will either confront them with how they are treating us now, if this is abusive in some way, or we will accept them for who they are and recognize the limitations of our adult child–adult parent relationship. We will let go of being stuck in hope, hope that we have used as a defense to protect ourselves from the overwhelming hurt of our parents not being who we needed them to be. We will have moved toward completing our growing up.

It is often helpful to observe how our parents are with our children. Sometimes we are triggered because they are much more loving toward their grandchildren than they were toward us; they are much better grandparents than they were parents. Sometimes we are triggered because we see them treat our children the same harmful way they treated us. We can use all of these triggers to become clearer.

It is not emotionally healthy for us to continue to take abuse in the present from anyone, and this includes our parent phoning us drunk, drinking too much in front of our children, putting us down or raging at us. Once we feel and process our voicelessness from our childhood, we realize that we do have a voice as an adult; we can tell our parent in a straightforward manner what we are willing to accept and what we are not. It is often surprising how much change our parents are able to make when challenged in this way. On the other hand, there are also those who are so entrenched in their self-righteousness that they would rather lose their connection with their children than change their unhealthy way of being. This is a sad truth that some of us have to face.

Sometimes as an adult recuperating from our childhood pain we can approach our mother or father and talk about the way it was for us. Sometimes this is a relief for our parent who has been silently suffering for how they were and what they did. Sometimes we can cry together. When this happens it is wonderful and both adults, child and parent, grow emotionally. This is quite different from dumping old anger on an aging parent instead of feeling it through. When we spew our old anger on our parents, we are acting out and not taking responsibility for what we need to feel. When we dump our anger on our parent in this way, nothing changes and our struggle continues.

On the other hand, if we as parents understand this, we can help our adult children by agreeing to talk with them about the past if that is what they want, but we will refuse to let them act out on us. It is not beneficial to anyone if we take abuse from our children.

If there is something we need to say about our parent's present behaviour and we put it off, we need to let ourselves identify and feel the fear that is stopping us. This will take us to our childhood fear. As we integrate this we can move forward, recognizing any fear that remains but still taking the risk of saying what we need to say. Fear that is felt loses some of its intensity and is less debilitating.

It is hazardous to stay numb to what is going on in our relationship with our aging parent. It is risky because this unfinished business will unconsciously spread out and affect our other relationships as well.

Adult parents

We often continue to look after our adult children in unhealthy ways, fixing things for them and rescuing them. This too is unfinished business. It is *our* need when we fix and rescue. It is really important to listen to ourselves now even if we never have before.

Stephanie wanted to know what she should do about her adult daughter who constantly expected her to babysit, never gave her adequate notice of this need and got angry if her mother was not available.

In the course of talking about this problem Stephanie revealed that her twenty-three-year-old son had returned home after university and it looked like he might be there to stay. Stephanie was very unhappy about this because she had really been enjoying having her own space and her own life since her children had left. It had not occurred to her that she could do anything about this. It also had not occurred to her that she did not need to take up where she left off with her son. Once again she was doing his laundry and preparing his meals.

As Stephanie felt what it was like to have all these expectations placed on her, she allowed herself to sink into the feelings of guilt engendered when she thought of not doing what her children expected of her. She started to feel more adamant about wanting her own life.

Stephanie connected with a childhood full of responsibility as the "good, responsible daughter" in a family of boys who were not expected to do anything around the house. She had wanted her own children to have a more carefree childhood than she had had but had subsequently unconsciously reenacted her childhood, always doing everything for them. In her therapy she wept for her lost childhood, felt her anger at her parents for their expectations of her and felt the fear she had repressed of losing them if she did not conform to their wishes.

As Stephanie felt more of what had happened to her as a child she got much clearer about what she needed to do in the present to look after herself. It took her some time to reach this point because she had confused loving her adult children with doing things for them, even when it meant denying herself. As she felt more of how she had been expected to deny herself as a child and to get her parents' love and approval by performing, she could feel her need, anger and hurt instead of guilt.

She was able to establish boundaries for herself by giving her daughter clear guidelines for babysitting requests. She told her what she was willing to do and what she was not willing to do. She told her son the same. We try to fix our need unconsciously through our children.

When we, as parents, continue to put our need on our children to make our lives meaningful, we are avoiding responsibility for our need and ourselves.

In-laws

In-law relationships are notoriously difficult.

> Sue came for therapy because she could no longer abide her mother-in-law and was furious with her husband because he would not stand up to his mother.
>
> Sue's mother-in-law, Peggy, was very controlling. She was always telling Sue and Blake what to do, and what was worse, she often ignored Sue. She would not acknowledge Sue when they arrived at her home and would often talk over what Sue was saying during a conversation. This was driving Sue crazy; she had stopped going to her in-law's house altogether.
>
> In her first session Sue was encouraged to go with her feelings about her mother-in-law. Her anger quickly turned to deep hurt at the rejection she felt. When I asked her if she had ever felt this way before she quickly said, "All the time as a kid, my parents never wanted me around."
>
> Sue had difficulty understanding that her present "battle" with Peggy had anything to do with her past, even though she could see that she had been hurt as a child. She wanted Peggy to change and she wanted her husband Blake to make this so.

It is very difficult to break the pattern of blame and victimization and to acknowledge that the strength of our feelings is ours. Sue had an opportunity here to feel, connect and integrate what had happened to her as a child. When we are able to do this, we feel differently about the people we have to deal with in the present. When the intensity of the feeling shifts and we feel better about ourselves, we have personal power that we did not have as a child. Instead of struggling as we did as a child, we can use our adult voice to solve our problems. When we approach the problem differently, we stop struggling about who is right and who is wrong and we work toward resolution. We also do not stop until we get resolution.

As Sue worked through her old pain, she connected with how alone she had felt as a child with no one to stand up for her. Both her parents had been too busy to notice her much and the only person she could think of who had ever encouraged her was a teacher who once told her she was very bright. She began to recognize that she was feeling like a little girl around her mother-in-law and that she wanted her husband to stand up for her in a way that she had so wanted her parents to do.

Sue was able eventually to talk to Blake without blaming him. She knew she needed to react to Peggy authentically herself whenever she was ignored. She asked Blake to support her in doing this, acknowledging that she did not want him to do it for her. She also asked him to deal with his own fear of crossing his mother. Sue noticed that the more she was able to simply tell her mother-in-law that they were doing something the way they wanted to do it without the old anger in her voice, the more Peggy seemed to just accept it and move on to something else. Even when Peggy gave one of her disapproving looks, Sue felt very differently about it; she felt a little smile inside herself as she was able to accept Peggy more.

The last two examples are cases where people have made enormous changes by connecting to the source of their pain and to their unentitled behaviour. Merely changing our behaviour in this kind of circumstance will not relieve us of our feelings and our need to struggle. Taking the time to make connections and to integrate them into our conscious experience will.

Adult siblings

I have had many clients who have had to grieve a lot because they could not connect with their adult siblings in the way they wanted to.

Fred had been the youngest in his large family. As an adult he was frustrated at the way he was being treated by his brothers and sisters. They would often get together and leave him out and would often make excuses not to come to his home when invited.

In his therapy, Fred recognized that his parents had been emotionally absent and in fact had had far too many children to ever meet their needs. He had transferred his need for them onto his older siblings. Not only had they rejected him, they had been jealous of him because from their perspective he was the baby and was getting more than they were. They still said things that indicated their jealousy, such as "You were Dad's favourite" and "You were the cute one." He was always baffled by these comments because they did not match how he had felt.

Fred connected time and again to how alone he had been in his family. Every time there was a family gathering he recognized how much he hoped things would be different. He felt how he yearned for his family to be what it had never been.

As Fred connected to his early need to have his older brothers and sisters like him and want him around, he grieved deeply. He remembered many times when he played alone when they were either not there or in another room with their friends telling him to "get lost." He felt his anger and his grief at not getting what he needed from his parents. The more he felt his early need and hurt, the more he let go of his need for his siblings in the present.

It is very common for one member of a family to be working on recuperating from childhood neglect and abuse while the other members remain in denial. This is painful and needs to be felt. When we engage our natural emotional healing power we always discover that the strength of the pain is coming from our past. We do not need our brothers and sisters in the present the way we did in the past, even if it feels as if it is about now. We can use any triggers that our siblings ignite to take us to where we need to go to heal. We will experience an internal shift that will allow us now to perceive these same people differently. Once we have felt, connected and integrated our past experience our feelings will not have the same charge on them.

We can use any current struggle with a sibling to feel to the past. The same struggles that we had as children will be repeating themselves in our present relationships with these same people if they have not been felt through enough. Understanding this will not change how we feel; completing the feelings from the past will. I have had many clients discover that the "sibling rivalry," the fighting that went on with their sister or brother, was really about not being able to tell their parents how they were feeling. These clients have grieved for how their relationship with their siblings was damaged because their parents could not listen to them.

It is much more difficult to acknowledge our underreactions; however, we are capable as adults of seeing them and feeling what they are protecting us from.

Pam always had everyone to her home for the big celebration days. One of her sisters was single, and hosting dinner just was not "one of her things." The other sister was always overwhelmed and in a crisis so nothing could be expected of her.

Pam would be exhausted and depressed for days afterwards. She felt that her family took her for granted and did not appreciate her efforts.

Pam entered therapy when she realized she was feeling depressed too much of the time. As she did her time line and started writing about how she was feeling, she realized more and more that she had a lot of resentment about what had been expected of her over the years.

As Pam connected with her fear of not doing what was expected of her, she opened to her anger and eventually to her hurt. She had a lot of grieving to do about not being appreciated for who she was as a child. As she felt her way through this, she began to take charge of her life more. She stopped making excuses for her sisters and informed her family of what she was and was not willing to do about family dinners in the future.

Pam realized that every time she felt depressed, she had an opportunity to identify what had triggered the depression and to dig for the feelings that she was depressing. She got very good at identifying when she was underreacting and kept using this as a door to go through to discover what she was protecting herself from feeling.

Friends

Many of us want a balance between lighter friendships that are based on mutual interest and friendships that are deeply satisfying. Most of us want an easy acceptance and a comfortable reciprocity. However, some of us persist with uncomfortable and even abusive relationships and do not know why, while others of us are blinded by unrealistic expectations. Unacknowledged, negative feelings and unacknowledged need leads to distress in our friendships. The more open, honest and real we can be with our friends, the more depth there will automatically be.

Claire was so angry she developed a splitting headache each time she met Charlene for lunch. When I asked her what she really wanted to say to Charlene, she yelled, "Shut up for once and listen to me."

Claire was encouraged to stay with her feelings about Charlene. She said Charlene made absolutely everything about herself and never seemed to care at all about what was going on in Claire's life.

Claire was encouraged to stay with her anger and keep looking at Charlene in her mind's eye.

When Claire came up out of her feelings in this session, she wondered why she kept trying to be friends with Charlene. I asked her to keep feeling that question until her next session.

Claire had no answer when she returned and I asked her what her relationship with Charlene felt like. She said, "A huge struggle." Claire stayed with the feeling of struggling with Charlene. She realized that struggling was a familiar feeling.

It took a long time for Claire to connect to how rigid her mother had been when she was a small child. She realized that her mother had needed things her way and had not adjusted her life much at all to meet the needs of her little daughter. When Claire felt the connection between her mother's and Charlene's self-centredness, she realized that she was struggling with Charlene, trying to get the recognition, acknowledgment and acceptance that she had needed from her mother. She began to feel the silent struggle and stayed with it until she broke through to the underlying hurt and sobbed out loud.

Claire decided she needed to tell Charlene how she was feeling. When she decided to do this, she felt scared. She stayed with her fear for several sessions, and in between sessions she kept imagining speaking with Charlene so that she could put herself up against her fear. She went back and forth between Charlene and her mother as she felt how afraid she had always been to tell her mother how she was feeling.

Claire eventually did tell Charlene how she was feeling and she decided not to try to continue the relationship when Charlene had no idea what Claire was talking about. She then grieved for the loss of the potential of this friendship and continued to grieve for her childhood losses.

There is an opportunity for us to move to emotional health when we recognize problems that surface in our friendships. This can happen when we find ourselves:

- Measuring ourselves in relation to our friends
- Self-doubting, self-blaming and feeling inadequate
- Gossiping
- Feeling that "there must be something wrong with me"
- Having unrealistic expectations of our friends; blaming
- Feeling responsible for others' feelings; feeling guilty
- Needing to be needed
- Helping others to our personal detriment
- Subduing ourselves for fear of being resented
- Seeking approval, pleasing, trying to be perfect
- Pretending everything is okay when it is not
- Afraid of conflict
- Fearful of hurting our friend
- Overlooking things that hurt
- Explaining and justifying ourselves
- Unable to talk about negative feelings

- Threatened by our friend's achievement
- Fearful that our friends will abandon us
- Feeling betrayed
- Confused by double messages
- Walking on eggshells; withholding
- Feeling unrecognized, discounted or closed off
- Continually thrown off balance
- Needing to be right
- Not taking responsibility for our negativity
- Finding fault as a basis of conversation
- Needing to put the other person down
- Being uneasy with silence
- Needing to use sarcasm
- Feeling locked in others' expectations
- Needing the other person to change
- Unable to be authentic

Peers, employers and employees

A great many of us work in toxic environments, in organizations that do not provide opportunity for us to redress problems adequately. We find that these organizations lack consistent, clear policies and follow-through in providing the elements of respect and fairness that make a healthy environment. Nonetheless, no matter how good or how difficult our work situation is, we still have choice about how we process the difficulties.

Aaron came for therapy when he felt he might lose his job. His anger was getting out of control; he had more than once come close to pushing someone.

As Aaron talked about all the things that triggered him—people standing too close for comfort, people coming into his office unannounced and people abusing the equipment—his voice escalated and his body tensed.

Aaron was afraid of his rage and worried that if he let himself feel it he might not be able to control himself at work or in the therapy room. He was encouraged to stay with his fear. As he stayed with his fear for a number of sessions he began to recognize that he had always been afraid of his rage. He acknowledged that if he had allowed his rage to surface when his parents were beating him, he would have had to kill them in order to save himself. This was an untenable bind and he chose passivity as his only defense. He recognized that his present rage was connected to the held, life-threatening rage he suffered as a child.

As Aaron felt the bind of his early, catastrophic fear, he was able to let his anger surface more in his sessions. As he used his triggers from work and kept feeling his rage, he connected it more and more to his abuse in the past.

Aaron learned to trust that he could control his anger at work as long as he knew he could go home and connect with it there. He used his punching bag a lot. It also helped him that he recognized more and more that his anger was about his past. His perceptions of his co-workers began to shift. He was able to deal with them differently, without the huge charge of his old feelings. Aaron had been severely physically and emotionally abused as a child. He was encouraged by the shifts that he felt in his work situation but realized he had deep wounds that he would need to keep feeling and connecting for some time.

Amanda was often put down by her boss. She complained about this all the time to her husband. He could not figure out why she stayed in the job, since she did have other options.

At first Amanda was defensive when Jon suggested something was keeping her there. She brought this to her group sessions to try to work through what was keeping her in this job.

She wrote in her journal every time her boss was verbally abusive. She would get up from her writing and wham the bed with her looped towel and yell at him. She knew he treated her a lot like her father had but she thought this was too pat a way to explain her taking this abuse and not just leaving the job. She had trouble feeling what it had been like to be the child she had been. One day her own daughter came home from school with a problem because the teacher had put her down, and the floodgates opened for Amanda.

She could feel her anger at Angie's teacher and then started to feel how desperately awful it would be if Angie were treated as she had been by her father.

Sometimes when we do not have easy access to our past, we find our way into our feelings by imagining what it would be like for children to suffer as we did. Amanda did connect enough with her childhood abuse and her powerlessness to be able to stand up more to her boss. She also felt her need around him and how much she wanted his approval. When she connected this back to her father and felt it deeply, she came to feel that she did have options.

We can be clearer about our work lives the more we notice and use our triggers and engage our natural emotional healing power. The more we recuperate from our childhood pain, the more we will want our work lives to be fulfilling and less of a struggle.

We have the opportunity to find our authentic self in any relationship.

EPILOGUE

Discovering and utilizing our natural emotional healing power can lead us toward a more positive future. Whether we are taking small steps to take responsibility and feel or whether we are in deep intensive therapy, we are moving in the direction of being a more emotionally healthy person. The more steps we take, whether they be small or large, the better off we are and the better our world will be.

Emotional fitness is a matter of degree. Living and growing is about continually moving towards wholeness; our human spirit inclines in this direction. We will not move in a linear fashion however; there will be many ups and downs.

There is a popular belief that our childhood trials and tribulations have made us strong. Although our survival behaviours may have fortified us, they often adversely affect us as adults, interfering with our ability to have close, satisfying relationships. What could be recognized is how much more potential we might have realized had we not had to struggle to survive.

When we feel the truth of our experience, we gain acceptance and empathy for ourselves and then for others. We do not need to be told to care about others in our world, we just do.

We can access our natural emotional healing power on our own. However, the deeper the wound, the more difficult it is to heal. Most of us were alone with our pain as children but now we can have a listening, supportive person with us while we feel through our old trauma. We can use our healing power in therapy and outside of therapy; it is ours to use when we need it. As we come to trust the internal shifts we feel inside, we come to trust ourselves and accept the truths of our lives. We come to trust the power we possess to know and heal ourselves and we relish this increasing freedom.

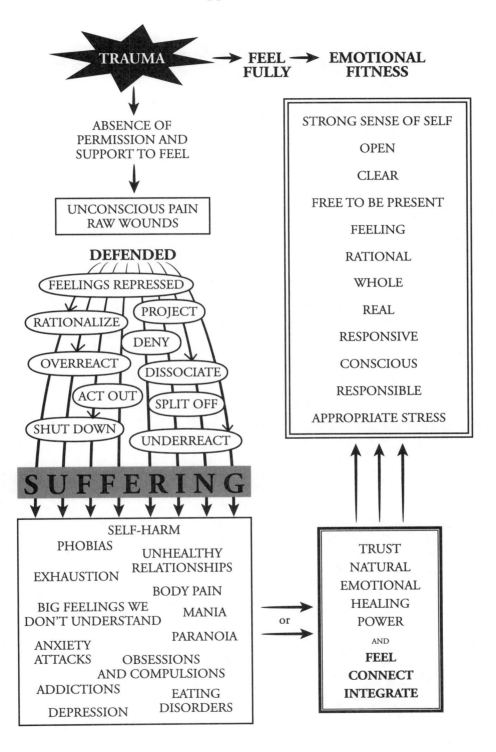

Continuum

All of us can move along the continuum toward emotional health and a more integrated life when we engage our natural emotional healing power.

Non-integrated/Split ——————⟶ *Integrated*

shut down ——————⟶ fully feeling
irrational ——————⟶ rational
unreal ——————⟶ real
outside ourselves ——————⟶ inside ourselves
unconscious ——————⟶ conscious
disconnected ——————⟶ connected
defensive ——————⟶ responsive
confused ——————⟶ clear
rigid ——————⟶ curious
withdrawn ——————⟶ expressive
closed ——————⟶ open
hidden ——————⟶ revealing
dishonest ——————⟶ honest
phony ——————⟶ authentic
blaming ——————⟶ responsible
driven ——————⟶ balanced
abusive ——————⟶ respectful
suspicious ——————⟶ trusting
incongruent ——————⟶ congruent

Glossary

Acting out Behaviours driven by unfelt, unconscious emotional pain

Authentic self Being genuine, real and without pretence

Clarity Feeling enough to be in touch with reality instead of illusion

Congruent Thoughts, feelings and actions are in agreement

Connection 1) The joining of our feelings to our experience; 2) joining or linking with others in a meaningful way

Conscious Knowing one's self, able to feel and be aware

Feeling fully Feeling our emotions to the fullest extent that we possibly can

Feeling Unentitled Feeling of not having the right to equal respect and dignity

Flashbacks A part of a memory breaks through repression to consciousness

Integrate To make complete or whole; when enough feeling and connecting has been done so that we no longer need to keep our feelings or experience of events split off from our consciousness

Knowing/feeling An integrated perception of our world

Letting go Feeling deeply and connecting enough to the sources of our pain until these experiences are integrated into our consciousness and we become free of their hidden drive; they no longer cause us a problem; we no longer obsess

Overreaction Feelings that are bigger than those appropriate to the current situation, indicating that accumulated pain is being repressed

Owning Acknowledging our responsibility for a thought, feeling or action

Processing Feeling our hidden pain to its source, connecting it and integrating it into our consciousness

Repression Our primary defense against pain; the unconscious blocking of any reality from our conscious awareness that is too painful for us to feel

Trigger Anything in the present that causes us to under or overreact, indicating that we have unfelt pain from our past

Unconscious The part of the mind containing cognitive information and emotional energy relating to past traumatic experiences that we have not yet consciously processed and felt to completion

Underreaction An absence of feelings where it would be appropriate to the current situation to have feelings, indicating that accumulated pain is being repressed

References

Bradshaw, John. *Bradshaw On: The Family.* Deerfield Beach, Health Communications, 1988.

Evans, Patricia. *The Verbally Abusive Relationship.* Holbrook, Adams, 1992.

Frey II, W. H. & Langseth, M. *Crying: The Mystery of Tears.* Winston Press, 1985.

Gordon, Thomas. *Discipline That Works.* New York, Plume, 1991.

Gordon, Thomas. *Parent Effectiveness Training.* New York, Plume, 1970.

Hendrix, Harville and Hunt, Helen. *Giving the Love That Heals.* New York, Pocket Books, 1997.

Janov, Arthur. *The New Primal Scream.* Wilmington, Enterprise, 1991.

Janov, Arthur. *Prisoners of Pain.* New York, Doubleday, 1980.

Janov, Arthur. *Why You Get Sick, How You Get Well.* West Hollywood, Dove, 1996.

Miller, Alice. *The Drama of the Gifted Child.* New York, Basic Books, 1980.

Miller, Alice. *For Your Own Good.* New York, Farrar, Strauss and Giroux, 1984.

Northrup, Christiane. *Women's Bodies, Women's Wisdom.* New York, Bantam, 1998.

Paul, Jordan and Margaret. *Do I Have to Give Up Me to Be Loved by You.* Minneapolis, CompCare, 1983.

Pert, Candace. *Molecules of Emotion.* New York, Scribner, 1997.

Real, Terrence. *I Don't Want to Talk About It.* New York, Scribner, 1997.

Solter, Aletha. *The Aware Baby.* Goleta, Shining Star, 1984.

Tavris, Carol. *The Mismeasure of Women.* New York, Touchstone, 1992.

Further Suggested Reading

Herman, Judith. *Trauma and Recovery.* New York, Basic Books, 1992.

Jenson, Jean. *Reclaiming Your Life.* New York, Meridian, 1996.

Kaufman, Michael. *Cracking the Armour.* Toronto, Penguin, 1994.

Miller, Dusty. *Women Who Hurt Themselves.* New York, Basic Books, 1994.

Roth, Geneen. *When Food Is Love.* New York, Penguin Group, 1991.

Schaef, Anne Wilson. *Beyond Therapy, Beyond Science.* San Francisco, Harper, 1992.

Viscott, David. *Emotional Resilience.* New York, Harmony Books, 1996.

Whitfield, Charles. *Memory and Abuse.* Atlanta, Health Communications, 1995.

Index